On the Cusp

On the Cusp
From Population Boom to Bust

Charles S. Pearson

OXFORD
UNIVERSITY PRESS

OXFORD
UNIVERSITY PRESS

Oxford University Press is a department of the University of Oxford.
It furthers the University's objective of excellence in research, scholarship,
and education by publishing worldwide. Oxford is a registered trade mark
of Oxford University Press in the UK and in certain other countries

Published in the United States of America by
Oxford University Press
198 Madison Avenue, New York, NY 10016,
United States of America

Library of Congress Cataloging-in-Publication Data
Pearson, Charles S.
On the cusp : from population boom to bust / Charles S. Pearson.
p.   cm.
Summary: "A comprehensive analysis of world population trends"—
Provided by publisher.
Includes bibliographical references and index.
ISBN 978–0–19–022391–5 (hardback)
1. Population. 2. Population—Economic aspects. I. Title.
HB871.P374 2015
304.6'2—dc23
2015014996

1 3 5 7 9 8 6 4 2

Printed in the United States of America on acid-free paper

To Su, who makes all things possible,
and to Pang, who draws the sting from aging

I wasted time and now doth time waste me . . .
—William Shakespeare, *Richard II*

CONTENTS

LIST OF FIGURES

LIST OF TABLES

ACKNOWLEDGMENTS

I thank Devon Swezey for excellent research assistance, and Lee Bramble and Mark Stephens for equally excellent technical help with the diagrams and much appreciated editing assistance. Thanks also to Tom Row for a helpful reading of the full manuscript. Ken Keller at SAIS, Bologna, and Werner Neudeck at the Diplomatic Academy of Vienna provided students and a forum when needed. Student feedback was as always most valuable—thanks to all!

C.S.P.

On the Cusp

CHAPTER 1

✧

Introduction

PRÉCIS

Within the span of half a lifetime, concern has shifted from population explosion to impending implosion....

In fifty years (1950–2000) population grew more than it had in the previous five thousand . . .

Since then the growth rate of population has been cut in half and is headed toward zero and below . . .

By the end of this century two-thirds of countries worldwide will be losing population . . .

Increasing life expectancy and decreasing birth rates inevitably lead to an older population . . .

The percentage of the world's population who are over sixty is projected to double from 11 to 22 percent in the next 38 years.

Humanity has undertaken a demographic voyage of almost unimagi-nable distance over the past 300 years. It was unanticipated, un-planned, uncharted, and unprecedented. And the journey is not yet over—we are entering new and unfamiliar waters. Whereas until now the defining characteristic of the voyage has been population growth, the future may well hold, for the first time, an aging and shrinking world pop-ulation. Within the span of half a lifetime, concern has shifted from population explosion to impending implosion. Global population is poised on the cusp where the arc of growth meets the arc of decline.

There is a compelling story here, even as the endgame is wrapped in uncertainty. The purpose of this book is to bring that story to light and to life. There is also a second, intertwined story to be told. Demographic variables are not independent of economic variables and vice versa. Since Malthus there has been a tension or contest between population and economic growth and the polarity of that debate has abruptly reversed. Yesterday's question was the interaction of population *growth* and economic well-being. Today's question is the interaction of population *stagnation and decline* and economic output. These stories are at the core of this volume.

THE BONES OF THE BOOK

Population Trends and Projections

As a preview, the major demographic changes are illustrated in figures 1.1 through 1.11. The first and most significant is the explosion of population

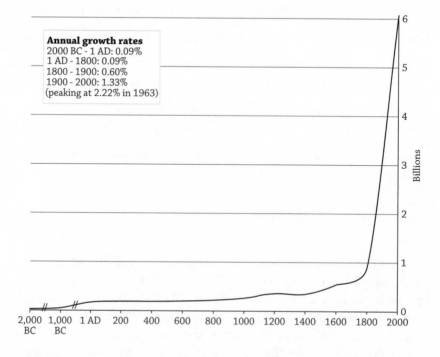

Annual growth rates
2000 BC - 1 AD: 0.09%
1 AD - 1800: 0.09%
1800 - 1900: 0.60%
1900 - 2000: 1.33%
(peaking at 2.22% in 1963)

Figure 1.1:
World population, 2000 B.C.–A.D. 2000
Sources: McEvedy and Jones 1978; US Census Bureau 2010.

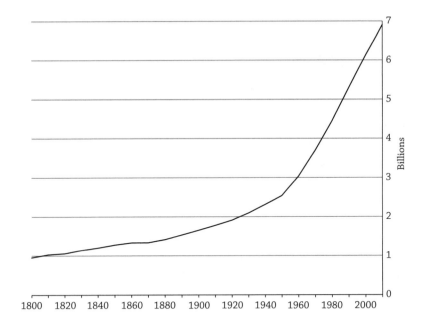

Figure 1.2:
The population boom years, 1800–2010
Source: Based on Goldewijk 2005.

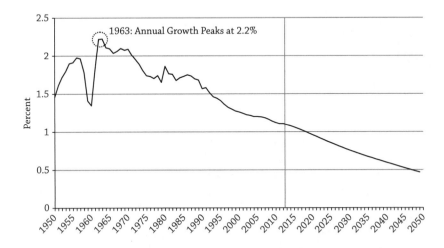

Figure 1.3:
World population growth rates, 1950–2050
Source: US Census Bureau 2010.
Note: US Census attributes the 1958 crash to the untoward effects of the Great Leap Forward in China.

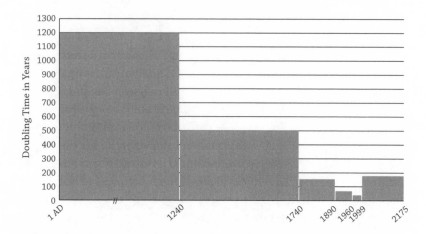

Figure 1.4:
Population doubling time
Source: Based on Lam 2011, figure A1.
Note: 1999–2175 at UN projected growth rate for 2050.

(figure 1.1). After a glacially paced increase for thousands of years, population increased in the nineteenth and twentieth centuries at rapid and accelerating speed. The result was a sixfold increase in world population in less than 200 years. The acceleration in the second half of the twentieth century can be seen in figure 1.2. In fifty years (1950–2000) population increased more than it had in the previous five thousand years.

While the raw numbers are impressive, they conceal a second trend of equal importance: The *growth rate* of population has topped out. Figure 1.3 shows that the *rate of growth* of world population peaked in the 1960s, has been cut in half to 1.1 percent since then, and is expected to be cut in half again by mid-century. All analysts project a continued slowdown, and some predict negative growth—a declining world population—later this century. For example, in a probabilistic exercise Sergei Scherbov and his colleagues (2011) estimate there is an 84 percent probability that world population will peak and start to decline in this century. (Recent data indicating a slowdown in fertility decline in Africa make this less likely). The United Nations projects that by the end of this century two-thirds of countries worldwide will be losing population.

Figure 1.4 reinforces this reversal in growth. Whereas the doubling time for world population fell from over a millennium in the early Christian era to less than 40 years at the end of the twentieth century, it has started to lengthen. At current population growth rates it will take 60 years to double again. But at the more realistic UN's median annual growth estimate of 0.38 percent for 2050, it would take 175 years to double. Indeed it is increasingly likely that world population will never double again.

Population projections over the next several decades are considered quite reliable. Most people who will be alive in the first half of this century have already been born, and even if the underlying birth and death rates change sharply, the aggregate effects will compound only slowly. Beyond 2050 the numbers become increasingly speculative. The United Nations has published a range of projections—high, medium, and low through 2100. Figure 1.5 shows the wide variation in these projections. The main sources of the variations are the fertility rate assumptions. The range at the end of this century is considerable: from a high of 16 billion people down to 6 billion, which is less than the 7 billion people alive today. The medium variant shows world population peaking early next century; the low variant shows the peak in just a few decades.

Previously the United Nations had entered deeper into the realm of speculation, publishing population projections to 2300, as shown in figure 1.6. As might be expected the range of population in 2300 is large: 2.3 billion to 36.4 billion with a medium variant of 9.0 billion, not far from what we have today. What is surprising is the power of small changes in assumptions concerning fertility rates. By the end of this century fertility rates in the medium variant are assumed to settle at replacement levels—defined as 2.1 births per woman, the rate that would keep overall population constant. Tweaking the rate up or down by a mere 0.25 children per woman generates the divergent 2300 population range of 2 to 36 billion. The track record in estimating future fertility rates is modest at best, suggesting some skepticism of long-term projections is warranted.

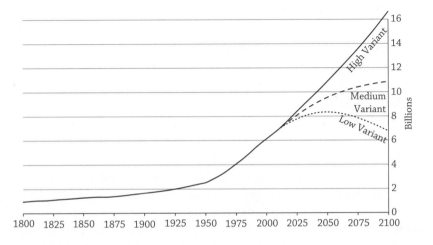

Figure 1.5:
World population, 1800–2100
Source: United Nations 2012b.

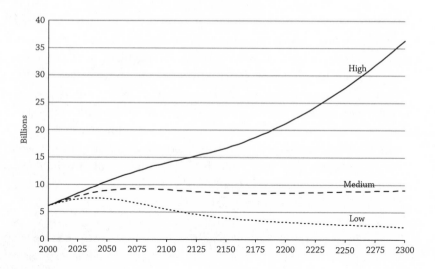

Figure 1.6:
Population projections to 2300
Source: UN Department of Economic and Social Affairs 2004.

The earlier explosion and the pending implosion of population is, of course, nothing more than the difference between birth and death rates. Death (mortality) rates are influenced by the age composition of the population, so a convenient alternative is life expectancy, with life expectancy at birth the most common indicator. *Ceteris paribus*, when life expectancy increases, population increases. The converse holds as well. Gains in life expectancy, while uneven, have been gratifyingly large. The life expectancy of a baby born in classical Greek and Roman times was about 28 years. Now, on a worldwide basis, it is about 68 years. (One must be careful in interpreting life expectancy numbers. In antiquity infant and child mortality rates were far higher than today, dragging down life expectancy at birth. One estimate is that in Rome if one survived to age 15 one could expect an additional 37 years of life.)

Ronald Lee (2003) has estimated the increase for the world for the period 1700 to 2000 to be 38 years, from 27 years to 65 years, and he projects an additional 14 years by 2100. See figure 1.7. The improvement in life expectancy (decline in death rates) started slowly in the eighteenth century in Europe and was a crucial initiating force in the demographic transition that we are now experiencing. The proximate causes are well known—better nutrition, sanitation and public health measures, and medical advances. Estimates for advanced countries in recent years, based on more solid data, confirm that the increase is continuing. Figure 1.8 charts the improvement in US life expectancy from 1900 to

2000 and makes projections to 2100. From 1900 to 2013 male life expectancy increased by about 30 years and is expected to increase another 7.4 years by 2100.

Birth rates are more complex and less well understood. Like death rates, simple birth rates are also affected by the age composition of the population. If the fraction of the female population in their reproductive years is unusually large, the birth rate is biased upward, and if the fraction is unusually small it is biased downward. To get around this demographers construct a synthetic measure, the total fertility rate (TFR). It is based on age-specific fertility rates in a woman's childbearing years and measures

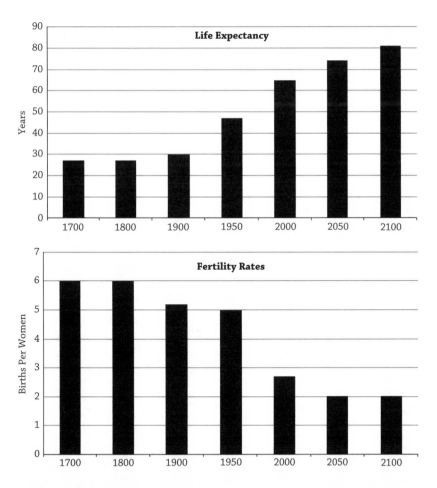

Figure 1.7:
Life expectancy and fertility rates, 1700–2100
Source: Based on Lee 2003.

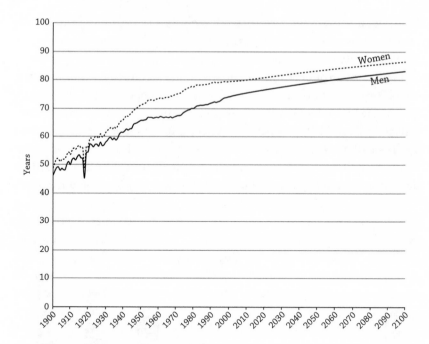

Figure 1.8:
US life expectancy at birth, 1900–2100
Source: US Social Security Administration 2010.
Note: The precipitous drop in 1918/1919 was a result of deaths due to the "Spanish Flu."

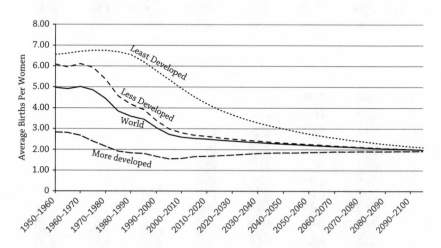

Figure 1.9:
Total fertility rates
Source: United Nations 2012b.
Note: More developed regions comprise Europe, Northern America, Australia/New Zealand, and Japan.
Less developed regions comprise all regions of Africa, Asia (excluding Japan), Latin America, and the Caribbean plus Melanesia, Micronesia, and Polynesia. The least developed countries are 48 countries, 33 in Africa, 9 in Asia, 5 in Oceania, plus one in Latin America and the Caribbean.

the average number of births per woman over her lifetime.[1] The movement of this rate has been as remarkable as population growth and life expectancy rates have been. On a worldwide basis, fertility was quite constant for the 200 years 1700–1900 at about 6 children, decreased modestly between 1900 and 1950, and then plunged from 5.0 to 2.7 in the second half of the twentieth century (see figure 1.7).

Figure 1.9 contains estimates and projections for fertility over the period 1950–2100 for the world and for three major subgroups. Although starting from very different bases, the United Nations projects a convergence by the end of this century close to the standard replacement rate, 2.1 children per woman. These aggregates conceal considerable variation among countries. For example in 2005–2010 some 75 countries with 45 percent of global population had fertility rates below replacement level. By mid-century this is projected to almost double to 132 countries and 77 percent of the world population. Fertility rates remain one of the great unknowns when contemplating long-term trends and the common assumption of convergence to replacement levels is convenient but hardly assured.

An Aging World

Increasing life expectancy and decreasing birth rates inevitably lead to an older population.[2] We are older today than ever before in human history and by conventional measures will continue to age at an accelerating pace. To date the world as a whole has aged noticeably but not radically, as some countries still have relatively high birth rates. This is changing in a dramatic fashion as shown in figure 1.10. The percentage of the world's population who are over 60 is projected to double from 11 to 22 percent in the next 38 years. This rapid change in age is unprecedented in human history. Europe, already the front runner, will continue to lead with more than one-third its population 60+. North America is spared the most rapid gain in part because of projected immigration but still winds up much older than today. Perhaps

1. The alternative to TFR is the cohort fertility rate (CFR) which follows an age-based cohort, say those born in 1970, through their reproductive years. The CFR indicates fertility trends only after a long lag (i.e., after the cohort has completed its reproductive years), and, although more stable, is not as useful in spotting recent trends. For more details, see chapter 6.
2. Aging is a tricky concept. The conventional view is that it can be measured by percent of population over age 60 or 65, or by increases in median age. An alternative view is that aging can be measured by the imminence of death, in which case rising life expectancy is relevant, and it is no longer clear that world population will dramatically age this century. See chapter 8.

the most remarkable implication is that developing countries will be almost as much caught up in aging as the developed economies. Asia, dominated by India and China, shows the largest percentage gain, with almost a quarter of its population over 60. Latin America will be almost as old as the United States. Even Africa, where population growth remains high, will experience an increase from 6 to 10 percent of those 60+. Figure 1.11 shows a dramatic inversion of the ratio of children to the elderly.

The data for the "super old" are equally compelling. A larger share of those over 60 will be 80 or more. For the world as a whole that share climbs from 14 to 20 percent. In the more developed countries the share of those aged 80 and older in the 60+ population will rise from 20 to 29 percent. The centenarians are on the march!

All this may be on the alarmist side. As discussed in note 4 and again in chapter 8, there is a strong argument that conventional measures of aging are flawed and "aging" projections are exaggerated.

The Key Economic Statistic

These figures illustrate core transitions that have taken place in the nineteenth and twentieth centuries and the further changes ahead in the

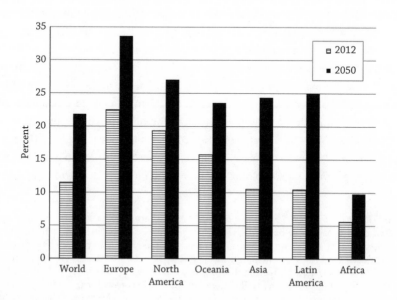

Figure 1.10:
Aging by region, as percent of population over 60, 2012 and 2050
Source: United Nations 2012a.

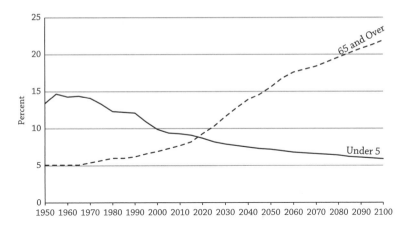

Figure 1.11:
Percent of population under 5 and over 65
Source: United Nations 2012b.

twenty-first—the demographic bones of the story. But that story is set within an equally dramatic economic transformation. During the 180 years when world population was increasing sixfold, world income and output increased by 52 times! This means that world per capita income increased almost ninefold, from an estimated $666 in 1820 to $5,800 in 2000. See figure 1.12.

Per capita income growth is the key *economic* statistic in the story. For two centuries population grew at unprecedented rates, but world output and income far surpassed those rates. This amounts to a burial service for Malthusian theory, in which food scarcity would check population and hold economic welfare at subsistence levels. While per capita income admittedly is an imperfect measure of welfare and living standards, especially as it neglects the distribution of that income, it *is* a measure of growth and economic vitality. This raises a number of crucial questions. What have been the interactions between population and economic growth? Are they complements? Does growth in one stimulate growth in the other? Or would per capita income growth have accelerated further if there had been fewer people? More important, what will be the implications for economic growth as population slows and starts to decline? Are the good times over? Do we face a long-term economic crisis? If the population surge in the past two centuries failed to crush economic growth, will population decline and accelerated aging manage to do so? Or, more optimistically, is stabilization and prospective decline of world population

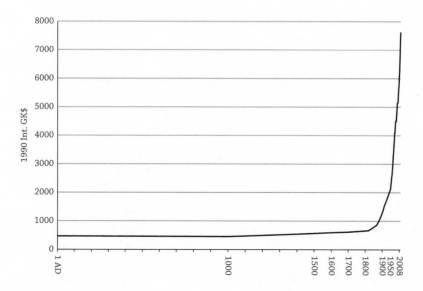

Figure 1.12:
World per capita income growth, A.D. 1–2008
Source: Maddison 2010.
Note: 1990 International Geary-Khamis dollars are a hypothetical unit of currency that has the same purchasing power as the U.S. dollar had in the United States in 1990.

an opportunity to simultaneously lay the ghost of Malthus, scotch an impending environmental crunch, and enjoy a bit more elbow room?

A ROADMAP

This book traces concern for population from uncontrolled growth to depopulation and aging. The upswing carries us through chapter 4. We pause in chapters 5 and 6 to consider the concepts of optimal population and demographic transition, and then continue by examining the prospective population downswing in the following four chapters. Chapter 11 presents concluding thoughts.

Chapter 2 starts in the late eighteenth century with Thomas Robert Malthus, the most influential of economic demographers through to the present day. To his credit Malthus's theory remains a plausible explanation of population dynamics in the centuries leading up to the publication of his essay in 1798. His "model" rested on two fundamental propositions: in the absence of checks, unbridled sexual passion would lead to rapidly increasing population; and population growth would exceed the capacity to expand food production. The truly depressing conclusion was that the vast majority of the population would be trapped close to poverty at a subsistence standard of living. Both of these propositions have proved to be spectacularly wrong over the past 250 years. The interesting question is why his dark views have continued to exert such visceral influence up to the present day. Chapter 3 addresses this question and concludes that the post–World War II concern for economic development in poor countries, together with an unanticipated acceleration of global population growth, revived flagging interest in Malthusian theory. This revival received major support as energy and environmental limits were added to food as constraints on population and economic growth.

Chapter 4 maps the shifting views of how population and economic growth interact. The thought is that if we understood how population growth and economic well-being interacted, we would be better prepared to assess the forthcoming economic effects of population stagnation and decline. Unfortunately, there has been little consensus in the past. Adam Smith saw a positive relation between the two, each supporting the other. Most classical economists foresaw a long-run stationary economy with population following a Malthusian path. Later, in the nineteenth century, growth itself was less studied as the discipline of economics shifted its attention to optimization, marginalism, and equilibrium analysis. Concern for the Malthusian devil, a term later used by Keynes, waned during the last decades of that century as the Malthusian propositions were being demolished by accumulating evidence of declining fertility and increasing productivity of agriculture. A geopolitical concern for depopulation took root, especially in France. By the 1930s, in the throes of the Great Depression, the threat of declining population became the issue in many industrial countries and was identified by Keynes and others as a cause of chronic unemployment. The post–World War II era was a jumble of views. Some held that runaway population was retarding economic growth in recently decolonized developing countries, but this concern faded by the end of the century as fertility plunged worldwide. Robert Solow developed his highly influential neoclassical economic growth model, but it had no essential explanation of or role for population. The new growth theories of the last decades of the twentieth century tend to reestablish a positive role for population via induced investment and technological change but the empirical basis remains weak.

The middle chapters, 5 and 6, examine two important economic-demography concepts: optimal population and the demographic transition. Optimal population is an attractive notion and implies that an active population policy may be desirable. But it turns out to be an elusive term.

It does serve, however, to introduce us to complicated ethical issues such as the Repugnant Conclusion and the Conclusive Conclusion; to the concept of ecological carrying capacity, widely used in the environmental literature; and to the idea of reproduction externalities. The last provides an economic rationale for a government population policy, but little clarity as to the direction it should take.

The demographic transition is the big news in economic demography and has major policy implications. Chapter 6 provides a quick sketch of its main features, reviews theoretical explanations for its most prominent features, declining fertility and increasing longevity, and discusses the recently discovered existence of a demographic bonus. The demographic transition has run at different speeds in different countries, but has nowhere run its full course and trend exceptions are explored. The end point for world population—projected to stabilize at somewhere between 2 billion and 36 billion in 2300—is a measure of our ignorance.

The following four chapters, 7 to 10, work within the current consensus on global population trends: deceleration and ultimately depopulation over the next century; further declines in fertility rates globally and sub-replacement rates in most countries; increases in life expectancy; and rapid and substantial aging in developed and most developing countries. Accepting this consensus may be rash. Population trends can reverse sharply and unexpectedly. The postwar baby boom and remarkably rapid declines in fertility in many developing countries demonstrate this. Chronic health challenges and modern lifestyle choices may reverse life expectancy trends in some countries. Think also of Malthus looking back when he should have been looking forward. Rash or not, these trends provide a typical framework for analysis.

Chapter 7 starts on a positive note, looking for the upside of population decline. It finds that note in the easing of pressures on natural and environmental resources—Malthus's old lament about land and food supplies and the more modern concern about global warming. But it quickly points out that rising income and consumption may swamp the beneficial effects of population stabilization and decline. It also points out negative interactions between food supplies and climate change.

Chapter 8 turns to the downside of population decline. The prospect of stagnant or declining economic growth (output per capita) underlies the more specific challenges. Accelerating aging is identified as the usual suspect, with loss of scale economies playing a very minor role. The negative economic growth impact is decomposed into two components: the shrinking size of the workforce and possible declines in our productivity as we age. The prospects brighten however with the discovery of a second demographic dividend (bonus) and with a novel approach to measuring aging.

Chapter 9 approaches the demographic transition and aging from the perspective of intergenerational transfers. These flow down from working generations to the young for education, health, and subsistence expenses through both public and private (intra-family) channels. The transfers also flow upward to the elderly for consumption and health expenses, again through public and private channels. Rapid aging can put severe strains on the inter-temporal and intergenerational "bargain" underlying these transfers. Fiscal strains on public pension schemes are examined. Health costs associated with aging are a second source of fiscal stress and the concept of healthy aging is introduced.

Chapter 10 evaluates a number of coping strategies for an older and more sparsely populated world. They include boosting fertility, increasing worker participation and productivity, reforming pension schemes, immigration, and a "de-growth" alternative.

The final chapter concludes that the threat of population aging and decline is serious but easily exaggerated. If managed wisely we can drop both the gloomy Malthusians and the equally gloomy depopulation pessimists as our guides, and (cautiously) follow Dr. Pangloss into a bright new and perhaps less crowded future.

CHAPTER 2

✃

The Long and Baleful Shadow
of Thomas Robert Malthus

The Malthusian forecast itself was wrong. Not just slightly off, but magnificently wrong.
—Goren Ohlin (1992)

Ideas matter. We learn from Adam Smith of the invisible hand and the magic of the market. We learn from David Ricardo of comparative advantage and the benefits of free trade. And we learn from Karl Marx about the economic class foundations of social structures and conflict.

What do we learn from Malthus? On one level, we learn very little. Malthus's fundamental thesis—that population growth is constrained by the availability of food, that this constraint produces vice and misery for the lower classes in the form of epidemics and famines, and that as a consequence there is little hope for sustained improvement in human well-being—has been refuted by events over the past 215 years. Contrary to his theory, world population has increased sevenfold from 1800 to 2010, food production has increased still faster, and life expectancy, perhaps the best single indicator of well-being, has increased by 40 years, from 27 in 1800 to about 68 today. What is remarkable is not the astuteness and accuracy of his thesis but that, despite a long period of eclipse, its influence today on population thought remains considerable. What we learn from Malthus is that, valid or not, ideas matter, and if convincingly expressed, can be surprisingly durable. And we also learn that in revolutionary times, as his were, good hindsight does not always make good foresight. The future did not turn out to be like the past.

Malthus (1766–1834) studied mathematics at Cambridge and subsequently was an Anglican cleric and professor of political economy. His most famous work, *Essay on the Principle of Population*, was published in 1798, with the sixth edition appearing 1826. It was initially presented as a response to the writings of the radical William Godwin and others on the perfectibility of society. It has remained controversial to this day.

This chapter and the next attempt to explain the attraction and staying power of Malthusian ideas. We first present a concise statement and critique of his views—the core of his thesis—followed by a sampling of nineteenth-century reactions. We then trace a series of developments from the mid-nineteenth to the mid-twentieth century that brought the Malthusian problem into eclipse—less refuted than bypassed. That brings us in chapter 3 to the post–World War II period, and the transformation and rehabilitation of Malthusian thought, or Malthus redux. We conclude by asking whether the prospective peaking and decline of world population over the next century will finally lay the ghost of Malthus to rest.

MALTHUS'S BIG IDEA

The Model

Malthus starts by observing that all animals, including humans, have the capacity to increase their numbers over time geometrically (i.e., exponentially).Thus, if the growth rate is 2.8 percent per year and the starting point is 1 billion, population would double to about 2 billion in 25 years and double again to 4 billion in the next 25 years. Malthus considers a doubling in 25 years to be a reasonable upper bound to the *capacity* (fecundity) for population growth *if left unchecked*.[1] His source for the doubling rate appears to be the United States, whose experience at that time he believed approximated an unchecked growth state. Note that, had a growth rate of 2.8 percent per year been maintained from 1810, when Malthus was still writing, to 2010, world population would have increased from 1 billion to 250 billion. In fact it reaches (only!) 7 billion in 2011, for an annual growth rate of 0.98 percent.

---

1. 2.8 percent is not outlandish. World population between 1965 and 1970 was growing by 2.07 percent per year, implying a doubling within 34 years had it continued. But as explained subsequently this was an artifact of the demographic transition and could not and was not sustained. Malthus (VI.5) attributes an astonishing 15-year doubling time and a 4.7 percent per year growth rate to population in the rural, backwoods sections of the United States. Unless otherwise noted all direct quotes from Malthus are from the first edition of his *Essay* (chapter, paragraph).

But Malthus goes beyond establishing a *capacity* to reproduce at exponential rates. He asserts that sex is so powerful a force that *unless checked*, population growth *will* rise to its exponential capacity. He knows by looking backwards from 1800 that European population had not doubled every 25 years, so he needs to identify a check—a reason why it had not, and indeed could not, rise to its reproductive capacity. He finds this reason in the incontrovertible postulate that man needs food to survive, and the *controvertible* assertion that because land is fixed food supply can only grow at an arithmetic rate—that is, linearly. Observe that he uses food and subsistence interchangeably. Clothing and shelter would not work as well because in his view there is no fixed supply of inputs to their manufacture, and exponential expansions of both are feasible. Malthus insists on a distinction between "food and wrought commodities, the raw materials of which are in great supply" and can be expanded to meet demand (V.18).[2]

With the two rates in hand, it is then easy work to show that even under the most favorable conditions exponential growth would outstrip arithmetic growth, food would become scarcer, and a check would be set on population growth. Although exponential growth is more powerful, the arithmetic rate trumps the exponential rate.[3] The shorter the doubling time the faster population overtakes food. These are the famous geometric (exponential) and arithmetic ratios that lent Malthus's theory an aura of scientific certainty.

It is worthwhile considering the two assertions in the argument thus far. Malthus attempts to nail down the first assertion, that the sex drive is continually pushing growth toward its capacity, by ruling out any diminution in sexual desire: "The passion between the sexes is necessary and will remain nearly at its present state." While this may or may not be true, it conflates copulation and reproduction, ruling out contraception. Malthus failed to see that we can eat the cake (sex) and still have the food. We return to this point later.

The second assertion—that food production cannot increase at more than an arithmetic rate—has been proven wrong over the past 215 years. Looking backwards from the perspective of 1800, it may have been a plausible conjecture, although it slights the eighteenth-century agricultural

2. Malthus acknowledges that with an unlimited supply of fertile land agricultural output could keep up with exponential population growth. When that supply is exhausted, however, output increases must come at an ever slower rate from improved cultivation, the familiar notion of diminishing marginal returns.

3. Starting from an index of 1 for both population and food, after a century population would stand at 16 and food at 4.

revolution in Europe. Should population dynamics reverse in the future and resume exponential growth, it may yet turn out to be correct. But for the past two centuries the Malthusian conclusion has been overturned— the growth of food production has *outstripped* the growth of world population. This has been a consequence of opening up new farmland, land-saving technological changes (e.g., fossil fuels replacing draft animal power, freeing up pasture land for food crops), irrigation, multiple and rotation cropping, artificial fertilizers, a host of technological improvements in plant and animal breeding, and so forth. What is perhaps more remarkable, the growth of food output has been accomplished while dramatically shedding labor from the agricultural sector.[4] In the United States, the share of the labor force in agriculture fell from 90 percent at the time of independence to about 3 percent at the start of this century (Johnson 1997).

The assumptions and conclusions of the Malthusian model are illustrated in figure 2.1. If we accept his two assertions, Malthus has a compelling argument. He acknowledges that improvement in the productivity of land is possible and states that through great encouragements to agriculture, output might be doubled in an initial 25-year period. Unchecked population would also double, leaving per capita food supplies unchanged. But in the following 25 years population would tend to double again to four times its initial level, while food would only increase by its initial amount to three times its starting level. Food per capita would be only 75 percent of its initial level in year 50, would fall to 50 percent of its initial level in year 75, and to 31 percent after a century. This is impossible. Somewhere in the second period the checks must be engaged, bringing down population growth to the sustained arithmetic rate of growth of food.

The empirical record confirms the error of his assertion regarding agricultural productivity. Figure 2.2 displays world population, food production, and per capita production trends from 1961 to 2011. This period includes both the peak population growth rate and the largest annual population increases. The conclusion is clear—food production outpaced population by a substantial margin.

The most distressing feature of the Malthusian framework is that the only long-term stable standard of living, measured by per capita food consumption, is at a subsistence level. Any temporary increase would trigger a surge in population and a subsequent fall in food per person. The remorseless workings of this system is not that starvation is inevitable, but that labor cannot aspire to sustained increases in standards of living

4. Total annual factor productivity growth in agriculture beat manufacturing 2.7 percent to 1.5 percent for OECD countries in the period 1960–1990 (Johnson 1997).

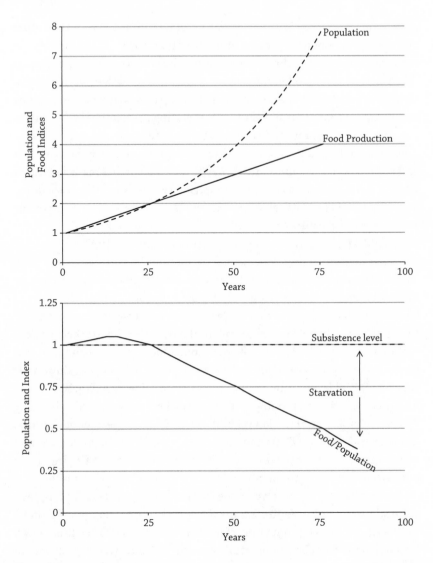

Figure 2.1:
Malthusian mistakes
Source: Author.

above subsistence levels. No wonder this has come to be known as the Dismal Theorem and economics dubbed the Dismal Science. The inevitability of the conclusion that income must always revert to subsistence level—the Iron Law of Wages—is disturbing, and in Malthus's initial framework at least, inescapable. Before we turn to the policy implications of this doleful conclusion, we need to consider the mechanisms underlying the model and especially the checks on population growth.

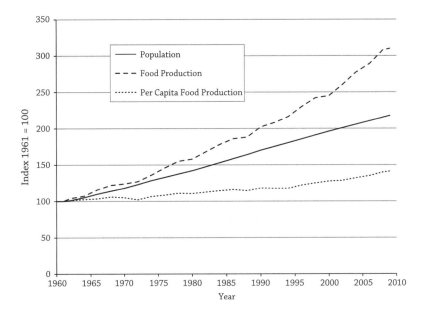

Figure 2.2:
World food production, 1961–2009
Source: Lam 2011, figure 4. With permission.

The Checks

Malthus argues that foresight and reason cause men to pause before yielding to the powerful urge to procreate. This is what he calls a preventative check. It is perhaps an unfortunate choice of words, as it excludes contraception, which is deemed a vice. The preventative check requires sexual restraint and is explained by Malthus as follows. At the highest social and economic ranks, some men (perhaps only a few) may recoil from the expenses they must retrench or the fancied pleasures they will deprive themselves of if they were to produce large families. We cannot expect many forgone births here. Going down the class ladder, the reasons for pause before procreation strengthen. An educated gentleman of limited income will consider whether a large family will lower his rank in life to the level of modest farmers and the lower classes of tradesmen, and, to his discomfort, place his wife, the object of his affections, two or three steps below her upbringing and anticipated station. Moving down another rung, a laborer may foresee that he will be obliged to work harder and perhaps still not be able to provide food for his family. Most poignantly for the poor, "may he not see his offspring in rags and misery, clamoring for bread he cannot give them?" (II.22) Note that for Malthus the responsibility for the well-being of children rests with the parents, not society. Note also that Malthus hints at an externality—that one family's decisions on children affect the well-being of other families—but he stops short of recommending coercive public measures to limit births.

These considerations act as a restraint, especially on early marriage. In turn this restraint on procreative sex "almost necessarily produces vice." Vice is a code word for Malthus. Although not explicit, he means all practices that inhibit or prevent live births: prostitution, venereal disease, homosexuality, onanism (masturbation), abortion, and all forms of birth control. Fornication outside of marriage fits in his thinking as a vice, but why it does not produce children is not clear. Perhaps the vice of abortion covers it.

We need not dwell on shifting views of "vice." It is sufficient to say that from our own perspective, 200 years later, certain Malthusian vices and especially birth control have gained widespread if not universal approval, while certain virtues, especially celibacy, have lost their luster. If Malthus had had a more "modern" conception of vice, his entire edifice would have been severely weakened. Specifically, with a more neutral view toward contraception, a little more vice and a little less virtue might have solved Malthus's dilemma, brought population into alignment with food, and avoided the inevitable distress arising from the second major check, the ill-named "positive" checks of disease, epidemics, famine, plague, and war.[5] But Malthus's model does not let vice have the upper hand. Instead, he insists, "Yet in all societies, even those that are most vicious [vice-ridden] the tendency toward a virtuous attachment [procreative sex] is so strong that there is a constant effort toward an increase in population" (II.23). A moral paradox in the making—more vice would bring less misery!

Malthus names the second check the "positive check," although it is difficult to see much positive in it, as it consists of increasing mortality and creating misery. The agents are disease, pestilence, famine, war, and the like, all presumably linked to scarcity of food. His language is flamboyant:

> The vices of mankind are able and active ministers of depopulation. They are the precursors of the army of destruction; and often finish the dreadful work themselves. But should they fail in this war of extermination, sickly seasons, epidemics, pestilence and plague advance in terrific array and sweep off their thousands and ten thousands. Should success still be incomplete, gigantic, inevitable famine stalks in the rear, and with one mighty blow, levels the population with the food of the world. (VII.20. Also cited by Dorfman 1989, p. 155)

---

5. Malthus opposed contraception as immoral and believed it would lead to underpopulation and indolence (Langer 1975).

There is little in the way of specifics, although he does say this check is chiefly confined to the lowest orders of society and especially children. Both urban and rural households are affected, but perhaps those in towns more severely.[6]

To be fair, in the second edition of his *Essay* (1803), Malthus attempts to soften the harsh conclusions of the theory by adding an additional element to the preventative check of delayed marriage—moral restraint.[7] This is not quite the prudential restraint of the first check and appears to be restraint from marriage that is *not* followed by "irregular gratifications"; that is by vice. It is a call for prolonged celibacy (a virtue) before a delayed marriage, which might be termed abstinence plus. In doing so, he accepts the critique that sexuality can be controlled by discipline and reason, and concludes that with sufficient restraint there may be some prospect for gradual improvement for the masses. This offers a bit of hope: "On the whole, therefore, though our future prospects respecting the mitigation of the evils arising from the principle of population may not be as bright as we would wish, yet they are far from being entirely disheartening, and by no means preclude the gradual and progressive improvement in human society" (2d ed., cited by Smil 1994, p. 283).

Nevertheless, Malthus has a low opinion of the poor's ability to exercise this moral restraint and continues to bet on vice and misery as essential to controlling population growth. The headnote to chapter 5 of the first edition remains operative: "All the checks to population [for the lower classes] may be resolved into misery and vice."

To complete the model, an increase in population brings distress and misery to the poor. The mechanism is excess supply of labor pushing down wages and a growing shortage of food pushing up prices. The adjustment comes when falling wages discourage marriages and reduce births. Also, cheap labor means more intensive use in agriculture, boosting output and relieving distress. When delayed marriage fails, the second check is engaged. Thus, population and food are brought into alignment at a subsistence level allowing the cycle to start once again. These oscillations are not short and sharp, but occur quite slowly. Malthus argues that their long

6. Malthus apparently believed that "in the modern countries of Europe" the preventative check of delayed marriage would generally dominate the positive check of famine, but the positive check would dominate in the East, especially China. Recent research has challenged this description of population control in China (Lee and Feng 1999).

7. In *Principles of Political Economy*, published in 1820, Malthus backtracked further, acknowledging that real income gains might lead to choosing improved living standards, not more children. For a generally sympathetic reading of Malthus, see Collard (2001).

period and their concentration in the lower classes, whose history has been largely ignored, make them difficult to detect.

Recent empirical research helps confirm Malthus's theory as it applies to the 250 years prior to the publication of his essay. It finds the long-term oscillations in England's population that Malthus wrote of. More important, in this more distant period food prices, an indicator of scarcity, tracked population growth, surging in periods of strong growth and stable or falling when growth halted (Schofield 1983). But the research also shows that relation collapsed in the first decades of the nineteenth century. Population boomed but food prices did not. As Schofield (1983, p. 271) comments, "By an ironic coincidence Malthus had given expression to an issue that had haunted most pre-industrial societies at almost the last moment when it could still plausibly be represented as relevant to the country in which he was born."

Malthus looked backwards when he should have looked forward.

Policy Implications

Immediately after identifying the positive check, Malthus launches into a spirited attack on England's poor laws.[8] His arguments have an ironically modern ring to them. And from the distance of the twenty-first century, they also display surprisingly little Christian charity. According to Malthus, poor laws governing relief for the destitute are calculated to eradicate a spirit of independence among the peasantry, and "hard as it may appear in individual instances, dependent poverty ought to be held as disgraceful" (V.13). The language gets rougher. "The quantity of provisions consumed in workhouses upon a part of society that cannot in general be considered as the most valuable part diminishes the shares that would otherwise belong to more industrious and worthy members" (V.11). After explaining that a fixed amount of food spread over a larger population means less for all, he concludes that "a laborer who marries without being able to support a family may, in some respects, be considered an enemy to all his fellow-laborers" (V.13). Poverty is not only shameful but it harms the worthy. Compare this to Gerald Hardin writing on population 170 years later in his great work, *The Tragedy of the Commons*: "Freedom to breed will bring ruin to all" (Hardin 1968 p. 1248).

---

8. The English poor laws were a compulsory, decentralized, parish-based system of poor relief initiated during the reign of Elizabeth I (1533–1603), administered by overseers, and financed by a property tax. Lindert (1998) estimates expenditures exploded from 1 percent of GDP in 1750 to 2.7 percent in 1818.

Malthus's complaints directed at the poor laws continued. One complaint makes considerable sense. A parish-based welfare system, as was then in effect, restricts the mobility of workers, and this is detrimental to all: labor, capital, and landowners. Other complaints may or may not contain kernels of truth but certainly sound familiar. Parish relief given to the poor saps their willingness to work. For those that do work, it saps their will to save and fattens the profits of the alehouses. The institutions for distributing relief are conducive to petty tyranny. Most important for Malthus, the poor laws then operating removed an inhibition on early marriages, resulting in population pressing on fixed food supplies and thus contributing to ongoing misery of the lower classes.

Malthus proposes a mix of remedies and palliatives. They include abolishment of then-current parish poor laws to free up mobility in the labor market; subsidies and trade protection for agriculture over manufacturing and for the more labor-intensive tillage over grazing, to maintain the demand for agricultural labor; and a crackdown on restrictive practices by corporations and apprentice systems that work to the disadvantage of agricultural wages. For cases of extreme distress he advocates the construction of county workhouses where the able bodied are obliged to work at hard fare. Other cases of extreme distress would be remanded to the benevolence of individuals. In the event, real reforms were delayed until sweeping changes were made in the Poor Law Reform Act of 1834. From an economic standpoint his policies are a mixed bag. Some might improve efficiency, others not. He did not propose an active and direct state role in population control. If there was to be family planning, it would be done at the family level, not the state.

Now we have come near the end of our explication of the Malthusian thesis.[9] It only remains to see how he, an Anglican clergyman, attempts to reconcile his dreary and dark-hued view of the inevitable suffering of the lower classes with the purpose and plan of the Creator. He does so in the final two chapters of his essay. The penultimate chapter asserts that "want" is a stimulant and keeps humanity from falling into a fatal torpor: "Had population and food increased in the same proportion it is probable man might never have emerged from the savage state" and even as the laws of population occasion partial evil, they tend to promote the general purpose of Providence. The final chapter completes his explanation by

---

9. The first edition of Malthus's *Essay* is only a sliver of his total writings, which include substantial revisions in later editions and his major work, *Principles of Political Economy* (2d ed. 1896). In the larger corpus, one can trace a more sophisticated theory of population, in which effective demand for labor and industrialization play a more central role. See Spengler 1945.

finding virtue in suffering: "The sorrows and distresses of life . . . seem to be necessary . . . to soften and humanize the heart, to awaken social sympathy, to generate all the Christian virtues, and to offer scope for the ample exertion of benevolence . . . the heart that has never known sorrow will seldom be alive to the pains and pleasures, the wants and wishes, of its fellow being."(XIX.1)

REACTIONS AND INFLUENCE

Malthus and his theory made a splash. His essay ran to six editions (1798 to 1826) in his lifetime and stirred up a debate that only dwindled in the latter decades of the nineteenth century. In general, it was given a warm welcome by supporters of the status quo, including the English landed gentry (to which his family belonged), as it relieved them of responsibility for the rural poor. His thesis on population was also taken up by the classical economists of the day—J. B. Say, David Ricardo, and John Stuart Mill in mid-century—and played a central role in the so-called "classical growth theory."

Ricardo

The personal and intellectual relationship with Ricardo was particularly intense. Ricardo relied on Malthus's population theory and its emphasis on pinning the real wage at or close to the subsistence level, later known as the Iron Law of Wages. He was less dogmatic, however, and granted that if sufficient investment were available wages could be sustained indefinitely above this level. But he was not optimistic. He adapted Malthus's concern for growing scarcity of food as an agent for stagnation. Malthus had argued that with limited agricultural land, population pressures would drive up food prices, drive down the real wage, and ultimately create the miseries of the positive check explained above. Ricardo added to this argument by noting that as population rises, cultivation is extended to progressively poorer soils. While rents on those lands are negligible, rents on existing fertile lands rise. This formalized the concept of diminishing marginal returns to land on the intensive and extensive margin. With wages held close to the subsistence level, an increase in the share of income going to landowners in the form of rent means a decline in the rate of profit, not only in agriculture but generally. Falling profits meant lower investment, less innovation, and slower productivity growth, laying the basis for a long-run equilibrium consisting of a stagnation of income to the three factors of production: land, labor, and capital. This is the core of the classical growth (stationary) model, and Malthus's assumptions of population growth continually pressing on fixed land lie at its heart.[10] Notice the absence of technical change as a driving agent for growth.

Limited returns in agriculture were a key for both economists. But they took opposing sides with respect to removing restrictions on imported grains, the Corn Laws.[11] Malthus, looking back on an agricultural past, concerned with maintaining the prosperity of landowners, and conscious of the plight of agricultural labor, supported tight restrictions on the importation of grain. He distrusted a shift from an agrarian to a commercial and industrial structure in part because rural poverty appeared less onerous than urban poverty, and in part because he feared that reliance on imported food and exported manufactures would eventually shift the terms of trade against England and contribute to its impoverishment. (Ironically a century later the influential if misguided Argentine economist Raul Prebisch used data on England's *improving* terms of trade in the latter part of the nineteenth century to argue that the terms of trade of natural resource exporting developing countries were deteriorating, and for them industrialization via import substitution was the solution). Ricardo, looking forward to a commercial and industrial future, advocated a free trade regime in which English manufactures would exchange for food and raw materials from abroad, an idea dismissed by Malthus as not suitable for England's circumstances. (Gilbert 1980). Ricardo argued that access to foreign food would hold down labor costs and facilitate the shift in labor from agriculture to industry. But his argument was resisted and it was another 30 years before the trade-restricting Corn Laws were abolished.

A second difference between Malthus and Ricardo concerned the possibility of insufficient demand for goods to fully engage the productive capacity of an economy. This is the famous "glut" controversy resurrected by Keynes a century later. Briefly Ricardo argued that an overproduction of goods would at most be a transient problem as Say's Law concludes.[12] Malthus disagreed, holding that a class of unproductive consumers with spending power was needed to provide demand, a role the English landed gentry were admirably well-equipped to perform (Dorfman 1989). Abolishing the Corn Laws would impoverish landowners and exacerbate the

---

10. See chapter 4, figure 4.1, for Samuelson's clear exposition of the classical model.
11. Enacted 1815 and repealed 1846.
12. Crudely stated, supply creates its own demand.

glut. Keynes, of course, found Malthus's position on the possibility of sustained insufficient demand more congenial and grumbled that if Ricardo had lost that debate the course of economic thought over the following century would have brightened: "The almost total obliteration of Malthus's line of approach and the complete domination of Ricardo's for a period of one hundred years has been a disaster for the progress of economics" (Keynes cited by Corry 1959, p. 718).

Darwin and Marx

Malthus was also famously influential outside the realm of political economy. In his autobiography, the biologist Charles Darwin gives credit to Malthus for sparking the concept of natural selection and survival of the fittest, the motive force in evolution:

> In 1828 . . . I happened to read for amusement Malthus on *Population*, and being well prepared to appreciate the struggle for existence that everywhere goes on from long-continued observations of the habits of animals and plants, it at once struck me that under these circumstances favorable variations would tend to be preserved, and unfavorable ones to be destroyed. The result of this would be the formation of a new species. (Cited by Seidl and Tisdell 1999, p. 398. Note the *'for amusement'* —strange fellow, Darwin)

Other reactions to Malthus's essay were considerably more hostile. It was vilified or refuted by many religious writers and by the utopians who correctly saw it as an attack on the ideas of progress and the perfectibility of man.[13] Marx considered Malthus an apologist for the status quo and offered an alternative theoretical construct employing the concepts of surplus value and a reserve army of labor. The latter originated from the operations of a capitalist system, not any uncontrolled urge to breed. Malthus had allowed for exploitation of labor but rejected it as an essential feature of his population model. Capitalists and farmers can grow rich from the cheapness of labor, and combinations among the rich and unjust conspiracies may delay the eventual restoration of wages in periods of distress. But Malthus is adamant in saying that a great part of mankind will exist in an almost constant state of misery in both a state of distributional

---

13. The intellectuals of the day, poets and men of letters, were also critical (Petersen 1979).

equality or inequality. Specifically, income equality or common ownership of property would offset moral restraint, reestablishing the miseries of the positive checks.

French Thought

In two long and heavily documented articles written in the 1930s, Joseph Spengler, the then dean of US economic demographers, assessed reaction to Malthus in French intellectual thought. The analysis is especially relevant because Malthus's essay had been written as a challenge to the English political philosopher William Godwin and the French philosopher and mathematician Nicolas Condorcet, both of whom were much taken by the perfectibility of man and society and who were deeply influenced by the Enlightenment and the ideals of the French Revolution.

One reaction was to accept Malthus's idea of population pressing on food supplies but to argue that with intelligence, foresight, and restraint the preventative check would dominate, with little need for vice, and even less need for the draconian positive checks. Education, prudence, and delayed marriage could free labor from misery and poverty. Others used Malthus to argue against collectivism as that would frustrate natural selection and have a dysgenic effect. French Catholic thought was mixed. Some condemned Malthus's theory as un-Christian, or promoting immoral behavior. Others found in Malthus a defense of the Catholic principles of morality, abstinence, and celibacy. Still others simply denied any problem and contended that Providence would see that all were fed.

One of the more radical views came from the utopian socialist philosopher, Charles Fourier. He argued that in a utopian society checks to fecundity and fertility would naturally become increasingly effective. Women would become more robust, with "their excess vigor rendering them more apt for pleasure, but much less for conception." Furthermore, the refinement of food (the "gastroscopic regime") would make "gluttony . . . the source of wisdom, intelligence and social accord" and reduce natural fecundity (Spengler 1936, p. 749). Perhaps the ultimate dismissal of Malthus was made by the French political economist Pierre Leroux who, in Spengler's words, asserted that "population growth could not cause poverty, since every man is a producer, who destroyed nothing and returned to the earth as a fertility-increasing fertilizer whatever he consumed" (Spengler 1936, p. 751). The night soil rebuttal!

MALTHUS ECLIPSED

Crumbling Empirical Support

In the second half of the nineteenth century, Malthus's population theory faded. It was not so much replaced as dropped from view. There are several reasons. The principal one is that the two main supporting pillars of the theory failed to materialize in England, the country to which Malthus had tailored his essay. First, despite substantial increases in population, real wages rose in a sustained fashion, lifting living standards for most workers well above subsistence levels. The population of England and Wales increased from under 8 million in 1801 to 32.5 million in 1901 for an annual growth rate of 2.2 percent. The most rapid increases were in the first third of that century. Contrary to Malthusian theory, this did not fix real wages and living standards at a subsistence level. From 1750 to 1813 real wage growth for the working classes had been essentially zero, but grew by 1.2 percent per year from 1813 to 1913 just before World War I. This represents more than a tripling of real wages over the 100 year period (Crafts and Mills 1994). Much of this gain can be attributed to repeal of the trade-restricting Corn Laws in 1846. According to one study (O'Rourke 1997, wheat prices would have been about 20 percent higher in mid-century and up to 90 percent higher in 1880–1913 had the Corn Laws not been repealed. He attributes up to one-half of the real wage gains in the late nineteenth century to cheap food enabled by falling transportation costs and international trade. As a result, living standards and population had been decoupled from land, undermining a fundamental Malthusian tenet.

The second tenet to fall was that sexual passions were such as to push reproduction rates to their maximum if adequate sustenance were available. Wrigley and Schofield (1981, p. 438), in their exhaustive examination of English population history, summarize the radical behavioral shifts that took place in the last decades of the nineteenth century:

> Neither improving standards of living nor the possibility of limiting fertility within marriage persuaded late-Victorian men and women to embark on marriage younger or more generally. They turned away from the marriage patterns of earlier generations, throttling back fertility by changes in behavior which all tended to produce the same effect—later marriage, a rising proportion never marrying, fertility control within marriage, even a fall in illegitimate fertility, and all this in a period when real incomes were rising steadily in secular trend. The whole represents a clear break with the nuptiality and fertility

patterns of earlier centuries, a demographic revolution to match the economic revolution three quarters of a century earlier.

In short, fertility defied prediction. The Malthusian trap had been sprung in England.

The trap was never properly set in France. For the 300-year period 1400–1700 French population had virtually no net increase (10 percent). Starting in 1700, it took 200 years for the population to double, and in the following 45 years, 1901–1946, it actually fell by 0.4 percent. One might argue that this is simply the Malthusian checks at work, but it seems implausible that over this 550-year period the scarcity of land allowed a mere doubling of population, from 20.2 million to 40.5 million. Rather it was France's head start on declining fertility at work.

Depopulation Fears

In the latter part of the nineteenth century, *depopulation* was perceived as the problem. In 1897 Dr. Jacques Bertillon, Director of the Paris Statistical Bureau, after noting several recent years in which births fell short of deaths, said, "It grieves me to say it, but I see firm proof of the imminent disappearance of our country."[14] Although death rates were falling, the concern for depopulation was fueled by rapidly declining birth rates. That decline started in the late eighteenth century, some 100 years before it was seen in England and elsewhere in Europe. Marital fertility dropped from an index between 0.8 and 0.9 in mid-eighteenth century to about 0.3 at the end of the nineteenth century (Cummins 2009).[15] Explanations for this radical break are inconclusive, but once again actual fertility departs from Malthusian logic.

Concern for a stationary or declining population was not limited to France and preceded the Keynesian unease about population stagnation and insufficient aggregate demand (discussed later). Writing in 1929, the British economist, Lionel Robbins predicted the early arrival of a stationary

14. Quoted by Tomlinson (1985, p. 405). Writing a century ago, the American economist Walter Weyl (1912, p. 343) stated: "In this year, 1912, less than eight hundred thousand living babies will be born to the forty millions of France. This is the problem of French depopulation in a nutshell. It is the most significant fact of French life."
15. The index measures actual fertility relative to an observed maximum (that of early twentieth-century Hutterites, a religious group who married early and prohibited contraception). A score of 0.3 implies fertility was only 30 percent of its potential.

population in Great Britain and anticipated many of the challenges we face today: flagging aggregate production; an aging population with possible declines in savings rates; and pension-related budget problems—"the money we spend on pensions is a dead weight on production" (1929, p. 76). In short, population trends were further undercutting Malthus's relevance.

While the gap between predictions and reality sharply reduced Malthus's influence, other factors also help explain the eclipse. Classical political economy, with its emphasis on theories of value, theories of growth and stagnation, and theories of how output and income were distributed in the form of rent, wages, and profits to the three factors of production (land, labor, and capital) gave way to the concerns of neoclassical economics. These included concepts of utility, marginalism, rational maximizing behavior, equilibrium, and the use of mathematics for research and expository purposes—the familiar components of microeconomic analysis. In effect, in its early years in the last decades of the nineteenth century, neoclassical economics paid little attention to issue of population and growth. The urgency of Malthus's message was lost in the general prosperity at the close of the century, and to a large extent neoclassical economics replaced political economy as the core of the discipline.

AN ABORTED REVIVAL

The period 1914–1945 saw two world wars and the Great Depression. The interwar period, 1918–1939, had mixed impact on Malthus's stature. His central thesis—population outstripping food and the consequent impoverishment of labor—had to compete with new population issues. These included the social movement based on eugenics (selective breeding to improve the species), which thrived in the 1920s, but was ultimately tarnished by its Nazi associations. Advocates of birth control were also active. In the United States, Margret Sanger founded Planned Parenthood and successfully fought for easing restrictions for contraceptives sale and use. Also in the United States, immigration reached a peak shortly before World War I but was throttled back with restrictive laws in mid-1920s. None of these policies were debated primarily in Malthusian terms of overpopulation, food, vice, and misery.

Despite this competition, Malthus did enjoy a temporary revival in the 1920s. One reason was the realization, made evident by the war, that England and much of Europe was "overpopulated" relative to its agricultural base, highly dependent on imported food, and thus vulnerable to higher international food prices, a point that had been made by Malthus. An increase in birth rates following the war was a second. But the revival was short-lived. The arrival of the Great Depression in the 1930s shifted attitudes once again and *depopulation* became the hovering specter.

The major economic figure of the era, John Maynard Keynes, illustrates this rapid shift of views. In his first great work, *The Economic Consequences of the Peace* (1919), he spoke of the "disruptive powers of excessive national fecundity" and highlights the Malthusian threat to Europe. Noting that prior to 1870 Europe was largely self-sufficient in food, he saw a turning point and an increasingly unstable situation around the turn of the century. Specifically, and contrary to Malthus, as population increased it became *easier* to secure food up to about 1900 as the terms of trade between agricultural imports from America and English manufactures exports moved in England's favor. Subsequently he detects an unwelcome reversal about 1900 as diminishing returns in agriculture set in—the Malthusian objection to free trade from a century earlier.[16] Keynes goes on to assert that in the golden but atypical era of 1870–1914, Malthus's melancholy message—the devil of population outstripping food—was lost: "For half a century all serious economical writing held that Devil in clear prospect. For the next half century he was chained up and out of sight. Now perhaps we have loosened him again" (Keynes, *Economic Consequences of the Peace*, as quoted by Petersen 1955 p. 229).

As circumstances changed, so did Keynes's perspective on population.[17] By 1937, when Keynes delivered a lecture to the Eugenics Society, he had recanted any immediate Malthusian population concerns. The title of the lecture—"Some Economic Consequences of a Declining Population"—said it all. His primary concerns were chronic unemployment and insufficient aggregate demand. (England's population growth rate was positive, but low and trending downward.) Keynes puts forward the argument that an increasing population is helpful and may be necessary to achieve full employment—with a declining population there is insufficient incentive for

16. The evidence for his terms of trade argument was later successfully challenged by Sir William Beveridge.

17. Even in his early career, Keynes was not an uncritical admirer of Malthus. In a manuscript written in 1913–14 but not published, he observes that a good deal of Malthus's essay should be discarded including the geometrical and arithmetic ratios, for which there was no justification; notes the muddied treatment of diminishing returns in agriculture; and also notes Malthus's flawed belief that an increase in economic well-being tends to bring about an increase in population. In the end Keynes simply concedes that at the core of Malthus are two pessimistic conclusions—to maintain the proper balance between population and food involves misery, and in most places material conditions would have been better if population had been less (Toye 1997).

investment to match full employment savings. Keynes utilized Malthus's theory of gluts (excess production), which he had championed while promoting his concern for overpopulation: "I only wish to warn you that the chaining up of one Devil [Malthusian population growth] may, if we are careless, only serve to loose another [unemployment] still fiercer and more intractable" (Keynes 1937, p. 523).

To summarize, Malthus rode high in the first half of the nineteenth century but faded in the second. The twentieth-century interwar period saw a concern for imminent depopulation that further displaced the Malthusian threat in Europe. But Europe is not the world. Although population issues outside the industrial countries had been given little attention, they were to revitalize Malthus in the post–World War II era.

CHAPTER 3

༒

Malthus Redux

As matters stand, the longer run prospect is definitely Malthusian, with man sitting on a demographic time bomb . . .
— Joseph Spengler, *1965 Presidential Address to the American Economic Association*
(Spengler 1966a)

Malthus took a beating in the century between 1850 and 1950, first from the failure of events to follow his theory during the heyday of the Industrial Revolution, and later from the depopulation threat that materialized in the Depression era. But the setback was not a knockout. After World War II and in the flush of the baby boom, Malthus's views made a comeback, albeit with significant modifications and redirection. Elements of Malthus's population theory remained a potent influence in postwar debates—the stacked race between food and population; population growth undercutting economic development and derailing higher incomes in poor countries; and natural and environmental resources (for Malthus, land) placing limits on economic growth. In short, the Malthusian doctrine was refashioned to address the population explosion in the South and as a prophet of limits to growth.[1]

This chapter recounts that comeback. It has two sections. The first explains how Malthus's analysis of early nineteenth-century European demographics

---

1. The terms "North" and "South" have come to denote industrial and developing countries.

was lifted up, tweaked, and put to a new task: understanding population issues in developing countries. The second section follows a related thread. It views Malthus as an early exemplar of the thesis that natural and environmental resources constrain economic growth, a proposition that has wide support today and one that helps reestablish his relevance for high-income, high-consumption countries.

MALTHUS AND DEVELOPMENT (MALTHUS TRANSPOSED TO THE SOUTH)

In the early post–World War II era, attention shifted to population issues in developing countries, the so-called South. Two underlying reasons were decolonization and the Cold War. Decolonization meant a large number of new states, many of which were only minimally equipped to deal with the basics of independence. To greater or lesser extent former colonial powers felt an obligation and/or saw an opportunity in assisting them. The United States joined them in part for humanitarian reasons, in part for long-term commercial and investment reasons, and in part to win allies or at least neutrality in the East–West conflict.

A Budding Crisis

At that time (1950–1955), the growth of population in developing countries (excluding China) was an extremely rapid 2.13 percent per year, sufficient for a doubling in 33 years.[2] This was considerably higher than the European growth rate of about 1.5 percent experienced a century earlier during its growth spurt. The population boom was mainly the result of rapid declines in the annual death rate, which had started to drop early in the century and fell from about 37 per thousand in 1937 to 24 per thousand in the 1950–1955 period. This was some four of five times faster than was experienced earlier in Europe. Birth rates were falling but remained relatively high at about 45 per thousand, ensuring rapid growth. While there was considerable variation by region, with growth highest in Latin America and lowest in Asia, it is fair to say the developing countries were in the early stages of the demographic transition (see chapter 6), a transition that turned out to be more compressed and dramatic than the

---

2. This and the following are data from a comprehensive survey by Allen Kelley (1988).

earlier one in Europe and North America. A key feature of the early transition stage is the age structure becoming younger, which sets up conditions for an upsurge in births one generation later and explains how population growth can accelerate even at later stages of the transition. One reason for the shifting age structure was that infant mortality rates were cut by an astonishing 56 percent in the 35-year period from 1950–1955 to 1985. The data show a relatively young population in the 1950–1955 period at 38 percent under age 15 (40 percent excluding China), and the population growth rate notching up from 2.13 percent in 1950–1955 to 2.25 in 1985–1990, despite a dramatic fall in the birth rate from 48 to 34 per thousand.

Thus, the North's interest in the successful development of both the newly independent countries of the South, and those in Latin America that had gained their independence somewhat earlier, coincided with what appeared to be the makings of a Malthusian crisis of historic proportions. Would sustained development be possible in those parts of the world where population was already doubling every 30 or 40 years? More dire, with the Malthusian devil loose for a second time, would the positive check of widespread famine be inevitable? The situation looked all the more critical as many countries did not have a tradition of the preventative check—delayed marriage—to bring about balance, and even Malthus had been skeptical about the powers of moral restraint.

Different Initial Conditions

This conjunction of interests and the unprecedented demographics was sufficient to breathe new life into Malthus's legacy. But in reality there were many important differences between conditions in Europe at the start of nineteenth century and in the Third World in the mid-twentieth century. First, despite the increased population, not all cultivatable land in all developing countries was under the plough. "Land" was not limited in acreage in most of Africa and Latin America, and indeed in some countries in Asia, for example, Thailand. One estimate was that only 50 percent of arable land was in use worldwide at mid-century (Kelley 1988). The limiting factor was not land per se but irrigation, transportation, the prevalence of debilitating diseases, land holding patterns (the latifundia in Latin America) and so forth. In other words, it was initial investment costs and institutional barriers, not Malthusian scarcity that prevailed. In cases where land was available to be developed, the bedrock assumption, Malthus's arithmetic ratio, loses force.

Second, changes in fundamental agricultural practices from land-intensive to more labor-intensive cultivation techniques were possible. One example was a shift from long fallow, slash and burn (swidden) agriculture to short fallow or annual and multiple cropping. The former is land intensive but may boast high labor productivity. The latter is land-saving but labor-using. When population pressures arise such a transformation may be rational as it leads to increasing rather than decreasing returns to land (Boserup 1976). By and large such a shift was not available in Europe at the time Malthus was writing.

Third, even though late marriages were not customary in most developing countries, pre-modern societies had evolved a number of other methods for controlling fertility and population. In Malthus's view, European countries made active use of the preventive check (delayed marriage); whereas, the positive check (famine and disease) was the principal control on runaway population in non-European societies. This was inaccurate. Lee and Feng (1999) have shown that in China, the major focus for Malthus, a combination of practices kept population growth to a snail's pace over millennia. These included: infanticide and especially female infanticide; delay or failure of males to marry due to shortage of brides and not necessarily due to "prudential" motives, as in the West; and relatively low marital fertility rates. Thus, the cultural and social bases from which the demographic transition was launched in the West and in the developing countries were quite dissimilar.

Fourth, Malthus saw the problem from a national standpoint and his analysis reflects this, especially his rejection of trading manufactures for food as a solution. By mid-twentieth century, international trade and transportation networks had revolutionized access to food supplies. Self-sufficiency was not the only option. Even more fundamentally, confronting the impending Malthusian challenge was considered an international problem requiring an international response.

Fifth, and perhaps most important, the very failure of Malthusian predictions concerning fertility and food supplies over the preceding century helped dissipate the pessimism and inevitability surrounding his analysis. The record showed clearly that even in developing countries food supplies could match and exceed population growth. Between 1960 and 1970 *per capita* food output increased 0.4 percent per year in developing countries and 0.8 percent in the world as a whole, with growth continuing in following decades (World Bank 1984). The second Malthusian pillar was also toppled in the South—copulation could be separated from reproduction, and sustained increases in living standards could be achieved. Rather than passive Malthusian acceptance, misery and vice could be averted by large-scale efforts at family planning, and by substantial efforts in agricultural research and development, infrastructure, outreach, and training.

Aspirations for economic development played a key role in all this. Not only was development a major objective of the international community and developing country governments but also it was recognized that population played a dual role in its attainment. The positive role was that economic development could be a powerful force for reducing fertility, a connection that Malthus got backwards. The negative role was that rapid population growth could thwart development efforts. Thus, there was room for a triple alliance: those who advocated rapid development (thought to entail industrialization), presuming that development itself was an effective contraceptive; those who advocated strong support for family planning, presuming that declining fertility was a prerequisite for rapid development; and those who advocated investments in transforming traditional agriculture, with an eye on staving off famine and malnutrition and improving the lives of the rural masses while industrialization took hold.

Although the ultimate objectives may have been broadly similar, the paths were not. Inevitably, disagreement on priority and funding arose between strategies and indeed between donor agencies and recipient governments. Differences also arose regarding the coercive element of family planning programs. In the late 1970s, China swallowed Malthus whole, decided that overpopulation was the cause of its poverty, and instituted strong collective control over family fertility decision-making. Whether it was necessary, in view of the sharply declining fertility rates elsewhere in Asia, remains an open question.

The important point for our narrative is that despite the substantial differences between Europe in 1800 and the South in 1950 there was little choice but to fall back on Malthus. However flawed the supporting evidence, it was the only demographic model around. Its main message was interpreted as avoiding population growth before it chewed up economic gains. The evidence from the North, that industrialization itself would play a powerful role in bringing about fertility decline, was not widely stressed.

The State of Development Theory

It is worthwhile to pause for a moment and consider the then commonly held view that rapid population growth could undo development efforts. As elaborated on in the next chapter, the principal channels were thought to be a dilution of capital and a dissipation of savings. Perhaps the most striking disparity between developed and developing countries at this time was the level of productive capital per person, generally thought of in terms of physical capital—transportation infrastructure, factories, machines, and so forth. It followed that rapid increase in capital available per worker and boosting its productivity were seen as the keys to growth. Increasing capital involves saving and investment. Savings were scarce and limited by low incomes. Rearing children diverted potential savings to current consumption and weakened capital formation. Moreover a large and growing population diluted whatever capital there was over a larger workforce, depressing per worker productivity. Lower productivity meant lower savings and investment. Controlling population growth appeared to be a powerful tool to break this vicious circle. This was not the Malthusian vicious circle of population pressures on food and diminishing marginal returns, but the implication for population growth policy was the same—less is more. This view was formalized in the famous Harrod-Domar growth model, originally a business cycle model but modified to investigate longer term growth; it is explained in the next chapter. Note that investment in *human* capital (i.e., education) played no positive role. Raising large families simply diverted family income from potential savings. The fact that children grow up to be workers and producers was mostly overlooked.

To summarize the conventional wisdom at this time, one could easily support family planning on the strict Malthusian grounds of averting malnutrition and famine,[3] but one could equally easily support it as conducive to rapid economic development. Not only was the Malthusian demographic model available but also there was general agreement among development experts that a strong investment performance fortified by robust family planning was needed to spur economic growth.

MALTHUS AS A PROPHET OF LIMITS TO GROWTH
The Concept of Limits

The postwar recognition of environmental limits to economic growth also helped revitalize Malthusian doctrine. One must be careful here. Malthus did not claim England was overpopulated. Rather, he argued that overpopulation would be automatically suppressed through the preventative

---

3. Spengler (1966b) wrote, "Unless the wings of the ['baby'] stork are clipped in the short Indian summer that lies ahead, at least one of the four horsemen, Hunger, will ride within the lifetime of our children."

and positive checks. Nor did he deny that aggregate economic growth (GDP in modern terms) could occur. Instead he argued that *per capita* income growth was not possible for the masses. The limit to population *and* income growth was the scarcity of land.

The literature on limits to growth is extensive. Indeed it has shown no limits itself. Malthus, whose thesis that population continually pressing on a finite resource, land, would bring about subsistence level incomes for most people, was an early contributor. Incorporated into the classical canon, the notion of limits became a pillar of the stationary economy. After a hiatus of a century, the idea of limits again flourished after World War II.[4] Population growth and increasing per capita consumption were thought to be the principal drivers. The limits notion was nourished by a growing environmentalism and concerns for sustainability. In this fashion, Malthusian ideas re-emerged in a way that was relevant for both rich and poor countries—the former because of their disproportionate consumption levels, and the latter because of their surging populations.

In this rediscovery of limits, land has become only one of many environmental and natural resource constraints. It is a crowded field: minerals, energy, fresh water, biological diversity, and various ecological constraints including carrying capacity have all contended for first place.[5] Nevertheless, thus far the curve of world income growth has not flattened. Recent data show world population grew by 1.1 percent in 2012 and world gross output grew by almost 4 percent per year from 2010 to 2012.

Nothing grows forever, and to say that global limits on economic growth have not yet been engaged is not to say they never will. Moreover our conventional measures of economic income and output are deeply flawed. To put it briefly, they fail to properly account for the depletion and degradation of natural and environmental resources and the associated dis-amenities. Depletion and degradation limit and diminish the capacity of the world's stock of productive capital—physical, human, and environmental—to produce income in the future. To reject out of hand natural resource and environmental limits to growth on the basis of conventional national income statistics would be a serious mistake. Still, even if flawed, economic growth is a goal for most of humanity. The decoupling of growth from environmental degradation remains an unresolved challenge.

---

4. Rapacious exploitation of resources such as timber and a desire to conserve nature's amenities did contribute to the Progressive Movement in the United States at the start of the twentieth century. The Dust Bowl of the 1930s highlighted the fragility of soils. But, in general, the issue was mismanagement, not resource limits.

5. Carrying capacity: the maximum population size of a species that an environment can sustain indefinitely. See chapter 5.

Energy Limits: The Case of Coal

Of all the proposed limits, energy ranks close to the top. An obvious reason is that it is central to a modern economy, as much as land is to an agricultural one. Another reason is that the past 200 years of economic growth has been mainly fueled by *stored, nonrenewable* energy in the form of fossil fuels, not by the renewable energy sources that had fueled the previous 2 million years of human existence. A proper depletion allowance for use of nonrenewable resources is needed to establish whether limits are or will be binding. (This is also true for renewable but potentially depletable resources such as soils, fisheries, and forests.) Finally energy and environmental degradation are obverse sides of the same coin, and to name one implies the other.

The British economist William Stanley Jevons wrote on the coal question half a century after Malthus and a century before the environmental challenges to growth that arose in the 1960s. His thesis makes an interesting bridge between the two. For Malthus land was a finite resource capable of renewable production of food. Growth of that production was possible through the application of capital and labor (e.g., fencing, drainage, liming) but subject to diminishing returns. Population growth was thus the destabilizing element. While Malthus exalted food as essential for human subsistence, Jevons exalted coal as essential to the British economy, calling his the Age of Coal, and stating "Coal in truth stands not beside but entirely above all other commodities" (Jevons 1866, chapter 1, paragraph 3).

Jevons analyzed a nonrenewable resource, subject to diminishing returns and increasing costs, as easily mined coal seams were played out. Increased extraction rates would only accelerate the problem. Industrial production, central to British economic growth and not population pressure per se, was seen as the driving force. Jevons was clear in his understanding of a difference between the food problem and the coal problem. He wrote: "A farm, however far pushed, will under proper cultivation continue to yield forever a constant crop. But in a mine there is no reproduction, and the produce once pushed to the utmost will soon begin to fail and sink to zero. So far then that our wealth and progress depend upon the superior command of coal we must not only stop—we must go back." The British standard of living could not be sustained.

Did Jevons predictions fare better than Malthus's? As regards the rising cost and price of coal he appears to be correct. Writing in 1941, Hans Singer calculated that the purchasing power of coal over all other goods, its real price, rose from an index of 100 in 1833/37 to 243 in

1933/37 (whereas the price of wheat fell from an index of 100 to an index of 62 over the same period). But Singer challenges two other predictions: that British standard of living would cease to rise and eventually decline; and that Britain would lose its economic supremacy. In a devastating analysis Singer demonstrates why King Coal lost its crown and became just another commodity. The reasons, which perhaps should have been predictable, were increasing efficiency in the use of coal in industry as its price rose, substitution by other fuels, notably petroleum, and a shift in the structure of production away from coal-intensive industries. Jevons appears to have been looking back to when the coal intensity of industrial output had been rising, instead of looking forward to when it might decline. Singer is stingy on evaluating the other predictions, that declining reserves of coal would cost Britain her economic supremacy. At most he acknowledges that there had been such a loss of since mid-Victorian days, but whether this was connected to dwindling supply of low cost coal is not established. To summarize, Jevons's contribution to the limits debate was not directly connected to population growth but instead spoke to the long-term management of a nonrenewable resource, an issue that, in the guise of oil, is of ongoing interest.

Coal, a nonrenewable resource subject to generally clear property rights, makes a convenient transition to modern concerns. Its deplorable pollution profile makes it a modern concern; its firm property rights attributes are similar to the property rights in land in Malthusian analysis. In the post–World War II period the environmental/resource limits argument rested in large part on the *degradation* of land and other *renewable* resources (forests, fisheries, pasture). This notion of degradation of productive capacity was absent in Malthus. (Ricardo went further and wrote of the "original and indestructible powers of the soil.") In the modern environmental limits perspective, population pressure may be the proximate cause of degradation but a more fundamental problem is free access to common property renewable resources—the tragedy of the commons explanation. This is a *property rights* failure and was definitely *not* an element in Malthus or Jevons, for whom property rights were complete and enforceable.

THE ENVIRONMENTAL ERA

It is useful at this point to say a few words about the intellectual atmosphere in the 1960s and the early 1970s that reinvigorated Malthusianism and applied it to contemporary issues. A series of remarkably influential books called attention to worldwide threats to the environment in rich and poor countries alike. These included Rachel Carson's *Silent Spring* (1962—chemical hazards to the environment, including notably DDT); Kenneth Boulding's *The Economics of the Coming Spaceship Earth* (1966—with finite world resources we must all hang together); Georgescu-Roegen's *The Entropy Law and the Economic Process* (1971—the impossibility of perpetual growth); Paul Ehrlich's *The Population Bomb* (1968—the title tells it all); Barry Commoner's *The Closing Circle* (1971—the geographic interconnectedness of economic and ecological systems); Donella and Dennis Meadows's *The Limits to Growth*, commissioned by the Club of Rome (1972—a gloomy computer-driven model of five variables headed for trouble: population, industrialization, pollution, food, resource depletion)[6]; E. F. Schumacher's *Small is Beautiful: Economics as if People Mattered* (1973—a plea to reorient toward "eco-development"); and Erik Eckholm's *Losing Ground: Environmental Stress and World Food Prospects* (1976—analyzing degradation of agricultural resources in developing countries). One way or another all were concerned with intergenerational equity and stewardship and all took a dim view of population growth.

At the same time, the United Nations became involved, launching the first of a series of major conferences on environmental issues. The 1972 Stockholm Conference on the Human Environment created the United Nations Environmental Programme, the first major UN agency to be located in a developing country (Kenya); and, in 1973, it hosted the third United Nations Conference on the Law of the Sea, which among other accomplishments created 200-mile exclusive economic zones for coastal states. And, of course, the background news for this flurry of activity concerning environment and natural resources was the massive oil price spikes and concurrent commodity price booms of the early 1970s. While many economists express skepticism about the most apocalyptic projections, there can be no doubt that the concept of limits to growth and a concern for sustainability flourished in these two decades, precisely the time when world population growth rates were close to their peak. Concern for population, concern for natural resources, and concern for a sustainable environment nourished one other.

The Malthusian doctrine of population pressure on limited land returned to relevance, but with a further ugly twist. A vicious circle composed of population, poverty, and environmental degradation was envisioned in developing countries, in which the fundamental resource

---

6. The aura of mathematical ratios in Malthus is echoed by the reverence for computer-based calculations in *Limits to Growth*.

base for food supplies was being degraded. Population growth in the context of poverty no longer meant simply more mouths to feed, but perhaps *less* food: shortened fallow periods, cultivation of steep hillsides leading to subsequent erosion, the burning of dung for fuel and not being used as fertilizer, salinization of soils by improper irrigation techniques, overfishing and destructive fishing practices (dynamite fishing!), overgrazing of pasture, and deforestation and desertification due to charcoal manufacture (the poor's fuel). All this went far beyond Malthus, who had implicitly relied on secure property rights to protect and promote the integrity of land. But it fitted neatly into a lengthy list of ecological catastrophes that dot history.

These pernicious effects were real but on a worldwide scale their impact on the population-food balance turned out to be limited. Excess food production in the West, the Green Revolution in Asia, and most importantly the dramatic decline in human fertility in developing countries managed to scotch a true Malthusian crisis.[7]

In the first decades of this century, climate change has emerged as a potential new limit to continuous population and economic growth. Agricultural accounts for 20–35 percent of all greenhouse gas emissions and its control will be expensive. At the same time a failure to control global warming could have catastrophic impacts on food supplies. An "atmospheric" limit may replace a Malthusian "land" limit on economic growth, but with much the same consequences. The connections between global warming, population, food, and fuel are considered in chapter 7.

DOES MALTHUS STILL SPEAK TO US?

This is not a simple question. The easy answer would be "yes," in sub-Saharan Africa, where the population growth remains high, and where a still uncertain demographic transition is in its infancy, and "no" in the ever-increasing number of countries that have sub-replacement fertility rates, and face depopulation. But this answer needs qualification. Even in Africa the strict Malthusian conditions do not hold—population outpacing food supply and the masses held to subsistence living. Moreover food trade is a backstop. The African question today is much like the population

---

7. This is not to say that malnutrition and hunger have been banished. They have not and remain with us today. International trade has an ambiguous impact. Food imports can relieve local shortages. But there are numerous examples in which exports have led to environmental degradation and reduced yields, especially when open access common property resources are involved. See Pearson (2000).

debates of the 1960s—would economic growth accelerate with lower population growth, and if so what population policies work best? These questions move well beyond Malthus's framework.

The "no" answer for most of the rest of the world, where fertility has fallen and population momentum is weakening, also needs qualification. If one moves from Malthus's fixation on land and takes a more expansive view of natural and environmental resources, a case can be made that there are indeed limits to economic growth. But instead of increasing population, these limits are engaged largely through increasing affluence. As argued in chapter 7, the interactions among climate change, climate change policy, and food supplies manage to keep Malthus relevant for this century.

CHAPTER 4

◦◊◦

Population and Economic Growth

If no restriction is placed on the rate of reproduction . . . poverty is the inevitable result.
—Aristotle in *Politics* (quoted by Feen 1996)

When goods increase, they are increased that eat them.
—Ecclesiastes 5:11

NOTE TO READERS

This chapter proceeds at two levels. The first level is the text, which gives an intuitive and nontechnical explanation of how population and economic variables have interacted in key models over the past 200 years. The second level is five analytical diagrams (figures 4.1 to 4.5), together with their explanatory legends, that describe the interactions in a somewhat more technical fashion. The text conveys the essential message and can be read without referring to the diagrams. The diagrams reinforce the text and may interest those who appreciate visual exposition. Figure 4.6 summarizes the evolution of views as to whether population growth is positive or negative for economic growth.

This chapter considers the interactions of population and economic growth. In some formulations, it is a one-way relation, either from population to economic growth or from economic to population growth. These are illustrated in the two quotes above. But in more elaborate models such as the Malthusian framework, the two are jointly determined within the model itself. Here we are mainly concerned with the effects of population growth on economic growth, deferring to chapter 6 a more detailed discussion of the effects of economic growth on fertility. We also defer to that chapter a fuller discussion of the age structure of the population and its effect on economic growth. The effects of population *decline* on economic growth are considered in chapters 7 to 10.

WORKING BACKWARDS: FROM THE CLASSICAL MODEL TO ADAM SMITH

Adam Smith published his masterpiece, *An Inquiry into the Nature and Causes of the Wealth of Nations*, in 1776. A little more than two decades later, in 1798, the first edition of Malthus's great work, *An Essay on the Principle of Population*, appeared. The works of the other classical economists, Jean-Baptiste Say, David Ricardo, John Stuart Mill, and Karl Marx, followed. All worked within the classical political economy canon and all shared certain fundamental assumptions. Nevertheless, there were important differences. A case can be made that only Adam Smith proposed a framework in which continuously rising real wages and real per capita incomes were possible, in effect an economic growth model. The others, except Marx, set forth long-run stationary (stagnation) models, with the masses more or less condemned to a subsistence livelihood.[1] Marx foresaw something more radical but equally erroneous—class struggle eventually leading to communism and the withering away of the state. In the event, Adam Smith proved to be closest to the mark in anticipating continuous increase in real incomes over the following 200 years.

Normally one would suppose that a newer theory, more consistent with the facts, would supplant an earlier, flawed, theory, and improvements could be traced chronologically. The opposite seems to have occurred between Adam Smith and his successors, concerning the theory of population and economic growth. The flawed theory of Malthus, built on the iron law of wages reverting to their subsistence level, and, as articulated even more clearly in Ricardo, the inevitability of a stationary economy emerging, largely displaced Adam Smith's analysis of two decades earlier. However messy, Smith presented a growth model, while the subsequent classical economists built a stationary one. As a result, it was 200 years

---

1. Ricardo acknowledged that continuous technological progress could postpone wage stagnation at the subsistence level.

before Smith's insights, which contemplated continuously rising real incomes, took center stage.[2]

Adam Smith was a mentor for Malthus but cannot be held responsible for the dark and dismal conclusions of the latter. Indeed Smith was an optimist and on the central question of securing a growing population with rising living standards, he, not Malthus, supplied what turned out to be the correct answer. As a consequence of this regression in thought, it is more productive for us to reverse the chronology and start with the classical model that incorporated Malthus, and then return to the question of whether Smith had a different and ultimately superior understanding of population and economic growth.

Elements of the Classical Model

According to the classical model, there are three inputs to production: land, labor, and capital. The latter can be fixed in the form of machinery and buildings, or circulating, such as raw materials ready for processing. Together the inputs produce the nation's output, consisting of consumption and investment goods. Capital and labor are used in fixed proportions in a particular sector, for example, one worker/one shovel and two workers/two shovels in agriculture, or one teacher/one classroom, and two teachers/two classrooms in education. Production is assumed to be affected by diminishing returns to land. This means that applying equal doses of additional capital, say fertilizer, and labor to a fixed amount of land would produce successively smaller increases in agricultural output. Ricardo clarified that if additional land could be brought under cultivation, it is likely to be of inferior fertility, and in these circumstances there would also be diminishing returns. This concept of diminishing returns had been the *bête noire* of growth theory until the last decades of the twentieth century, as it forces per capita output growth toward zero.

Classical economics is not only about production. It contains a theory of how output and income are distributed among the three productive inputs in the form of wages to labor, profits to the owners of capital, and rent to the owners of land. In the long run, the labor wage rate is assumed to equal a subsistence level and is pinned there by labor's supply response to increasing or falling real wages. If wages temporarily rise, births increase, labor supply increases, and wages are driven back toward subsistence levels. This is the so-called Iron Law of Wages and is Malthus's

---

2. Paul Samuelson (1977) gives grudging tribute when he says that Smith is "less guilty" than Ricardo, Malthus, or Marx in believing in a subsistence-wage supply of labor in the short and medium run.

contribution. It relies fundamentally on the assumption of diminishing returns in agriculture and, as elaborated in chapter 2, is the byproduct of unbridled sexual passion. In the long run, the rate of return to capital, the rate of profit, is just high enough to call forth savings and investments by the owners of capital sufficient to maintain the stock of capital at a constant level (i.e., cover depreciation) but not so high as to have positive net investment and growth of that stock. Rent is a residual after labor and capital receive their share of national output and income.

These components form the bones of a long-run economy in which land, labor, capital, output, income, wages, profits, and rent are constant, a stationary state that Smith had earlier called "dull." With wages and profits at their minimal levels, rent, as a residual in the distribution scheme, would be at its maximal level. The classical economists recognized that an economy could depart from its long run stable equilibrium during a transitory period but argued that forces would arise to nudge it back toward the stationary state. For example, if at a point in time labor and capital are below their equilibrium levels the sum of wages and profits will be above, and rent below, their equilibrium levels. With real wages above subsistence, population will grow. With profits above their long-term level there will be positive net investment and the stock of capital rises. This is the progressive or growth state, but it would not last. The increased inputs and fixed supply of land trigger decreasing returns; population growth is cut off by wages falling to subsistence level, competition forces the profit rate down, and net capital accumulation ceases. The stationary state emerges once again. For a diagrammatic exposition based on Samuelson (1978), see figure 4.1.

While the post-Smith classical economists acknowledged that inventions, innovations, and technological progress could extend a transient growth phase, this was not their central concern. Indeed, whereas Smith had lauded the progressive state, calling it the "cheerful state," John Stuart Mill clearly preferred a stationary economy. He wrote: "I cannot, therefore, regard the stationary state of capital and wealth with an unaffected aversion so generally manifested toward it by political economists of the old school. I am inclined to believe that it would be, on the whole, a considerable improvement on our current condition" (J. S. Mill, "Of the Stationary State," 1848, IV 6.5). He goes on to lament the loss of solitude and nature consequent to rapid economic growth and declares he is not charmed with the struggle to get on with "the trampling, crushing, elbowing and treading on each other's heels" that industrial progress requires.[3]

3. The steady state mentality has made a strong comeback in modern times. See, for example, the environmental economist Kenneth Boulding, who coined the term "Spaceship Earth" and who wrote, "The 'shades of the prison house of earth' are closing in on us" (1973, p. 90).

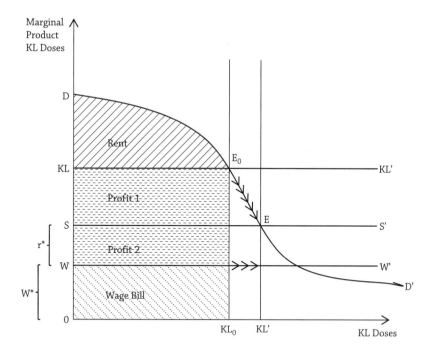

Figure 4.1:
The classical model: Long-run stationary state

Source: Based on Samuelson 1978, figure 2. With permission.

Note: The curve DD′ can be thought of as the marginal product of successive doses of labor and capital (in fixed proportions) applied to a fixed supply of quality-adjusted land. Area under the curve represents total output/income. The long-run supply of labor is fixed along WW′ at the subsistence wage W^*. The supply of labor plus the long-run supply of capital at a profit rate r^*, where r^* is that rate that will replace depreciating capital but not attract additional capital, is fixed along SS′. If the initial supply curve of capital plus labor is KL-KL′, the initial equilibrium is E_0, and KL_0 is the dose of capital and labor applied to the fixed land input. Total output is the area under the DD′ curve up to E_0. If the short-circuited version of rapid labor-market adjustment is used, total output is distributed as the rectangle labeled Wage Bill which is paid at subsistence levels to workers, profit consisting of rectangles Profit 1 and Profit 2 to the owners of capital, and as a residual, the triangle Rent goes to the owners of land. This is not a long-term equilibrium. Total profits and the profit rate are sufficiently large to lead to capital accumulation. The output point then starts to slide down the DD′ curve from E_0 toward E (see arrows) and, with fixed land, triggers diminishing marginal returns to the higher doses of capital and labor. Labor supply increases rapidly in response to temporarily higher wages (see arrows). Long-term equilibrium arrives when the profit rate is driven down to r^*, capital accumulation stops, and the labor force ceases to grow—the stationary economy. Output is now the area under the DD curve up to E. The wage bill is the lowest rectangle and profits are the next rectangle. Rent is now the area SDE and is at its maximum.

A Smithian Growth Model

Adam Smith was well aware that a stationary economy lurks in the shadow of every growing economy. The issue in his view was whether economies could operate in a continuous growth mode, indefinitely putting off stagnation. If so, he can be credited with leapfrogging classical and neoclassical growth theory, and landing squarely in the "new growth" literature of the last decades of the twentieth century.

At a superficial level, Smith and his successor Malthus were addressing different questions. Smith was seeking the wellsprings of economic growth; Malthus, in his essay, put forth an explanation (and justification) for poverty. But, of course, these are two sides of the same coin. In a crude but accurate sense, economic growth is increasing income per capita; poverty is the failure of income per capita for the masses to rise above subsistence level. Smith tackled the numerator, increasing income through productivity increases; Malthus fretted about the denominator, increasing population facing limited food. Adam Smith's core recommendation is to unleash economic man from the shackles of government restrictions on production and exchange, and allow self-interest and the universal desire of men to better themselves to be given free rein in a condition of "natural liberty." In contrast Malthus's core finding was to hold the poor responsible for their plight through excessive procreation. Malthus is blunt: the common people need to understand "they are themselves the cause of their own poverty" (1798; 2d ed., 1803). His central recommendation was for the laboring classes to adopt late marriages and practice moral restraint if they are to avoid the positive checks of pestilence and famine. Abolishing the poor laws was, for Malthus, a step in this direction. One could say Smith's view on population growth was the opposite of Malthus's: "The most decisive mark of prosperity of any country is the increase in the number of its inhabitants" (I.8.23).[4]

The difference between Smith's emphasis on increasing output and income vs. Malthus's stress on curbing population growth is illustrated in their views toward universal education for children of the lower classes. Smith argues for public support as the parents could not afford it and, once working, the children lacked time for studies. The window of opportunity for schooling was therefore early childhood. Although brief, Smith claims it to be sufficient time to acquire "the most essential parts of education, to read, write and account." Moreover, Smith disparages the teaching of Latin in such schools as not useful, but proposes the inclusion of elementary geometry and mechanics, stressing their practical value and as a foundation for subsequent on-the-job "learning by doing": "There is scarce a common trade which does not afford some opportunities of applying to it the principles of geometry and mechanics, and which would not therefore gradually exercise and improve the common people in these principles" (V.1.183).

---

4. The quote is from Smith (1776). Citations are by book, chapter, and paragraph. It is echoed by the political philosopher Jean Jacques Rousseau: "Other things being equal, the government under which . . . the citizens do increase and multiply the most is infallibly the best. The government under which a people wanes and diminishes is the worst" (*Social Contract*, Book III).

Because education is beneficial to society, as well as the individual, public support is justified. In short, Smith sees education as building human capital and increasing individual and societal productivity, which is a very modern view. He elaborates on this elsewhere by including labor's acquired and useful abilities as "capital fixed and realized, as it were, in his person" (II.1.17).

Malthus also supports public education for the children of the lower classes, but he sees it playing a quite different role. He rejected as without value the inclusion of geometry and mechanics in the curriculum for children of the poor, but instead plumped for the simplest principles of political economy, by which he presumably meant his own principles of population. Education would thereby help "promote peace and quietness . . . and prevent all unreasonable and ill-directed opposition to the constituted authorities" (1798; 6th ed., 1826, IV. IX.10). For Malthus, education would root out pauperism by teaching the poorer classes to exercise moral control and serve as a means of social control.

Smith did not directly challenge the contention that higher real wages spur population growth, but he was considerably more nuanced than Malthus was to be, avoiding the latter's controversial use of ratios. He starts his argument by acknowledging that "every species of animals naturally multiplies in proportion to their subsistence, and no species can ever multiply beyond it" (I.8.38). But he also notes that in situations of deep poverty fertility indeed might increase, using an example of poverty-stricken women in the Scottish highlands with 20 or more births, and observing that a luxurious life might be a disincentive to childbearing. In any event Smith does not say the link between higher real wages and population is a bad thing—it is simply another example of increasing demand, in this case for labor, stimulating a (lagged) supply response. He also said that those who questioned high wages had it backward—high wages are a consequence of, not an impediment to, economic growth. "The liberal reward for labor, therefore, as it is the effect of increasing wealth, so it is the cause of increasing population. To complain of this is to lament over the necessary effect and cause of the greatest public prosperity" (I.8.41). And economic growth is, for Smith, an unalloyed good: "The progressive [growing] state is in reality the cheerful and the hearty state to all orders of society. The stationary is dull; the declining melancholy" (I.8.42).

Smith goes beyond merely saying that high wages reflect prosperity: they contribute to prosperity by encouraging effort and promoting a healthy and productive workforce: "The liberal reward of labor, as it encourages propagation, so it increases the industry of the common man." . . .

"A plentiful subsistence increases the bodily strength of the laborer and . . . animates him *to* exert that strength to the upmost" (I.8.43).

These assertions by Smith concerning the positive roles of good wages in the progressive state, and his concern elsewhere for educating workers through at least literacy and arithmetic so that they have a foundation for learning from their work experience, provide hints at how the link between wages and population growth, which played such a central and pernicious role in Malthus, can be overcome. Economic growth, meaning rising income per capita, can be self-sustaining. To achieve this happy day, however, it is necessary to deal with diminishing returns, the *bête noire* that plagued growth theories from Ricardo in the first half of the nineteenth century to the Solow-Swan model in the second half of the twentieth. Smith attempts to do so by "endogenizing" technology—explaining technological progress by the workings of the model itself and not as the result of some unexplained outside force. In doing so, he attempted something very modern indeed. He is also very current in his emphasis on institutions and policy setting the framework for growth. Figure 4.2 sketches Smith's sustainable growth theory.

The core of Smith's insights into growth is found in the first chapters of the first book of *The Wealth of Nations*. Improvements in the productivity of labor have their origin in the division (specialization) of labor. Three sources for productivity gains from specialization are identified: increasing dexterity of workers as they concentrate on increasingly specific tasks; time saving as workers do not need to shift location and tools from one task to another; encouragement to innovate machines that "facilitate and abridge" the use of labor.[5] He states that division of labor and specialization takes place both within firms and among firms that specialize in one specific phase of the production process. Smith then introduces as a fundamental human attribute, the propensity to "truck, barter, and exchange one thing for another" in markets. Given this propensity, he asserts his famous theorem that the division of labor is limited by the extent (size) of the market. The extent of the market is positively related to the size of the economy. From this flows his advocacy of "natural liberty" and free markets in which government is relieved of responsibility for guiding, supervising, or regulating most private economic activity. A free and extensive market is the fecund matrix for division of labor and ultimately for economic growth.

5. Smith credits both workers and those who manufacture the machines for innovative activity.

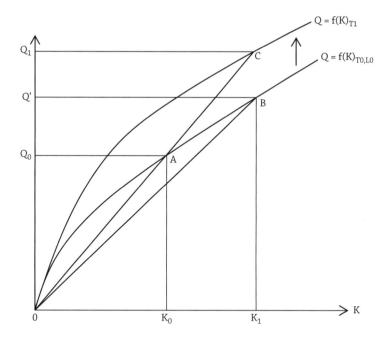

Figure 4.2:
A Smithian growth diagram
Source: Author.
Note: Smith endogenizes technology to overcome diminishing marginal returns. Consider the production relation between capital and output, $Q = f(K)$, holding labor and technology constant at L_0 and T_0. With initial capital at K_0 output is Q_0 and the slope of the ray 0A measures capital productivity, Q/K. With capital increasing to K_1, output increases to Q' but the productivity of capital falls, shown by the slope of OB less than the slope of OA (diminishing marginal returns). Further capital accumulation would further depress capital productivity. Smith's key argument is that as a result of capital accumulation the production relation shifts up to $Q = f(K)_{T1}$ for two reasons. First, increased output expands the market, intensifies specialization and increases productivity. Second, specialization is an inducement to innovate and install more productive machines. The expansion path is then 0AC, output is at Q_1 and diminishing returns are defeated. Growth can be sustained.

Smith was aware that growth was not inevitable. China is cited as a stationary economy, and by implication its laws and institutions, including international trade restrictions, are held responsible. Bengal is identified as a declining economy and blame is placed on its mercantile company overlords. The issue for us is not whether in Smith's framework a growing economy could slip back to a stationary state or worse with poor policies, but whether a transitional growth phase would inevitably grind to a halt in the face of diminishing returns.

Haim Barkai (1969) makes a spirited attempt to tease a formal growth model with endogenous technological change from Smith's writings.[6] The

6. An exogenous variable is an input to a model; and endogenous variable is an output.

key mechanism is that an increase in capital increases output directly but also, by expanding income and the extent of the market, indirectly induces further productivity improvements, including the innovation of new machines that facilitate and abridge the use of labor. The technical efficiency of the new machines is thereby associated with capital accumulation and an increasing capital–labor ratio. In this fashion a favorable change in one of the exogenous institutional variables that is holding an economy mired in the stationary state—for example, relaxing restrictions on foreign trade or improved protection of private property and stimulating savings—can trigger a self-sustaining increase in real output per capita. Diminishing returns to capital hiding beneath a falling profit rate, the Achilles Heel of the classical model, is still there. But it is trumped by *increasing* returns arising from extending the market and induced technological change. Smith's growth optimism and his view that an increasing population was a mark of prosperity and good governance is in sharp contrast to the growth pessimism of his immediate successors and especially Malthus.[7]

MID-TWENTIETH-CENTURY MODELING

As noted in chapter 2, interest in the interactions of population and economic growth waned between the middle decades of the nineteenth and twentieth centuries and, with it, the notion of diminishing returns leading to economic stagnation faded. Why? A number of reasons can be adduced. International trade relaxed the agricultural constraint; agriculture's share of output shrunk; Jevons's panic over running out of coal evaporated; neoclassical economics was otherwise engaged in building the foundations of microeconomics; despite increasingly severe business cycles and the disruption of World War I, growth in the West was robust; fertility was falling in Europe and concern for population *decline* replaced the Malthusian threat.

Growth economics was not totally abandoned, of course. In part, it survived in debates on increasing returns to scale—whether a doubling of the inputs to production might more than double output. That concept is perfectly congruent with Adams Smith's view of growth arising from specialization, but without strenuous tinkering, is incompatible with the

---

7. To be fair, Smith focused on capital and did not directly confront the possibility of fixed agricultural resources.

then prevailing dominance of neoclassical equilibrium theory.[8] Going against the grain, the case for increasing returns was revived and defended by Allyn Young in the 1920s (and revived a second time in the "new growth theory" of the mid-1980s), but was neglected in the subsequent depression years. Along a different path, the foundations for modern optimal growth theory were laid down by Frank Ramsey in 1928, but that analysis was silent on population. Joseph Schumpeter also made a major contribution to understanding growth through his work on innovation and entrepreneurship, but had little to say about population. In fact progress on long-term growth theory sputtered and quickly succumbed to the urgency of unemployed resources in the Great Depression. And in any event, none of these theoretical threads linked economic growth to population.[9]

Ultimately the aftermath of the Great Depression and the debates surrounding Keynesian economics combined with post–World War II decolonization to revitalize the population/economic growth issue. One thesis was that a stagnant population might undercut aggregate demand and tend to make recession or depression chronic—see chapter 2 for Keynes's about-face on this issue. A second and quite different thesis was that rapid population growth in developing countries would dissipate efforts to save, dilute the stock of productive capital, and hence depress economic growth.

Harrod-Domar: The Model that Switched Roles

The HD model, first put forward by Roy Harrod (1939) and followed by Evsey Domar (1946), occupied a pivotal role in both the extension of Keynes's work from a short period to a longer term model, and as an influential, if flawed, development model.[10] Looking back, it is more than a little ironic that the same theory used to investigate chronic insufficient aggregate demand and unemployment in industrial countries would become equally or more famous for analyzing insufficient supply and inadequate capital accumulation in poor countries. In a nutshell, the former were

8. The sticking points in the neoclassical framework are the assumptions of perfect competition and marginal productivity pricing of inputs to production (the assumption that inputs are paid the value of marginal product they produce). Both assumptions were needed for equilibrium theory.

9. Alfred Marshall, the dominant figure in economics at the turn of the century, also struggled with increasing returns. See Lavezzi (2003).

10. Domar subsequently disavowed his contribution was either a growth or a development model (Easterly 1999).

thought to be burdened by excessive savings and insufficient investment opportunities; the latter were suffering from *insufficient* savings to fund *abundant* investment opportunities.

HD did convert static Keynesian concerns into a longer model but of an unstable sort. Along the way it was hijacked and misappropriated as a development tool. As it turned out, no single model was adequate to both turn the Keynesian model into a modern growth theory and provide an adequate blueprint for development of poor countries.

Harrod-Domar Building Blocks

The fundamental equation of the HD model consists of four variables—per capita income growth (g^*), the national savings rate (s), which is the fraction of national income saved and invested, the ratio of the stock of capital to the output of the economy (v), which is a measure of the productivity of the economy, and the rate of growth of the population (n).[11] They are arranged as follows:

$$g^* = s/v - n$$

Some numbers can illustrate this. If the savings rate is 12 percent (0.12) and the capital output ratio is 4, and the population and labor force are growing at 2 percent per year (0.02), per capita income is growing by 1 percent per year.

A central problem arises when viewed from the Keynesian aggregate demand perspective. In this rigid structure s, v, and n are independently determined and there is no mechanism through which the rate of growth of capital, s/v is brought into equality with the rate of growth of the labor force. If the rate of growth of capital, s/v, is less than the growth rate of labor, n, one winds up with chronic Keynesian unemployment. This is illustrated in figure 4.3. This rigidity creates an unstable growth path, sometimes termed a knife's edge equilibrium. One way to overcome this is to drop the assumption that labor and capital are used in

---

11. The model is built on five critical assumptions:
   (1) national savings are a fixed fraction of national income (i.e., s is fixed);
   (2) the ratio of capital to output, v, is fixed;
   (3) labor and capital are used in fixed proportions in production;
   (4) population and the labor force grow at a fixed exogenously determined rate, n;
   (5) the national income accounting identity that savings equals investment.

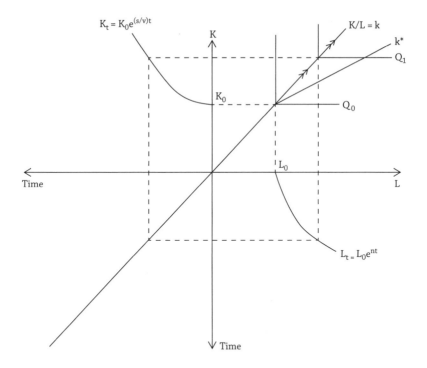

Figure 4.3:
Harrod-Domar model; Knife's edge character
Starting from initial levels of labor L_0, capital K_0, and output Q_0, and if L and K grow at equal rates, $n = s/v$, full employment output expands along the K/L path to isoquant Q_1. If n exceeds s/v, the expansion path is along k^* and chronic and increasing unemployment results.

fixed proportions and to allow them to be substitutes in production. This in fact led to the neoclassical (Solow-Swan) model considered later.

Harrod-Domar as a Development Policy Model

By mid-century the threat of inadequate investment opportunities and secular stagnation had lost its sting in the industrial countries and a new challenge of accelerating development in poor countries emerged.[12] The HD model is the point at which the economic growth/population literature diverges. One stream addresses the problem of development in poor countries. The second and main stream flows to the neoclassical growth

12. It is difficult to disentangle the controversy over the role of population in development from the highly contentious and politicized issue of appropriate population policies. The latter ranged from advocating active and sometimes coercive family planning programs to the view that economic development is itself the best contraceptive.

model, and there to the so-called "new growth theory" (endogenous growth). We first follow the development stream and then return to the second stream.

The simplicity and powerful policy implications of the HD model for labor-abundant countries became irresistible to the development community. Consider the fundamental growth equation as a framework for development policy:

$$g^* = (s/v) - n$$

While suppressing the nuances of modernization and development, this formula cuts through to what many believed was the heart of the problem, increasing per capita income, g^*. Moreover, it identifies the range of policies that could make this a reality. First gin up the savings rate, s. This might be accomplished by tilting income distribution toward high savings groups, or toward government income, which presumably is invested at a higher rate than in an underdeveloped private sector. Second, seek out high productivity investments (low value for v), which at this stage of development thinking were often associated with capital infrastructure, especially irrigation and transportation. Third, and most relevant for us, use measures to slow down n, the rate of growth of population. Thus, when migrating from industrial country analysis to guidance on development policy, the HD lost its initial justification for a growing population—as a stimulus to investment to mop up excess savings, but took on the opposite mission, to slow population growth.

The negative view of population growth in this early period is easy to understand. A growing population meant diluting capital over a larger population base and reducing capital per worker, a process known as capital shallowing. There was a further attractive feature to HD. It offered a convenient and defensible procedure for estimating and allocating foreign aid. An aid agency or development bank could set a target for per capita income growth of, say 3 percent, assess the domestic savings capacity at 12 percent of national income, estimate the capital output ratio at 4 from previous years (or simply borrow estimates for similar countries), observe population growing at 2 percent, and immediately see that there was a financing gap amounting to 8 percent of national income (i.e., 20 percent savings rate was required but only 12 percent available domestically). Easterly (1999), writing more than half a century after Domar, demonstrated and criticized the tenacious role the financing gap approach still maintained in international financial institutions, despite its death in the academic literature, and despite the lack of rigorous empirical testing.[13]

Other Development Models

Development models critical of rapid population growth started to pile up. Three are worth noting. Richard Nelson (1956) built a plausible theoretical model in which per capita income is trapped at a low level when the rate of growth of capital and hence the rate of growth of income falls short of the rate of growth of population. The population assumptions are critical. Nelson assumed that death rates would fall with an increase in per capita income through improved medical access.[14] But he explicitly calls his a short-term model and omits any impact of income growth on fertility and birth rates, either positive (Malthusian) or negative (in keeping with historical evidence). Hence, population is only partly endogenous, but still manages to work against escape from the low level "trap." The intuition is that an increase in income triggers an increase in population via a decline in mortality. The capital–labor ratio deteriorates ("capital shallowing") and per capita income is capped near subsistence levels. Unlike Malthus, the mechanism works through income's effect on mortality rather than fertility. The trap would be sprung if fertility declined with increased income.[15]

Coale and Hoover (1958) took a different approach from Nelson. They constructed a simulation model of the Indian economy at the time and then make two projections over the following 25 years. The first projects fertility at the then current (high) rate and the second projects a 50 percent

13. The financing gap approach took on renewed life with the publication in *The American Economic Review* of a "Two Gap" model of development by Hollis Chenery and Alan Strout (1966). One was a savings gap and the other a foreign exchange gap. Chenery was later to become Vice President for Development Planning at the World Bank and Strout was Chief, Policy Planning at US AID. Population growth was neglected in this model. Growth targets were expressed in GDP and not per capita terms. The supply of labor was not considered a significant limitation on growth. And there were no feedbacks from income growth to population dynamics—birth and death rates.

14. He does not investigate if the reduction of deaths would occur among infants, working age individuals, or the elderly, which would be important in determining the labor force impact. To his credit he includes the fraction of uncultivated arable land in determining net capital formation. He is also careful to note that the basic assumptions are for short-run analysis of an economy with subsistence level per capita income.

15. Times change. As discussed in chapter 6 "depopulation trap" models are now being introduced with *declining* population the trigger.

reduction in fertility phased in over the period. This comparison identifies changes in the level and age structure of the population under the two scenarios. The idea was to test whether a steep reduction in birth rates has a significant effect on economic growth and related variables. The assumptions were that during the 25-year period the size of the labor force would be relatively unaffected due to lags between birth and labor-market participation, and that natural resources (forests, agricultural land, mineral resources) would also be unaffected by the decline in births. In principle, however, the accumulation of the third factor of production, capital, could be accelerated. Fewer births would mean a reduction in the number of children and thus would make it easier to divert a part of current output from consumption to additions to the capital stock.[16] Fewer births meant fewer mouths to feed, and fewer children to school.

Indeed, their simulations indicated that after 30 years the income per head under the reduced fertility regime would be 40 to 50 percent higher than with no reduction in fertility. The study is significant not only for its results, but for its pioneering analysis of changing age structures and dependency ratios, issues also relevant for declining populations in this century. With a 25-year time span their central model could not capture the subsequent benefits of a rapid growth in the labor force in the high fertility simulation (the demographic bonus), nor indeed the even more distant demographic burden of an aging population. They did however investigate an extension of another 25 years but found that their initial results stood, presumably because the initial income benefits from declining fertility in the first period would be available and would compound in the second period.

We complete this roundup of pessimistic models of rapid population growth by considering Stephen Enke's contributions. In a series of academic articles published in *The Economic Journal* (1966, 1971, 1974), he builds on Coale and Hoover's approach of using high/low fertility growth scenarios to tease out the impact of reducing birth rates, and their view that by reducing the child dependency ratio, fewer births free up current output for additional savings and capital accumulation. The focus is clearly on the impact of fertility on economic growth, not the reverse. His findings are similar to Coale and Hoover's and his conclusion is blunt: "An increasing [population] growth rate, especially when due to a declining death rate, is economically disastrous. A decreasing population growth rate, because of declining fertility rates, is a major source of economic development" (Enke 1971, p. 807).

---

16. Coale and Hoover treat expenditures on children for health and education as consumption, not investment—a quaint notion today.

Enke's most controversial contribution was his 1966 article in which he calculates an illustrative cost-benefit ratio for birth control. His illustration uses $5 as the cost of a birth prevented (not just postponed) using a mix of control methods. The net benefit is calculated as the difference between the consumption and output streams of the phantom individual whose birth was prevented, and is calculated to be $263.[17] In effect, the excess of the phantom's lifetime consumption over his (her) lifetime production is considered the benefit of preventing his (her) birth. With the cost of a preventing a birth assumed to be $5, this yields a benefit-cost ratio of 263/5 or about 53, an apparently extraordinarily high return on birth control expenditures. Valuing a life on the basis of earnings minus consumption is, of course, very controversial. The ethics of valuing births, and births prevented, arise again in discussions of an optimal population in the following chapter.

Surplus Labor

A common thread in this early development literature was the assumption of surplus labor. This can be interpreted casually in the sense that the availability of labor was not a binding constraint on economic growth or, more technically, as an assertion that the marginal product of labor—the incremental product produced by the last worker—was close to zero. Both Arthur Lewis (1954) and John Fei and Gustave Ranis (1961, 1964) saw this not as a problem but as an opportunity to propel a stagnant economy into self-sustaining growth. This insight did not directly support high population growth rates, but was an early acknowledgment that a large population relative to agricultural land need not be an absolute barrier to economic development.

These development economists built dualistic, two sector models of the economy consisting of a traditional, mainly agricultural economy in which labor was in surplus, with zero or minimal marginal product, and a nascent, more modern capitalist industrial sector. The essence of successful development was to shift labor from its nonproductive role in the agricultural sector to the modern industrial sector, where it could make a positive contribution to output (the analytics are explained and illustrated in figure 4.4). This is a "something for nothing" strategy and has proved to be highly attractive to labor-abundant countries, especially when labor-intensive, industrial exports were later added to the mix. Unemployed labor in the agricultural sector could potentially fuel an industrial boom.

17. Both streams discounted to the time of the birth averted. The illustration uses a very high discount rate of 15 percent.

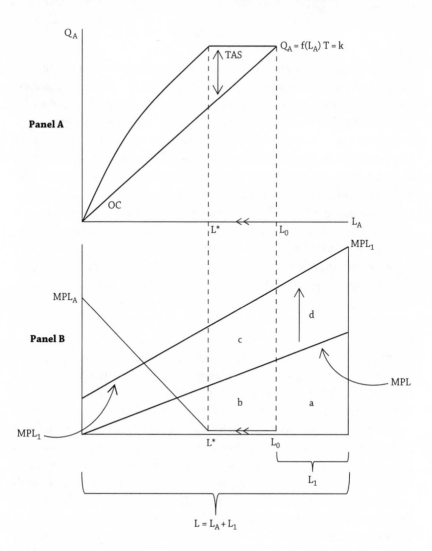

Figure 4.4:
The labor-surplus model

Source: Author.

Note: Agricultural output (Q_A) is a function of labor (L_A) and land (T), which is fixed at k. There is limited substitutability between them (Panel A). Industrial output is a function of capital and labor (L_1). The initial allocation of labor between the two sectors is at L_0 (with L_1 measured right to left). Panel B displays the marginal product of agricultural labor declining left to right and becoming zero at L^* over the range L^*-L_0. The kink in MPL_A at L^* is exaggerated but aids the exposition. The marginal product of industrial labor (MPL_1) declines right to left. Total initial agricultural output is the area under the MPL_A up to the point L^*. Total industrial output is the area under the MPL_1 curve up to the point L_0 (area a in Panel B measured right to left). With MPL_A at zero a market determined wage in agriculture would be zero (i.e., below subsistence level). The model assumes a positive, institutionally determined wage in agriculture set somewhere close to the average product of labor in agriculture (slope of the ray 0C in panel A).

If L_0–L^* labor were gradually reallocated from agriculture to industry, there would be no decline in agricultural output and an increase in industrial output as measured by the area b in Panel B. If additionally the real wage in agriculture were kept constant, surplus production in agriculture, measured by TAS in Panel A, would arise and be available to feed relocated workers in the industrial sector. Again, if the agricultural wage were held constant, rent to land owners would increase. If this rent were invested as capital in the industrial sector the MPL would shift up to the line MPL_1 and the total gain in industrial output would be the area b + c + d. Industrialization is based on an elastic supply of labor at initially low wages. This view of surplus labor is consistent with the demographic bonus concept discussed in chapter 6.

According to the more detailed Fei and Ranis version, in the initial phase the payment to labor in the agricultural sector is institutionally determined and workers are paid the value of their average product, not their marginal product, which would be a zero wage. With zero marginal product, some labor could initially be withdrawn from agriculture and wind up as productive workers in factories with no decline in total agricultural production, but with a shift in the balance of the economy toward a growing industrial structure. So long as the institutionally determined wage in agriculture was maintained at its initial level and so long as surplus labor in agriculture existed, the modern industrial sector could thrive and grow on the basis of a steady (elastic) supply of low-cost labor. Ultimately, surplus labor would be exhausted and wages would start to rise in both sectors. At this point, when the inefficiency of unproductive labor in agriculture has been squeezed out of the economy, one would expect growth to become self-sustaining. On the other hand, continued rapid population growth, weak productivity growth in agriculture, or prematurely increasing real wages could disrupt this process. In that event, the rebalancing of the economy from the traditional subsistence sector to the modern industrial sector would falter, as would economic growth. In short, high population *growth* remained a drag on economic growth.

Recap

To summarize this section: in the early postwar years, economics was caught with an embarrassingly empty toolbox with which to address the newly pressing challenge of development in poor countries. It was able to salvage from classical economics the notion of unlimited supplies of labor at subsistence wages. But unless savings and investment could be jumpstarted that in itself was of little help. The Lewis and Fei and Ranis twosector reallocation approach offered an escape but required holding wages constant in agriculture and extracting a food surplus to feed workers in the expanding industrial sector, all of which would be more difficult with a population explosion. In the scramble to build suitable development theories, a principal policy conclusion emerged that also tracked classical economics—control of runaway population growth was necessary. The rationale for family planning was not only the Malthusian race between mouths to feed and food supplies, but the need for capital deepening—to release output from current consumption and direct it to savings and capital accumulation. By and large the perspective was the effects of population on economic growth, and less attention was paid to the impact of income growth on fertility.

SECOND THOUGHTS IN SUBSEQUENT DECADES

The almost universally negative and often alarmist view of rapid population growth[18] did not last, and a reconsideration was inevitable (Birdsall 1988). When it came, it was multifaceted and not merely a superior theory replacing a defective one. The weaknesses of existing models showing a negative effect were exposed. Examples included the failure of the Coale approach to consider expenditures on children as investments, Nelson's unwillingness to link declining fertility to higher incomes, and exaggerations in Enke's cost-benefit calculations.

New, positive links between population and economics growth were proposed. Some were plausible but of perhaps limited relevance. Ester Boserup (1976), for example, advanced the idea that population growth can force a transformation from land-using practices such as swidden agriculture to higher productivity, labor-using agricultural technologies when population density becomes sufficiently high. While correct, this had surely occurred long before in labor-abundant regions such as Egypt, South Asia, and East Asia. Nevertheless, her broader thesis, that population pressures can trigger technological and management strategies to increase productivity, was borne out with the arrival of the Green Revolution. Land-yield ratios were radically changed, and with them so were demographic constraints.

Density and scale arguments were considered. Density, as measured by population per km^2, may well be important for efficient transportation systems and to secure economies of scale in infrastructure investments such as irrigation and communications, but its aggregate significance on growth can be questioned.[19] Scale economies in some manufacturing operations can be important, but they can be captured with an open trade regime and do not necessarily require a large home population.

Some arguments were flimsy. Julian Simon, one of the most well-known of the population optimists, used a model in which output is produced by three inputs, capital, labor, and "social overhead capital." The last was assumed to grow at a fixed fraction of the rate of growth of the labor force, so that population growth automatically leads to economic growth.[20] Moreover, his analysis showed that moderate population growth produces

18. Robert McNamara, president of the World Bank in 1973, "the greatest single obstacle to the economic and social advance of the majority of peoples in the developing world is rampant population growth," quoted by Kelley (1988 p. 1685).

19. Whether density (proximity) promotes innovation remains unclear. Major productivity increases in US agriculture in the twentieth century suggest not always.

20. See Warren Sanderson (1980) for a highly critical evaluation of Simon.

better economic results in the long run (120 to 180 years), whereas a slower growing population produces slightly better results in the "shorter" run (up to 60 years). Such long-run analysis does not inspire confidence.

Two other factors contributed to the reassessment. The first and most important was the failure to find strong and pervasive empirical evidence of the negative effect of population growth (Kelley 1988). Second, the initial proliferation of development models and development planning exercises ran its intellectual course, and policy attention shifted to efficient allocation policies (including open trade), improving institutions, and good governance.[21]

The conclusions reached by the National Research Council (NRC) of the National Academy of Sciences (1986) reflect the emergence of a more measured and temperate view of population growth and economic development. On the question of whether reducing population growth would relieve stress on nonrenewable resources, the NRC concluded that it might delay exploitation somewhat but would be unlikely to improve living standards over the long run. Market forces would be sufficient to encourage conservation and the development of substitutes. On renewable resources (air, water, species), the NRC favored slower population growth: "Slower population growth . . . is likely to lead to a reduced rate of degradation of renewable common property resources." This nuanced view of nonrenewable vs. renewable resources reflects the increasing attention to common property based market failures, the pernicious links between poverty and exploitation of the renewable resources, and the beginnings of the sustainable development movement. On the question that dominated many of the earlier debates, the link between population growth and per capita income via the accumulation and productivity of capital, the NRC concluded that slower population growth would likely raise the capital–labor ratio, thus increasing output per worker, but that this result may be relatively modest and would not necessarily exert a decisive influence on economic growth. Their reasoning was that slowing population growth would promote capital deepening directly and *might* also increase savings and investment rates. The most general conclusion, stated in cautious and qualified language, supported slowing population: "On balance, we reach the qualitative conclusion that slower population growth would be beneficial to economic development for most developing countries" (National Research Council 1986, p. 90).

21. Not entirely. Population growth, especially in Africa, still commands attention. See Sinding (2009) and Turner (2009), and chapter 6.

GROWTH AND POPULATION: BACK TO THE MAIN STREAM

We have noted that the HD model marks a watershed in thinking about economic growth. One stream leads off into the complexities of development economics, but despite its superficial attractiveness for setting growth targets and allocating foreign aid, the HD model was ultimately bypassed in the development literature. The second and main stream leads to the neoclassical model, often identified as the Solow-Swan model.[22] It became the dominant growth model in the post–World War II era. The new model shakes off the remnants of the Keynesian aggregate demand dilemma, which was the original motivation for HD-type models. In particular, it avoids the knife's edge instability in HD. It does so by dropping the assumption of fixed input coefficients between labor and capital, and instead assumes neoclassical style substitution between the two in producing aggregate output. This makes all the difference. Presto, the knife's edge disappears, and full employment of capital and labor rule! Blunting the instability at the knife's edge, however, comes at a cost. One must be prepared to accept the neoclassical structure in which the proportions of capital and labor are adjusted via markets—specifically that both inputs are paid the value of their marginal products, that they exhibit diminishing marginal returns, and that input markets are competitive. These assumptions allow *long-run* growth of aggregate (GDP) but are in conflict with *long-run* growth in per capita income.

For the mechanics of the stripped-down neoclassical model, see figure 4.5 The basic intuition is that per capita income can grow in the short run if savings exceeds the investment needed to offset depreciation and to equip a growing population. But at some point diminishing marginal returns to capital bring investment and savings into equality. Competitive input markets take care of this automatically. At that point all of the relevant variables—capital, aggregate income and output, savings, investment—are growing at the same rate, the rate of growth of population and labor.[23] If capital and labor are growing at the same rate, productivity—output per worker—is constant. Alternatively, if total income and population are growing at the same rate, per capita income is constant.

The key result of the model is that in the absence of technological progress and in the long run, per capita income stops growing. An increase in

---

22. Solow (1956) and Swan (1956). The models were independently developed but came to similar conclusions. There were analytical differences however. Solow worked with the capital-labor ratio; Swan worked with the output-capital ratio, which made it easier to incorporate technological change.

23. The model assumes that the labor force is a constant fraction of population.

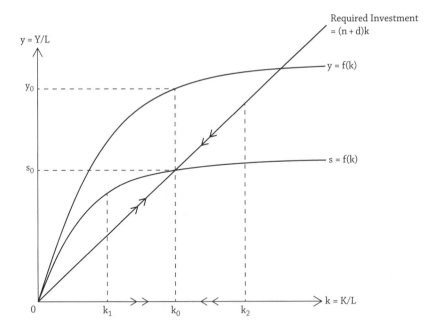

Figure 4.5:
Basic Solow model

Note: The axes measure per capita income, y, and per capita stock of capital, k. The line $y = f(k)$ traces the output (income) per worker. Note the diminishing marginal product of k. Assuming a constant fraction of income saved and invested, $s = f(k)$ is a savings and investment function. The diagonal Required Investment $= (n + d)k$ is the amount of investment required for each k given a depreciation rate d and a population growth rate n. At k_0 required investment equals actual investment and the long-run steady state per capita income is y_0. If the initial point is at k_1 savings exceeds required investment and the accumulation of capital drives k toward k_0, where it is halted by diminishing marginal product. At initial point k_2, savings are inadequate and k is drawn down to k_0 via depreciation to the stable long-term equilibrium. See arrows. The diagram is useful in thinking through comparative statics; changing savings rates, depreciation rates, population growth, and production technology.

the savings rate will bump up the ratio of capital to labor (capital deepening) and move per capita income to a higher level during a transitional period, but it will not support continually increasing per capita income and standards of living. Diminishing returns to capital drag per capita income growth down to zero. Also, starting from the steady state, an increase in the population growth rate will depress the capital–labor ratio, and over time will depress per capita income to a lower level, where it will stabilize with zero growth. Conversely, a decrease in the population growth rate brings capita income to a higher level, but will have no long-term effect on per capita income growth, which will remain zero without technological advance. The implication of this model for the modern era, in which depopulation is in prospect, is that a smaller population might enjoy a higher standard of living, but should not expect that standard to grow over time in the absence of (unexplained) continuous technological progress. This reconfiguration of the model to a shrinking population should be taken with a large grain of salt.

The neoclassical model, and especially the Solow version that is widely taught, appears more appropriate for modern industrial countries than poor developing countries. The core model does not deal with either a dualistic economy or surplus labor; land or natural resources are not integral components; countries are assumed to have access to the same production technologies; population growth is exogenous; and the age structure of the population is ignored. Most important for a poor country, the steady state solution, in which (absent technical progress) per capita income growth is zero, is likely to be far in the future. In the meantime, there is much work to be done in increasing savings, accelerating human and physical capital accumulation, and controlling population growth, all of which will leave the country with a higher per capita income when that long-run steady state arrives. Sato (1964), for example, calculates that the long-run steady state may take up to a century to materialize. If so, the conclusion that increasing savings rates will not yield increased growth rates in the long run is a message for the rich, not the poor.

All told, this appears to be a queer sort of growth model. Technological progress is the only remaining source for long-term economic growth, but is left unexplained. Population, which determines the long-run level (not growth) of per capita income, is also not unexplained.

This assessment may be too narrow however. First, if we read the original articles rather than textbook synopses, we see the model as providing a platform, ready for elaboration. Swan in his extensions considers making population growth a function of the standard of living; investigates the implications of adding land as another input to production; and notes but does not pursue Adam Smith's idea that technical progress may be positively related to the rate of capital accumulation. Solow in his extensions also considers how the size of the workforce might respond to the real wage, and how population growth itself may respond to income levels. The authors were fully aware that richer variations were needed to capture alternative population and other assumptions.[24]

Moreover, the sober conclusion that capital accumulation cannot increase living standards in the long run, and that technological progress holds the key for sustained growth, was a welcome corrective to the HD

---

24. For population assumptions, see Accinelli and Brida (2007), and Cellarier and Day (2011). Solow himself (1974) made a major contribution in extending the model to include nonrenewable resources.

focus on savings and investment in physical capital. Still, it is safe to say that the neoclassical model made little direct impact on our particular focus of interest, the connections between population and per capita economic growth.

NEW GROWTH THEORY

Eventually the temptation to provide endogenous explanations for population growth and technological progress proved irresistible. Starting with Gary Becker in the 1960s, work was underway to give an economic interpretation of population and its principal driver, fertility rates. This is considered in chapter 6. Explaining technological progress, not capital accumulation, is at the core of the new growth theory. Adam Smith sensed the key role of technology when he spoke of expanding the market and paving the way for productivity-enhancing innovations that conserved labor. In the 1940s the Swedish economist, Ingvar Svennilson, makes much the same point, arguing that capital accumulation is the mechanism for introducing innovative ideas and technology into production. Arrow (1962) picked up the idea, building a model in which technological improvements were embodied in new capital goods. In this fashion, gross investment becomes the vehicle through which advances in knowledge were incorporated into production (learning by doing). Moreover, with full employment, a rapidly growing labor force (population) would permit more rapid introduction of new machinery and stimulate productivity growth and rising per capita incomes.

The idea that investment involves more than just duplicating existing assets is also central to Maurice Scott's (1992) explanation of growth. Investment generally, not only investment in education or R&D, is the vehicle for technological progress. In his view, investment advances knowledge and creates positive spillovers (external economies) throughout the economy. In turn, this implies that, although specific firms can exhibit diminishing returns in their investments, there is no reason the economy as a whole need confront diminishing returns.[25] If correct, this permits sustained increases in per capita incomes and, by implication, suggests that the optimal social rate of savings and investment is higher than the market determined rate. Increasing knowledge is the centerpiece and

---

25. Although some new knowledge is privatized through patents, copyrights, etc., it is widely believed that property rights are incomplete and the full benefits accrue more broadly.

gains in one sector can drive growth in other sectors. Gale Johnson (1997 utilizes this insight. Advances in agricultural technology in the eighteenth and nineteenth centuries supported both increasing population and increasing per capita income. The availability of these substantial resources, facilitated by the growth of cities and universities, provided the conditions for a virtuous circle for the further creation of knowledge and further growth. In the United States, the federal government played a major supporting role, funding land grant colleges and agricultural extension programs.

Viewing increasing knowledge and knowledge spillovers as the wellspring for technological progress and growth has two advantages. As noted above, it helps resolve the troubling issue of diminishing marginal returns. Knowledge has "non-rivalry" characteristics (e.g., unlike a glass of wine, my use of the calculus does not preclude your use) and its usefulness does not diminish with widespread use. In principle, the larger the population, the greater the benefits. Unlike conventional inputs to production—traditionally defined as physical capital and labor—increasing knowledge is consistent with permanently increasing real wages and incomes. Knowledge externalities (positive spillovers) offset the tendency for diminishing marginal returns. Second, the emphasis on knowledge and technology opens up new approaches to understanding the sources of growth—the contributions of education, research and development activities, organizational structures, the introduction of new products, trade, and so forth.

Paul Romer (1986), a major figure in the new growth theory, constructed a model in which, despite diminishing returns to the *activity* of creating knowledge (research and development), the "materialization" of that new knowledge via investment creates production externalities for other firms throughout the economy. In this fashion, the neoclassical assumption of competitive markets could be salvaged, and the economy as a whole would still enjoy increasing returns.[26] Population growth neither adds to nor subtracts from long-term growth, but in this model large countries have better growth prospects than small countries, presumably because productivity-enhancing externalities are spread over a larger number of producers.[27] This conclusion is fragile however. In a subsequent contribution, Romer (1990) investigates technological progress arising

26. In Romer's words, "the creation of knowledge by one firm is assumed to have a positive effect on the production possibilities of other firms because knowledge cannot be perfectly patented or kept secret" (1986, p. 1003).

27. It is helpful to keep in mind the distinction between the size of a country's population and the rate of growth of that population.

from profit-seeking R&D activities set in a monopolistic competition framework. He concludes that the growth of product variety is the key variable to overcome diminishing returns. Grossman and Helpman (1994) also drop the perfect competition assumption when considering research and development expenditures. They find the effect of population size on economic growth to be ambiguous. To round out the offerings, Charles Jones (1995) constructs a model of endogenous growth based on research and development, but one in which the long-term growth rate is determined by an exogenous population growth rate.

None of this should be considered dispositive. Externalities are hard to measure empirically. In a globalized economy the size of the national population fades in importance. Scrapping the assumption of perfect competition for monopolistic competition had important implications for international trade theory, but offered little direct insight into the nexus of population and economic growth. These strands of the new growth theory are also incomplete, as they do not trace back the impacts of economic growth on demographic variables. Lucas (1988), for example, in a major article centered on building a theory of development, takes population growth as given. He admits this is a serious omission but "hopes" that development can be usefully considered separately from demographic issues.

While the level and growth of population plays a modest role in most of the new growth theory—sometimes positive as offering greater scope for externalities and by accelerating the capture of technological advances via new investment, sometimes negative if it diverts resources away from human capital to physical capital accumulation—one strand of the literature does put demographic developments at center stage. In a series of articles Gary Becker and his coauthors pioneered the microeconomic optimization approach to family decisions, including fertility. In specific applications (Becker et al. 1990, 1999), he weaves together a story in which population is endogenous (as in Malthus), human capital is the principal source of economic growth, and the rate of return to human capital *increases* as the stock of that capital increases.[28] This puts the analysis squarely under the new growth theory umbrella. Coupled with the assumption that families maximize their well-being by equalizing their returns with respect to the number of children they have and the amount

---

28. The reasons given are that the production of human capital is itself human-capital intensive, giving rise to increasing returns, and that the benefits from embodying additional knowledge in a person may depend positively rather than negatively on the knowledge he or she already has, at least up to some point.

invested in each child's education (the "quantity vs. quality" trade-off), and the further assumption that the opportunity cost of having more children is high in rich countries due to the time commitment of raising a family, the model yields two stable equilibriums. Poor countries with low stocks of human capital will have low returns and little incentive to invest in their children's education. With the opportunity cost of additional children relatively low, they will tend to have large families. In contrast families in rich countries will observe high returns on education (building human capital) and high opportunity costs for large families. The result is low fertility, small families, and low population growth. But in these countries the principal source of economic progress, human capital, is growing and indeed the returns to that capital are increasing. This analysis looks less relevant today as the era of large families and low investment in human capital has passed for most (not all) developing countries. In hindsight, this low-level equilibrium has (thankfully) not proved very stable for a large number of developing countries.

SUMMING UP: TRAPS AND ESCAPE MECHANISMS

Post–Adam Smith, and until quite recently, the majority opinion has been that rapid population growth works against increasing living standards. The main exception was a brief period during the Great Depression and its immediate aftermath in the 1930s, when population was thought to be a stimulus to investment and aggregate demand.

The negative relation has often been described in the language of "traps." Malthus was quite adamant that, for the masses, income would fluctuate

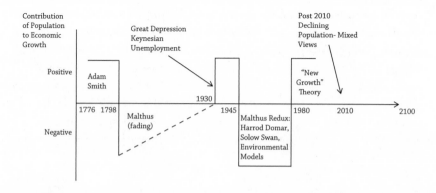

Figure 4.6:
Three centuries of positive and negative views on population and economic growth
Source: Author.

around subsistence levels, pinned there by undisciplined copulation and limited food—the Malthusian trap. The other classical economists—Ricardo, Say, and Mill—were guardedly optimistic, seeing possible escape from the trap through a combination of technological progress, foreign trade, expanding markets, and economic liberty.

The challenge of growth in poor countries after World War II was also seen in trap terms. The HD model was simple and clear (if inadequate). Low incomes meant low savings which meant low investment which meant low productivity growth which meant low incomes. The model did, however, provide a blueprint for breaking out of Malthusian stagnation by working directly on population control, and by pumping up savings, seeking high productivity investments, and via foreign aid. Nelson described a low-income trap arising from income growth leading to declining mortality and a surging population, but he also shows how to break free, as do the Chenery-Strout two-gap models. The dualistic labor-surplus models by Arthur Lewis and Fei and Ranis carry this one step forward by describing an explicit mechanism through which the transition from stagnant to modern labor markets can be accomplished by reallocating and more fully utilizing rural labor. As described in the previous chapter, a trap built on poverty, population pressure and the subsequent degradation of natural and environmental resources—an "eating the seed corn" style snare—was debated in the 1960s and 1970s. In the West the neoclassical model downplayed population growth and technological progress was seen as the sole escape from zero long-run per capita income growth. But that progress was left unexplained, a task later taken up in the new growth theory contributions. Only then did a more positive view of population growth emerge. It is noteworthy that in this large body of work virtually no attention was given to the age structure of the population. It was not until the 1990s, when the concept of a demographic bonus was elaborated on, that the effect of age structure on the size of the labor force relative to population was recognized as an important determinant of economic growth.

CHAPTER 5

✧

Optimal Population

An Attractive Chimera?

Does human society want 10 to 15 billion human beings living in poverty and malnourishment or 1 to 2 billion living with abundant resources and a quality environment?
> —Pimental et al. (1994)

One of the most sterile ideas [Optimal Population] that ever grew out of our science . . .
> —Gunnar Myrdal as quoted by Gottlieb (1945)

At first glance Myrdal's judgment appears churlish and unwarranted. To the contrary, striking a balance between numbers, aspirations, and resources has been pursued by societies for millennia, and maximizing well-being is a laudable goal. But on closer inspection the concept of optimal population has endured more than its share of controversy and remains on the periphery of economic analysis. Myrdal may not be so far off the mark.[1]

This chapter starts with a quick look back to earlier views, and then considers optimum population from three related perspectives: the welfare/ethical approach; the resources approach, which injects carrying capacity and sustainability concerns; and the divergences between private and social costs and benefits—the externalities approach.

---

1. For an exhaustive and generally sympathetic review of the optimal population concept through mid-twentieth century, see Gottlieb (1945).

EARLY VIEWS

Antiquity

Scholars have provided us with fascinating insights into how optimal population was viewed and practiced in antiquity (Fenn 1996; Wilkenson 1978). Some views are surprisingly modern. For example, it was recognized that population expansion could be a cause of war. The lure or necessity of colonization was present in ancient Greece and again in nineteenth-century Europe. In the twentieth century, the concept of *lebensraum* played a central role in Nazi ideology.[2]

Plato argued that excessive increase in population and intemperate desire for greater luxuries (fine furnishings and meat to eat) would lead to either aggressive wars for territory and resources or to poverty and domestic instability and civil unrest, as the balance between resources (mainly food) and population was disrupted. He foreshadows Malthus in pinpointing land: "A suitable total of the number of citizens cannot be fixed without considering the land" (Plato, Laws, 470 BC, as cited by Desvaux at Population Matters).

According to Plato, a stable population for an ideal city-state, enforced by state controls, would be the foundation for a well-ordered, prosperous, and quasi self-sufficient society. The controls would include a small number of households, set at 5,040, via fixed land plots of the same number. There would be restrictions on marriage and children, and in extreme circumstances, forced emigration through the establishment of new colonies.[3] Infanticide was condoned and practiced.

A small stable populace may have been the Athenian ideal, but successful defense, victories, and subjugation required soldiers. Sparta, in contrast to Athens, had a larger subject population to control and a continuing need for soldiers. *Underpopulation* was the issue and the Spartan response was severe penalties for celibates and rewards for childbearing. Nor would Rome, in subsequent centuries, have any patience for Greek intellectuals and their support of small, stationary city-states. For the Romans, a great state was a large, populous, and expanding state. And in the Roman world failure to breed by the upper classes was chronic and publically deplored.

The limited carrying capacity of the land was clearly an issue in Classical Greece. As they are today, deforestation and soil erosion were considered

---

2. Briefly, territorial expansion by a "superior race" to displace an "inferior race," in order to relieve its overpopulation.

3. The 5,040 households, including women, children, and slaves, would be about 50,000 persons, typical of Greek city-states of the time. The number 5,040 is convenient because it is divisible by every number up to 10.

evidence of overpopulation, and the ecological costs were noted. Plato lamented the losses: "What is left now is like the skeleton of a body wasted by disease; the rich soil has been carried off and only the bare framework of the district is left" (Fenn 1996, p. 453). The churchman Tertullian writing in about A.D. 200 in North Africa also hints at exceeding carrying capacity (and foreshadows Malthus) when he writes, "our numbers are burdensome to the world, which can hardly supply us from its natural elements. . . . Pestilence, war, famine and earthquakes should be regarded as a remedy for the nations, a pruning the luxuriance of the human race" (Wilkenson 1978, p. 440).

Modern Era

The more modern concept of optimal population started to crystallize in the latter part of the nineteenth century, when it was evident that the Malthusian model was falling apart, and the inevitability of a subsistence living standard for the masses was being refuted. Knut Wicksell provides a good example. Despite a sharp increase in population and distressed conditions including repeated crop failures in his native country, Sweden, and despite massive emigration in which almost 7 percent of the population left the country within a single decade, Wicksell forsook the gloomy Malthusian view and considered a better world once the tools for controlling population were perfected.[4] The optimal population question was clearly framed: "If we take a country with specific economic conditions and a given size, location, fertility of the soil etc., and also an average of level of technical knowledge of its population, then the question arises as to what population size and density would then guarantee everyone the maximum share of well-being and would thus, economically speaking, be the best"[5] (Wicksell 1910, translated by Overbeek 1973 p. 208).

This is a helpful formulation. It is based on the then conventional view that an optimal population balanced the force of increasing returns, which dates to Adam Smith and his linking of scale, specialization, and productivity to the force of diminishing returns from limited resources,

---

4. Wicksell was a Neo-Malthusian who rejected Malthus's recommendation of postponed marriages in favor of birth control through contraception. Gottlieb (1945) provided a literate and positive review of the concept at a time when depopulation concerns were widespread in Europe.

5. Note the absence of traditional nineteenth-century arguments supporting a large population: colonization, manning an industrial revolution, and raising and maintaining a large army.

which was the fixation of Malthus and other classical economists. It is intuitive and easily comprehended in diagrammatic fashion. See figure 5.1.

In regions of low population density and abundant natural resources, especially fertile land, each additional worker could draw on underused

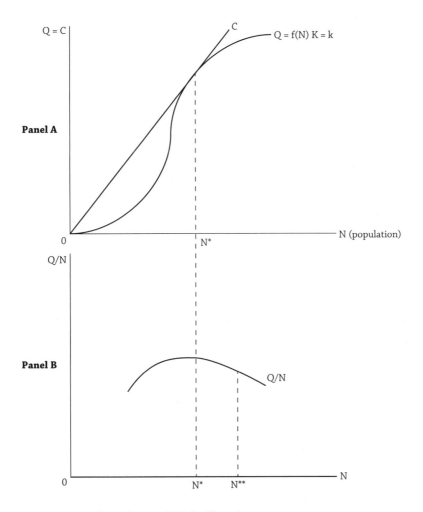

Figure 5.1: Optimal population: A Wicksellian view
Panel A displays a production function for labor assuming a stationary economy in which other inputs are constant (K = k) N is population and a constant fraction of the population is in the labor force. Q is total output and equal to total consumption (C). The slope of rays from the origin such as 0C measure average product. At low levels of population resources are abundant and economies of scale available, but at higher levels resources are stretched and diseconomies of scale set in, explaining the approximate "S" shape. Directly below, in Panel B, the average product of labor (Q/N) is plotted. It also measures per capita consumption. (Static) optimal population is at N* where the average and marginal product per person are equal and the average product is maximized. Note that N* does not maximize total output. In Panel B, an increase in population from N* to N** increases the area under the average product curve Q/N. The percent increase in population exceeds the percent decrease in average product.

resources. Industry could look to economies of scale in production. Via Adam Smith's specialization and productivity gains, the incremental output would pull up average labor output and provide the basis for increasing wages and living standards. But at higher population densities productivity gains would tend to weaken, the resource base would be stretched over greater numbers, and diminishing returns would come to dominate. The declining marginal product of labor would drag down the average, and per capita output and income would decline despite increasing total output. This would be the hallmark of overpopulation.

This formulation has other advantages. It sets the optimum in economic terms—output and income as conventionally measured. Other desiderata such as economic security or privacy or even further afield, spiritual values, which would have muddied the concept and its measurement, were generally not considered. (Wicksell did add an aesthetic provision that population should not be so dense as to preclude enjoying the beauty and grandeur of nature, but he did not elaborate.) The formulation also finesses the issue of inequality in distribution.[6] Moreover, it is centered on *per capita* economic well-being and not the maximization of total output and income, with Wicksell declaring that the densest population (the maximum) is the most *unfavorable*. This last point did not go down so well with the welfare theorist, Arthur Pigou, who wrote, "provided the average working family attains in the whole period of life any surplus of satisfaction over dissatisfaction, an increase in numbers implies by itself an addition to human welfare"(cited by Dalton 1928, p. 32). The merits of average vs. total utility or well-being resurfaced more than half a century later in the form of the so-called Repugnant Conclusion and are not yet resolved. We turn to it in a moment.

In spite of its attractive qualities, troubling features of Wicksell's formulation remain. The early proponents of optimal population struggled with a static formulation of what they themselves admitted was essentially a dynamic concept, a moving target. Economic conditions and especially technology are never constant. Natural resources are discovered, depleted, and occasionally recover. Physical capital can be replicated and labor productivity enhanced. It follows that today's optimal population, if it could be computed, would not be optimal for tomorrow. While some proponents recognized that today's population casts a shadow forward on

---

6. This was later assisted by the Kaldor-Hicks hypothetical compensation test, which hives off distributional considerations from efficiency analysis, leaving the former to politics and the latter to economics. Atkinson (2014) has attempted to rectify this in the context of utilitarian analysis of optimal population.

future resources and production and thus the future optimum, they did not offer a method for intergenerational aggregation of economic well-being. This is most evident in models including exhaustible resources and the need to balance one generation's welfare against another's. Partha Dasgupta (1969) got it right when he asserted that population and savings (the capital stock) have to be jointly determined, and it is the discounted welfare of all generations that is at issue. This, of course, greatly complicates the analysis, requiring as it does anticipating technological change, establishing the social rate of time discount, and considering the relative welfare of existing persons and potential persons not yet born.[7]

Inadequate Tests

Despite the agreeable simplicity of viewing the optimal as a balancing of increasing and decreasing returns, finding a reliable test for under-, over-, and optimal populations was difficult. Dalton (1928), a proponent of the concept, proposes three tests and rejects them all. (Surprisingly he does not consider immigration/emigration trends.) The first indicator considered is the time trend of per capita income. It had been suggested that if rising, underpopulation is indicated; if falling, overpopulation is at work. The weakness of this test is that many forces determine per capita income and the conjunction of these forces may easily obscure the role of population.[8]

The second candidate is rather surprising—changes in a country's international terms of trade—with a deterioration indicating overpopulation, improvement indicating underpopulation, and constant terms of trade presumably indicating optimal population. Modern trade theory has not picked up on this test of population optimality, although it has long embraced the concept of an optimal tariff. The size of that tariff is indeed linked to the size of a country, but size is measured as its share of world trade and not its population per se.

The third suggested test was the volume of unemployment, an important issue in the interwar period, and an idea that was revived in the postwar analysis of population in developing countries under the rubric of surplus labor (see chapter 4). Dalton, writing in 1928, dismisses this test

7. Samuelson (1975, 1976) investigated the optimal *rate of growth* of population. Slow growth has the advantage of minimizing capital dilution but sets up the intergenerational problem of diminishing support for the elderly.

8. Improvement in econometrics and data brought back this test when population and economic growth were considered in developing countries after World War II.

of overpopulation, arguing that unemployment was mainly a result of a mismatch between supply and demand for specific skills and occurred in very local labor markets. Interestingly, a decade later Keynes and others were arguing for *increasing* a falling birth rate to stave off chronic unemployment, an argument that resonates in Europe today.

At this point, having dismissed proposed empirical tests, Dalton (1928, p. 42) shrugs and passes the problem on to others: "The discovery of reliable tests remains an unsolved problem, difficult but not necessarily insoluble." As discussed later, much the same can be said today.

To close this section, it is useful to note dimensions of optimal population that are currently of concern, but that were either ignored or glossed over in early contributions. These can be grouped in two categories: the globalization of ecological stress and sustainability. The realization that the ecological basis for economic activity could be stressed and degraded by population growth was, of course, not new and can be traced back to antiquity. But those were viewed as local collapses. Even in the early post–World War II period, the problem was thought to be geographically concentrated in poor countries. And in that era there was minimal concern for the "effluents of affluence," the contribution the populations in rich countries were making to global environmental despoliation. It was not until the landmark 1972 UN Conference on the Human Environment that the contributions of both poverty and affluence to environmental stress was made clear (Pearson and Pryor 1978). This paved the way for an emerging analysis of population, sustainability, and the well-being of future generations. We examine this later in the chapter but first consider some tangled ethical arguments.

POPULATION ETHICS AND THE REPUGNANT CONCLUSION

The concept of optimal population involves comparing populations of different sizes to determine if one is "better" than another. Better as used here is an ethical term. It would be useful to have a secure ethical framework on which to make these judgments. We need some guidance grounded on moral principles.

Utilitarianism

Utilitarianism appears to fill the bill. It is a well-established doctrine with roots back to the nineteenth century. On the face of it at least, it is easy to understand—the morally right course of action is one that produces the greatest balance of benefits over harms, or in shorthand, the greatest good for the greatest number. In the issue at hand, a population policy that maximizes total utility or well-being—i.e. the net of benefits less harms—leads to the optimal population. This is the total utility version sometimes called classical utilitarianism. As an alternative, one could suggest the maximization of average utility, total utility of the population divided by the number of people it comprises. This is the average utility version, the one favored by Wicksell. For elaborations, see Razin and Sadka (1995).

Unfortunately the utilitarian framework can conflict with what our intuition and our common sense tell us about optimal population. There are two main problems. The first is that it leads to the so-called "Repugnant Conclusion" (RC). This appears to undermine utilitarianism as a moral foundation for population theory and policy. The second is the gnarly problem of valuing "potential" lives—lives that may or may not be brought into existence by policy actions. We take these one at a time.

The Repugnant Conclusion

The RC was formulated by the British philosopher Derek Parfit in the 1980s and has unleashed a growing literature. Cowen (1996), for example, states that it is the most serious issue which normative population theory must face. Moreover, it has spawned a growing family of unattractive, if inventive, offspring: The Very Repugnant Conclusion, The Reverse Repugnant Conclusion, The Sadistic Conclusion, the Absurd Conclusion, and the Conclusive Conclusion (aim for human extinction and be done with it!).[9] As argued later, however, its importance for practical population policy appears overstated.

As set forth by Parfit, the RC states, "Compared with the existence of very many people—say, 10 billion—all of whom have a very high quality of life [the A population], there must be some much larger number of people [the Z population] whose existence, other things being equal, would be better, even though these people would have lives that are barely worth living."

It is the assertion that a mere increase in the number of people can offset deterioration in the quality of each life that is counterintuitive and

---

9. Contributors include Arrhenius (2003), Blackorby and Donaldson (1984), Mulgan (2002), Parfit (2004), Renstrom and Spataro (2011).

which many people find repugnant. Moreover the popular interpretation is that the classical utilitarian version favors very large populations existing at very low levels of well-being. Neither implication appears attractive. Nevertheless, under the conditions specified by Parfit, it has been difficult to navigate around the RC.

It would be tedious to rehearse the various responses to the RC in detail. But three deserve mention.[10] The first is to stick with utilitarianism and claim that the Z life is not all that bad, and the large Z population *is* in fact better. This is easier to swallow if we set the "barely worth living" threshold a little higher. A variation to this response is to challenge what we, the well-to-do, anoint as a life "barely worth living." Those living such a life may see things differently and it is their valuation, not ours, that counts. A second approach involves "critical level utilitarianism." In essence, it sets a base of individual level utility of zero and a somewhat higher value, the critical level of utility or well-being. People with utility falling within the zero to critical level range do not add to total utility (and indeed may be assumed to reduce it); only the addition of persons whose lives surpass the critical level contribute to aggregate utility. In this fashion, it is easy enough to dump large numbers of additional people who have low but positive levels of utility into this range and conclude that a movement from the base case A of 10 billion with a high level of well-being is *not* dominated by Z, with its masses of nearly wretched souls. The RC is neutralized. But it appears highly arbitrary—to first acknowledge utility of the poor but then to exclude it from aggregate utility. A third approach is to start to pick apart the conditions Parfait laid out. An obvious stating point is the "if other things are equal" clause. Virtues and vices such as injustice and liberty may not be equally prevalent in populations A and Z. These are moral values as well and if they were considered they may negate the RC.

The Repugnant Conclusion Defanged

These responses chipped away at the RC but did not demolish it. The prevailing view has been that utilitarianism is ill-suited as a guide to optimal

---

10. A switch from total to average utilitarianism is not very satisfactory. If we start from population A of 10 billion at a high level of well-being and assume conventional utility functions, the subtraction of one person would raise average utility for those remaining. The downward spiral in optimal population toward zero would continue until the loss of companionship comes to dominate utility. Even God recognized that it is not good to be alone and He created a helpmate for Adam.

population policy, as it favored very large populations existing at wretched stands of living. This view is a mistake and arises from an unfounded assumption that total utility would continue to rise with ever larger populations. When real world conditions are introduced, including limited natural and environmental resources, the notion of unbounded utility collapses and takes the RC down with it.[11]

Shiell (2008) investigates the effects of bounding total utility with reasonable restrictions based on limited resources, the law of conservation of matter and others, and concludes that the problem of the RC may be overstated. Razin and Sadka (1995) show that by adding an activity subject to economies of scale such as public goods and a fixed input such as land, total utility increases, reaches a maximum, and then declines. Under these conditions choosing a population based on maximizing utility does *not* lead to an unduly large and poor population. Moreover the purported weakness of average utilitarianism—that it points to the smallest possible population as best—is shown to be false. We are back close to the Wicksellian concept of optimal population arising from a balancing of forces.

Valuing Potential Lives

Utilitarianism confronts a related and equally gnarly problem, the valuation of potential lives. The concept of optimal population implies choice—otherwise it is rather sterile. Choice implies *potential* lives, lives that may or may not be brought into existence by policy actions. How are potential lives to be valued? There are conflicting views. Classical utilitarianism directs us to take actions that will increase good (utility) in the world. If potential lives are brought into existence, and these lives enjoy positive utility or well-being, do we have an obligation to do so? We clearly have moral obligations to existing people and to future people who are actually brought into existence. Our obligation to the latter is to bequeath an environment and sufficient resources to support a good life, with positive utility. But do we have an equal obligation to the potential lives that *could* be brought into existence? To whom is this obligation owed? Perhaps to ourselves if we were so thinly populated that we lacked companionship. But surely we cannot have an obligation to the un-conceived and unborn that

---

11. In technical terms, for utility to be unbounded (have no upper limit), it is necessary that the elasticity of average utility with respect to population size must be less than one in absolute value.

do not yet and may never exist. To put it bluntly, the un–conceived have no moral standing and no claim rights on us.

The basis for a positive valuation must be that adding a good life to the existing population is an intrinsic good, and this is what classic utilitarianism seems to suggest. However, this view conflicts with another strand of population ethics, the "neutrality intuition," which holds that adding people who are expected to lead "good" lives with positive utility is an ethically neutral act, neither good nor bad in itself. (This intuition is not symmetrical. Bringing into being lives that are likely to be filled with nothing but pain and misery is not neutral but is morally bad.)

However, the neutrality intuition is not universally accepted. Partha Dasgupta (1998), for example, suggests that the weight given to potential lives could be positive, but less than the weight given to existing lives. John Broome struggles to reconcile the neutrality intuition with various theories of valuing population and has argued that it is deeply flawed. He suggests that for full evaluation of actions affecting such things as global warming it may be necessary to trace demographic consequences deep into the future.[12] Elsewhere he notes that arguments in moral philosophy are rarely conclusive because of inconsistencies in intuitions. The population ethics literature amply demonstrates this. Finding an acceptable ethical framework for assessing optimal population policy remains a work in progress.

RESOURCES, CARRYING CAPACITY, AND SUSTAINABILITY
A Ubiquitous Concern

The moral philosophy approach to optimal population described above pays little attention to the natural resource and environmental base of economic activity.[13] This is surprising as resources are at the center of most discussions of population size. The concern for resources traces to Plato and land, quoted above; it continues with Malthus and food supplies; surfaces in Mill as he extols nature and solitude in a stationary economy; switches in mid-nineteenth century to a prospective energy shortage (UK coal) with Jevons; re-emerges in 1972 with the influential, if flawed, Limits to Growth computer modeling exercise; is a centerpiece of the poverty-population-environmental degradation vicious circle thesis that

---

12. Broome (2005). See also chapter 7.
13. Partha Dasgupta is an exception.

arose at the same time; is integral to the sustainability debates starting in the 1980s; has embraced threats to specific resources (e.g., fresh water, soil, forests, fisheries, genetic diversity, coral reefs); confronted peak oil in the first years of the twenty-first century; and, in its most recent incarnation, enlivens the global warming debate.

The resource-population imbalances in earlier times were mainly local or regional in nature. Certainly the conflation of environmental stress and population on Easter Island in the fifteenth century, or collapse in the Chaco Anasazi settlements in the US Southwest in the thirteenth century, or the much earlier examples in Mesopotamia, were traumatic for residents, but they were not global events. The modern issue is framed differently. The internationalization of trade, capital, technology, and knowledge, and the emergence of global threats such as climate change and loss of genetic diversity has diminished the issue of local resource balances and focused attention on the global question—optimal world population in light of global environmental resources.

This does not mean that local and national data and analysis are not needed. Overfishing is often site-specific. An efficient regime for restricting greenhouse gas emissions must respect national differences in abatement cost. And, of course, global and trans-boundary environmental resources are managed, if managed at all, by national governments. But in the modern era a comparison of environmental resources and population at the national level misses the mark. We may wish to know the "ecological footprint" of, say, the Netherlands or Singapore, for reasons of determining responsibility for corrective policy, but it is the sum of the world's footprints that is the main issue.

Carrying Capacity

It is useful to start with the term "carrying capacity" and the distinction between its use in ecology and its use in discussing human populations.[14] Environmental carrying capacity in a nonhuman context can be thought of as the maximum number of a species that can be supported indefinitely without damaging the integrity of that environment. Sustainability is an essential aspect, with stability and resiliency of ecosystems (their integrity) directly related to biodiversity. It is tempting to lift this definition and apply it to the human condition. It would anchor our view of population on an upper bound, not necessarily at the optimal level but at a level

---

14. See the excellent review by Blake Alcott (2012).

that is feasible and sustainable. We might then work the numbers downward toward the optimal level. The ecologist Garrett Hardin (1986), famous for his work on the tragedy of the commons, believes that the concept of carrying capacity can be adapted to human populations with little change. But it is not so simple.

First, even in its nonhuman context, carrying capacity is not a precise concept. Variations in exogenous conditions (weather, disease), interactions with other species and competition with them for food, changes in reproductive behavior, and adaptive learning may significantly alter carrying capacity. Second, far more than most species, humans are continually altering their environment, sometimes intentionally, sometimes not. In doing so they change its carrying capacity, and that capacity is no longer fixed by biological factors, but through social institutions. It is not reasonable to seek the maximum human population from an estimate of carrying capacity, let alone an estimate of optimal population, if the environment itself is manipulated.

There is another problem. Even if we could calculate a precise human carrying capacity by fixing known resources and known technology, at best we would be estimating population at mere survival or subsistence levels. No one writing on optimal population aspires to this. To use the concept of carrying capacity productively in a human context we must say something about the material quality of life that environmental resources and technology permit. The result is a hybrid and has been called cultural or social carrying capacity. This step transmutes what was initially a biophysical concept into a social/institutional construct. And it suggests a range of optima as broad as our range of acceptable living standards. Presumably an optimal population size would fall within that range, but that hardly narrows the search. But adding "social" does transform the analysis to one that is normative and institutionally determined. That, in turn, underscores the ethical nature of the concept. Social carrying capacity cannot be objectively established.

Searches and Estimates

The barrier to an objective determination of social carrying capacity has not discouraged search for bio-physical limits. Writing in 1679, the Dutch scientist, Antonie van Leeuwenhoek, estimated the maximum world human carrying capacity to be 13.4 billion, well above the current UN medium projection for 2100. He found this number by applying the Netherlands population density (population per km²) to an estimate of the world's inhabited land area.

The search to reveal carrying capacity and social carrying capacity that flourished in the last decades of the twentieth century was one-sided. It was mostly an effort to document existing or prospective over-population and the urgency of population control. Very few saw underpopulation as the problem, and certainly not as a consequence of underutilized natural and environmental resources (Julian Simon is the main exception). Van den Bergh and Rietveld (2004) have conducted a meta-analysis of some 51 studies containing 94 estimates of maximum world population limits.[15] The majority of them were published in the second half of the twentieth century and reflected the then newly found interest in limits to growth. The results are of some interest. The median estimate was 7.7 billion people, not far from the actual value in the year that this meta-analysis was published. The minimum estimate was 0.5 billion and the maximum was 1×10^{21} billion people. The latter is certainly not plausible as it assumes all carbon on earth is incorporated in human bodies. More enlightening is that all studies published before 1940 found the population limit to be well above the then current level, while in subsequent years 21 of 94 estimates indicated that the then current population was already *above* the earth's carrying capacity. This shift is surely related to the population explosion in the post–World War II era but also the explosion of concern for the environment.

At a broader level, it is not clear that studies purporting to identify population limits address sustainability, especially sustainability in the context of global warming, acidification of the world's oceans, and biodiversity losses. They certainly do not provide much insight into social carrying capacity and optimal population.

Environmental Indicators of Overpopulation

A seemingly straightforward way to document overpopulation is to examine the existing and prospective draw on natural and environmental resources to see if they appear sufficient and sustainable. If not, the draw is deemed excessive and either population or living standards needs to be scaled back, or technological fixes found. In practice, it is not so simple. Economists and ecologists often have very different understandings of sustainability. The former tend to focus on maintaining or improving the standard of living and the latter look to the diversity and resilience of

---

15. For an earlier effort, see Cohen (1995).

ecosystems.[16] The difference in focus between economists and ecologists is not unbridgeable. Many of the former would acknowledge that economic activities are sustainable only if the life-supporting systems on which the activities rely are resilient (Arrow et al. 1995).[17]

Careful investigation of current and prospective global consumption patterns can shed light on sustainability in both its ecological and economic meanings, without resorting to crude carrying capacity estimates or assertions of optimal population. For example, a rising price trend for those natural resources that are marketed suggests increasing relative scarcity and the need for conservation and substitution in production. Also, in principle, if the market rate of return on risk-free investments exceeds the social rate of discount on consumption, inadequate savings (excessive consumption) are indicated. (However, a lack of relevant market data and unresolved ethical disputes plague the social rate of discount and limit the usefulness of this indicator.) If depletion and depreciation of natural, physical, and human capital exceeds new investments, sustainability is in question. Finally, if market prices are known to be below real values due to externalities and defective property rights (e.g., open access fisheries), exploitation is likely to be unsustainable. Using the available data together with adjustments for population growth and technological change, Arrow and his colleagues (2004) find evidence of unsustainable eco-economic conditions in sub-Saharan Africa and the Middle East/North Africa. In these regions investment in human and manufactured capital does not offset depletion of natural capital.[18] Not coincidentally, these two regions display high fertility rates as compared to global averages.

Optimal Population or Optimal Affluence?

Adding a concern for living standards introduces another complication when considering optimal population. If the draw on nature's resources is shown to be excessive and unsustainable, how do we separate the contribution of population from the contribution of affluence? The allocation of

16. Economists are further divided between proponents of "weak" vs. "strong" sustainability—a controversy over how easily physical and human capital can substitute for environmental "capital" in production and consumption activities.

17. It is interesting that the meeting of experts that attempted to bridge gaps did not include any demographers.

18. Natural Capital is a term for nature's assets and their role in providing natural resource inputs and environmental services for economic production.

responsibility between the rich and the poor for an impaired or declining global resource base is a hot political issue. It is also central to an effective policy response if overpopulation/overconsumption is implicated. As discussed in chapter 7, it becomes especially fraught in discussions of global warming and the relative contributions of the rich North and the poor but populous South. How much weight should be given to population size in the allocation of access to international common property resources?

A final facet of the natural resources/population puzzle deserves mention. The dominant limiting resources have long been identified as food and energy. Sometimes they are considered separately—Malthus and food, Jevons and coal. But sometimes the interaction of all three—population, food, and energy—is at issue. As argued in chapter 3, there were localized cases in many developing countries in the latter half of the twentieth century, when energy prices spiked and population growth was at its highest. (Africa today is not immune.) Food and energy are again in conflict, but at a global level and in the context of climate change. Chapter 7 examines whether the slowdown in population will ease this conflict.

This section has concentrated on the interactions of population, living standards, and natural resources in the hopes of salvaging the optimal population concept. It appears to be a quixotic effort.

REPRODUCTIVE EXTERNALITIES

Having looked at ethics and resources, we turn to a third approach to optimal population: social vs. private interests in reproduction.[19] In general, economics is content with letting the private sector provide an optimal supply of popcorn or gravestones or economics textbooks. Does it also supply the optimal number of babies? Can we thrive with a laissez-faire procreation policy? The answer depends on the prevalence of *reproductive externalities*: the divergence between private and social costs and benefits of bringing children into the world (Birdsall 1988). If externalities from childbearing are positive, it suggests considering pro-natalist policies to nudge up birthrates. If negative, social restraints on procreation are indicated. Even if the externalities cannot be exactly calculated, they may point the direction in which optimal population lies. The sign and size of

---

19. An externality can be defined as the incidental but not necessarily unanticipated effect caused by the actions of one economic agent on the welfare of another economic agent in which the effect does not pass through markets, but is directly felt. Externalities can be either positive or negative. Industrial pollution is a common example (Pearson 2000).

reproductive externalities is likely to vary among countries, and especially between rich and poor.

It is useful to go beyond a simple positive/negative notation and discuss two classes of externalities: those having to do with population and the mismanagement of natural and environmental resources, and those arising from flows between individuals and their governments, sometimes termed fiscal externalities. Both may have intergenerational implications.

Population-Environmental Externalities

The birth of another citizen is not a purely private affair if its use of natural and environmental resources generates negative externalities. Many such resources exist as open access, common property resources (e.g., fisheries, genetic resources, the atmosphere). If these are unregulated or improperly managed, as is likely to be the case where private ownership is technically difficult or disputed, open access invites excessive exploitation and externalities, the classic "tragedy of the commons." *Ceteris paribus*, the larger the population in such situations, the more severe the negative externality and loss of social welfare. Because the externalities are frequently international and intergenerational, they are that much more difficult to control. These costs are not fully internalized by the parents of a newborn and indeed are often ignored completely.

The first best policy is to correct the mismanagement, generally through restriction on access to the resources. For example, if there is overfishing of open access fisheries or overgrazing of communal lands "stinting" the commons has been a traditional response. But if that is not available, population control measures may be considered. Moreover, even if the resources are optimally managed, a population externality may remain if the resources are communally owned. Adding a child reduces the per capita yield or harvest that the resource can optimally generate and is thus an external cost imposed on others that is not borne by parents. Two corrective taxes may be needed—a tax to limit access to the resource and a childbearing tax to help maintain the per capita yield. But one must also be careful to also consider possible positive externalities associated with an expanding population.

Efforts have been made to quantify reproductive externality costs in the context of global warming. The methods, assumptions, and conclusions vary widely. We summarize two for illustration. Brian O'Neil and Lee Wexler (2000) set out to estimate the cost of an additional birth if atmospheric CO_2 levels are eventually stabilized by emissions caps or taxes.

In the analysis emissions are held constant along a predetermined path.[20] Thus, the additional cost of birth is measured by the additional abatement cost of maintaining the cap, not the damages that that person's emissions would cause over her lifetime. The costs are also assumed to include abating the emissions of the descendants of the new-born.[21] Moreover the authors seek only those costs not borne by the prospective parents—that is they seek the costs borne by society at large. The externality cost of a birth in a more developed country (MDC) is estimated separately from a birth in a less developed country (LDC) under the assumption that emissions per capita vary with income, although a birth anywhere will create costs for all. This means the model must specify the allocation of abatement effort and timing between the two regions, and also their respective marginal abatement costs. The cost is measured as the difference in net present (discounted) value of consumption with and without the birth for persons living in MDC and in LDC regions. (It is helpful to remember that a ton of CO_2 emitted from a poor and a rich country are indistinguishable once they reach the atmosphere and they create the same damage, although the damage will vary widely among countries).

The results show substantial but not dramatic externalities. As displayed in table 5.1, in the base case the externality cost of a child born in the rich world is $4,420 for citizens of MDCs and $470 for citizens in LDCs. If the child is born in an LDC, the costs are $1,510 for the MDCs and $360 for LDCs. These can be explained as follows: If born in an MDC the child can be expected to have a high income and create high emissions. Thus, the abatement costs to hold emissions at their predetermined levels will be high. The allocation of this cost as between MDCs and LDCs will depend on the specific cost allocation rule in the prevailing international climate agreement. If, instead, a child is born in a LDC region, emissions and hence abatement costs will be lower. The division of the abatement costs between MDCs and LDCs depends on the abatement effort allocation rules, the marginal abatement costs in the two regions, and ultimately on their relative populations. The analysis considers a number of

20. Abatement costs can be thought of as the cost or reducing greenhouse gas emissions, mainly CO_2, through conservation or the use of more expensive renewable energy.

21. In other words, a birth today sets up a dynastic line of descendants, each of whom would emit greenhouse gases. It is a bit of a leap to go from optimal population today to optimal population for all time. Without denying that fertility decisions today have long run consequences, is it not enough to accommodate new persons arriving today, leaving long-run birth decisions and their environmental consequences to future generations? See chapter 6.

assumptions concerning abatement costs and their allocation. (Please note that it may be inappropriate to simply add the externality costs to MDCs and LDCs to get a global total—for example, for a MDC baby, $4,420 plus $470 equals $4890. Because of their lower level of income it is customary to weight a dollar of cost to the poor more highly than a dollar of cost to the rich).

Table 5.1 also shows externality costs for the two regions under alternative assumptions. As expected in climate economics, the discount rate, which transposes future values to the present (an exchange rate over time), is critical. The base case uses a discount rate that is 3 percent per year higher than the Low Discount Rate scenario.[22] The results were significant. The externality cost of a MDC birth rises from $4,420 to $28,200 for residents of MDCs and from $470 to $4,810 for developing countries. Even larger percentage increases arise from a birth in a developing country. There is no mystery. The present values of future abatement costs are highly sensitive to the discount rate.

Population growth, which in this model is exogenous, is also important. Using lower UN population projections, the externality cost of an additional MDC birth is about 40 percent lower for residents of MDCs and 70 percent lower for residents of LDCs as compared to the base case. The externality cost of a birth in a developing country drops by about 75 percent. Again there is no mystery. A lower assumption about population growth means lower emissions and lower abatement costs to comply with a fixed emissions trajectory. And a lower population projection means fewer descendants and fewer emissions from the descendants of an additional birth.

Finally, the introduction of an effective international greenhouse trading system, which is highly desirable on efficiency grounds, can dramatically affect the distribution of the externality cost between MDCs and LDCs. For example, and assuming greenhouse emission permits are distributed internationally in a fashion that favors LDCs, the externality cost of a MDC birth increases over the base scenario cost of $4,420 to $5,800, but the cost to LDCs reverses and becomes a net benefit of $2,300!

---

22. Specifically and technically, in the base case the pure rate of time preference, which is one component of the discount rate, is set at 3 percent, and in the Low Discount Rate scenario it is set at 0 percent. Opinion is divided as to the appropriate number for the pure rate of time discount and a zero rate is often defended on ethical grounds. The second component of the discount rate adjusts for expected increases in income over time and the diminishing marginal utility attached thereto. This component of the discount rate is assumed to be the same in the base and the low discount rate cases.

Table 5.1. POPULATION-GLOBAL WARMING EXTERNALITY COSTS

Scenario	Regional greenhouse externalities to 1995 birth (USD 1990)			
	MDC birth		LDC birth	
	On MDCs	On LDCs	On MDCs	On LDCs
Base case	−4,420	−470	−1,510	−360
Low population	−2,650	−140	−850	−80
Low discount rate	−28,200	−4810	−11,460	−4,380
Emissions trading	−5,820	2,300	−2,050	−70

Source: O'Neil and Wexler 2000, table 1. By permission.
Note: MNC = More Developed Countries; LDC = Less Developed Country.

The explanation is that emissions trading results in an efficient allocation of abatement *effort* but the allocation of the monetary costs of that effort is determined by whether a country becomes a net buyer or seller of permits. In this particular example, the LDC's additional abatement costs were more than offset by its receipts from sale of permits to MDCs in the emissions trading markets.

The second illustration, from Henning Bohn and Charles Stuart (forthcoming), takes a different approach and reaches much more dramatic conclusions. The authors attempt to estimate the tax on children which, if assessed on parents, would equal the global warming externality cost of an additional child.[23] In this model the *environmental* externality of greenhouse gas emissions is controlled with an emissions cap. Controlling the higher emissions from a larger population, while retaining the cap, requires lowering per-person emissions. This imposes a cost on everyone. Thus, the private decision to have a child does not reflect the full social costs of doing so. That is the externality that the tax on children is designed to correct. Note the similarity to the basic Malthusian model in which population growth confronted a fixed factor land—in this case the emissions cap—leading to reduced real incomes for all, and ultimately restraining population growth. In the absence of the tax, and with the costs of children partially socialized, the incentive for prospective parents is to have children. This implies that actual population will exceed optimal population.

The tax is measured in units of parent's consumption. The base case results are striking. They show the optimal tax per child to be about

23. Taxes to correct an externality are called Pigouvian taxes and were first discussed by the welfare economist, Arthur Pigou in the 1930s.

20 percent of a parent's lifetime income in steady state. Moreover, the optimal (long-term) steady state population is only one-quarter its untaxed size.

Neither of the two studies described above is sufficient to establish an optimal population and certainly not an optimal population below its current level. Positive population externalities as described in the new growth theory (knowledge spillovers) and fiscal externalities described below may dominate those associated with climate change. Nevertheless, the two studies do suggest that restrictive population measures might be a useful adjunct to a serious climate policy. Short of that, they suggest that the current global *pattern* of declining fertility, with the lowest levels mainly in the most affluent countries, is supportive of environmental objectives. The main task, of course, is to deal directly with greenhouse gas emissions, not population.

Fiscal Externalities

It is something of a relief to find potentially substantial positive reproductive externalities in fiscal matters, although negative externalities may also present. The positive and negative effects arise in a number of ways. First, an additional birth dilutes the per capita ownership value of collectively owned assets such as mineral rights on public lands (or sovereign wealth funds). This cost is not borne by parents and is a negative externality.[24] Second, an additional birth dilutes the per capita public debt, spreading it over a larger tax base. If the debt is ever redeemed, which it may not be, this benefit is not captured by parents (or the child) and thus is a positive externality conferred on society at large.

Third, after a lag to reach maturity and enter the workforce, an additional birth will spread the burden of financing public goods over a larger tax base. This too is a positive benefit not captured by parents and hence is another positive externality. But to be genuine, they must be true public goods in which the use by one individual does not reduce availability for others (non-rivalrous). National defense and basic research qualify as genuine public goods. Quasi-public goods like streets do not qualify if they are subject to congestion, but in general higher population density does tend to reduce their per unit cost, a plus.

---

24. By symmetry every death would create a benefit for the remaining population. Note that increasing deaths are *not* considered in the same light as decreasing births. This is another example where we draw an ethical distinction between the rights of existing people and the weaker or nonexistent rights of the unborn.

Fourth, net intergenerational transfers through government taxes and government benefit programs (education, health, public pensions) resulting from an additional birth are potential positive or negative externalities, as these fiscal transactions are not borne by parents of newborn children. The logic here is that an addition birth lowers the country's age profile. Because intergenerational transfers mediated through governments in advanced countries are tilted toward the elderly, a positive externality, benefiting the elderly, results (Lee and Miller 1990).[25] As currently structured, most public pay- as- you-go pension schemes discourage the capture of this externality. Prospective parents are not compensated for many of the costs of rearing children and most pension schemes fail to "reward" them for parenting by adjusting their subsequent pension benefits upward. The result is to discourage parenting (Ehrlich and Lui 1997; Meier and Werding 2010). This bias away from parenthood could be corrected by structuring higher benefits for those who contribute children who, after maturing, will contribute to public pension schemes. Still this solution is somewhat dodgy. It merely postpones the problem by a generation as the additional children will at some point be additional retirees.

In a pioneering study, Ronald Lee and Tim Miller (1990) attempted to quantify fiscal population externalities for the United States and four other countries. For the United States in 1985, expressed on a per birth basis, they found: a negative externality of $4,611 for dilution of public assets (mainly mineral rights); a positive externality of $10,013 for dilution of government debt; a positive externality of $74,950 for spreading the burden of paying for public goods; and a positive externality of $24,688 as a consequence of intergenerational transfers. The net grand total is $105,040. By comparison, per capita income at that time was $16,757. A similar but more recent study (Wolf et al. 2011), which took account of fiscal differences between parents and childless adults, found the net fiscal externality of becoming a parent to be positive at $217,000.

The implication of these two fiscal externality studies appears to be that the United States has yet to reach its optimal population and pronatalist (and perhaps pro-immigration) policies are indicated. But before

25. See also chapter 8. In a country such as India where support for the elderly is more likely to be provided privately, and where the government has substantial obligations to educate youth, the externality resulting from an additional birth might be negative. Note that at this point we are slipping away from the notion that an externality arises from some technical consideration—CO_2 emissions when fossil fuel is burned or the characteristic of non-rivalry. The intergenerational transfer externality described above is the result of institutional and policy conditions. A change in policy could wipe out the externality and avoid any need for a childbearing tax or subsidy.

reaching that controversial conclusion, the limits of the approach are germane. First, neither incorporated environmental externalities, which may be strongly negative and point to the opposite population conclusion. This is doubly important as such externalities are often international or global in scope, and the fiscal externalities can only speak to population issues at the national level. Second, the positive intergenerational transfer externality has the hint of a Ponzi scheme and is a questionable justification for pro-natalist policies. It is true that transfers from young to old are facilitated by increasing the number of younger workers. But the young wear out and grow old and ever more young contributors to pension schemes are needed. Third, the positive effects identified in the studies are largely attributable to the *descendants* of the newborn (and would be wiped out with a sufficiently high discount rate). It seems questionable to rely on the fiscal role of the stream of descendants in justifying a subsidy to prospective parents today. It is a bit like borrowing from the unborn. Finally, in this study a new birth amounts to providing society with an asset generating net revenues which have a present value of $217,000. But that value is contingent on tax and benefit policies in place in future years, which cannot be pre-committed today. A baby in the buggy is not money in the bank.

CONCLUSIONS: THREE STRIKES AND THREE MISSES

The optimal population has slipped away from us again. Three approaches were tried: ethical, based on moral philosophy; resource constraints, based on environmental and ecological concepts; and reproductive externalities, based on economics. There is a singular lack of agreement within and among the three approaches. Each had something to contribute but none were successful in developing a robust theory and measurement of optimal population. It may be more productive to consider the rise and fall of populations, rather than launch a direct attack on finding the optimal level. That suggests we pay attention to the so-called demographic transition.

CHAPTER 6

☙

Demographic Transitions

Development is the best contraceptive.
—Dr. Karen Singh, *World Population Conference, Bucharest, 1974*

A QUICK SKETCH

The so-called demographic transition (DT) is a well-known concept and does not require a detailed description.[1] There are however several features that cast light on aging and declining population, the subject of subsequent chapters. These features merit greater attention and are the focus of this chapter.

The centerpiece of the DT is a society's passage from a semi-stable equilibrium of high birth rates, high death rates, and a stable or very slowly growing population, toward another potential equilibrium of low birth and death rates and relatively stable population size. This is accompanied by classic demographic markers: first increasing, then decreasing, and then possibly negative population growth, dramatic increases in population size during the first phases of the transition, and subsequently, as fertility rates fall, an equally dramatic and protracted aging of the population. The driving force for population growth is that declines in birth rates start later than declines in mortality (although France and the United

---

1. See Bloom, Canning, and Sevilla 2003; Bongaarts 2009; Demeny 2011; Lee 2003; Reher 2011.

States were exceptions). Consequently, the population growth rate initially spikes upward but then decelerates and aging sets in.

Key Descriptive Statistics

It should be emphasized that this is an idealized description of the DT and that no country has fully completed it. Some countries, mainly in sub-Saharan Africa, have just begun and will have rapidly increasing populations in coming decades. Many countries, more advanced in the transition, have not yet found equilibrium in their birth and death rates and the proposed endpoint, a smaller but stabilized population, is unclear. Figure 6.1 captures the main features of the transition but the end stage remains speculative. Figure 6.2 uses changes in Korean population age pyramids over an 80-year time span to illustrate the remarkable shifts in the age distribution profile. Note also the gender imbalance in higher age brackets.

The prominent demographer Ronald Lee (2003) has provided global estimates and guesstimates of the transition. See table 6.1. Comparing 1700 and 1800 shows the stability of demographic variables in the eighteenth century. But over the 300-year period 1800–2100 the classic features of the transition are all there and tell a riveting story. Average global life

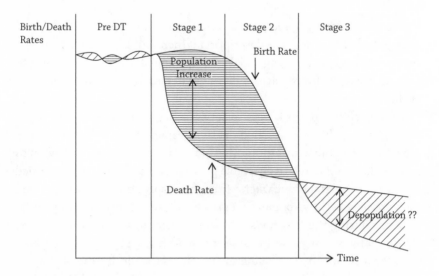

Figure 6.1: Demographic transition
In the pre-DT period birth and death rates are high and population is relatively steady. In Stage 1 death rates fall, birth rates remain relatively stable and population surges. Stage 2 is marked by declining birth rates and slower population growth rates. Stage 3 is uncertain and may include depopulation.

Pyramid A

■ Male □ Female

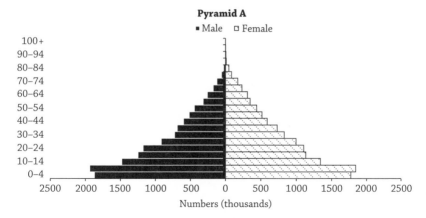

Numbers (thousands)

Pyramid B

■ Male ⊡ Female

Numbers (thousands)

Pyramid C

■ Male □ Female

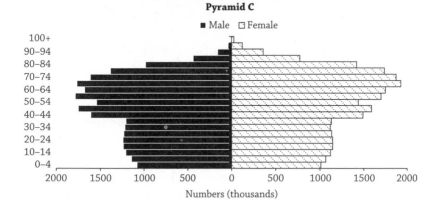

Numbers (thousands)

Figure 6.2: South Korean age structure
Pyramid A: Korea 1960
Pyramid B: Korea 2000
Pyramid C: Korea 2040
Source: UN 2012.

Table 6.1. THE DEMOGRAPHIC TRANSITION IN NUMBERS

Year	Life expectancy (years at birth)	Total fertility rate (births per woman)	Population size (billions)	Population growth rate (% per year)	Population <15 (% of total population)	Population >65 (% of total population)
1700	27	6.0	0.68	0.5	36	4
1800	27	6.0	0.98	0.51	36	4
1900	30	5.2	1.65	0.56	35	4
1950	47	5.0	2.52	1.80	34	5
2000	65	2.7	6.07	1.22	30	7
2050	74	2.0	8.92	0.33	20	16
2100	81	2.0	9.46	0.04	18	21

Source: Based on Lee 2003, table 1. By permission.

expectancy at birth, a measure of mortality, increases from 27 years in 1800, to an expected 81 years in 2100. The average increase in life expectancy is 0.18 years per year, which means that if a newborn could delay its conception and birth by one year, it would earn a bonus—additional longevity of two months and five days. Annual bonuses for those of us well along in years are also positive, but smaller. Indeed life expectancy has a certain elastic quality even if mortality rates remain unchanged. Life expectancy for a US male of 65, the once traditional retirement age, is currently almost 17 years. If he can hang in there until age 82 (65 + 17) his life expectancy is an additional 7 years. It may or may not be comforting to know that one's life expectancy does not drop below a single year until one reaches the age of 112.

The global total fertility rate, which measures the average number of births a woman would experience by the end of her reproductive years, fell from 6.0 births in 1800 to 2.7 in 2000. Subject to considerable uncertainty, it is projected to fall to 2.0 births in 2100. This is just below the replacement rate of 2.1 births, the rate needed to maintain a stable population in the very long run.[2] Some small fraction of declining fertility in recent years may be due to increasing infertility—difficulty in conceiving. But a global analysis of 277 surveys found little evidence of changes in infertility over two decades, 1990–2010 (Mascarenhas et al. 2012).

2. If infant and youth mortality rates fell further, the replacement rate would approach 2.0 as a limit. In high-mortality countries, the replacement rate may exceed 3.0.

The rate of growth of population in 1800, the pre-Malthusian world, was 0.5 percent per year. It rose to 1.8 percent in 1950 (peaking at 2.2 percent in 1963), slowed sharply to 1.2 percent by 2000, and it is expected to plunge to near or below zero (0.04 percent) in 2100. World population increased from fewer than 1 billion persons in 1800 to 6.1 billion in 2000 and currently exceeds 7 billion. It is projected by the UN to be 9.5 billion in 2100, close to a tenfold increase over the three centuries. Aging also casts its shadow. The percent of world population over 65 increased from 4 percent in 1800 to 7 percent in 2000, and may reach 21 percent by 2100. Lee estimates that over this period the ratio of the elderly to children in the world will have increased tenfold, a sobering thought.

Two Waves

These data are helpful in illustrating the dramatic demographic changes that have taken place in a relatively short interval of human history. But they conceal a major dimension of the story. The demographic transition has come in two waves, consisting of two distinct sets of countries, and initiated a century apart.[3] Global data as displayed in table 6.1 merge these two waves, although they started at different times, have proceeded at different speeds, and are currently at different points in the transition. The merging can muddy their distinctive features.

The first wave consists of European countries and other countries with deep European roots (e.g., Argentina, Chile, United States, Canada, Australia, and New Zealand). It started in the late eighteenth century with declining mortality rates (increasing life expectancy) followed almost a century later by declining fertility. The latter decline has either continued to this day or has stabilized at unprecedentedly low levels. The second DT wave consists primarily of developing countries, which historically and today contain the bulk of world population. For most of them, the pronounced decrease in mortality did not start until the twentieth century and major fertility declines are concentrated in the post–World War II era. Both waves exhibit the same fundamental features identified above: falling mortality rates preceding falling fertility rates, initial increases but subsequent decreases in population growth rates, and actual or prospective pronounced

3. The second wave of the DT should not be confused with what is sometimes called the second demographic transition. The latter refers to changing twentieth-century cultural characteristics such as cohabitation, births out of wedlock, and non-marriage, all increasingly prevalent in the West, but less so in Asian societies. See pp. 125 below.

aging of a much larger population. But there are major differences between them as well.

The starting conditions for the two waves were different. First, the birth and death rates in Europe in 1800 were generally lower than those prevailing in developing countries in the early 1900s. Total fertility rates have been estimated to be four to five children per women in Europe and perhaps six or more per women in the underdeveloped countries. Life expectancy was 30–35 years in pre-industrial Europe but 25–30 years in low-income countries in the 1920s. Europe was also richer, especially at the starting points of fertility decline in the two waves. Second, the knowledge base and technologies available for both mortality and fertility control were greatly different. Mortality decline in Europe has been a long process stretching over more than 200 years. The early sources were reductions in contagious diseases, improved public health measures, and better nutrition. The biggest gains were made in reducing infant and childhood mortality. This is important as it increases the number of women of childbearing age a generation later. The second wave also relied on these sources, but by the post–World War II era there was considerable assistance in improving public health through international institutions such as WHO and the World Bank, and increasing international access to modern medicine. Fertility decline in Europe, when it first came, was achieved through condoms, the rhythm method, and *coitus interruptus*. Developing countries in the postwar era had increasing access to modern birth control methods, including the pill.

The third, and perhaps most important, difference between the two waves is the compression, speed, and severity of the second wave transition. In hindsight the European wave looks almost leisurely with its long lag between mortality and fertility decline, and the continuation of both trends well into the current century. In contrast the key demographic changes were accelerated and magnified in many of the second-wave countries. Although starting almost a century later, fertility declines in some have caught up with, and in a few instances exceeded, first-wave Western countries.

A Contemporary Example

Thailand is a good illustration. Over the half century 1960 to 2010, life expectancy has increased by 18.5 years, from 55.1 years to 73.6 years; the crude death rate has fallen from about 13 per thousand to 7.2 per thousand; the infant mortality rate has fallen from 130 per thousand in the early 1950s to 12 per thousand today; the crude birth rate has fallen from 42.5 per thousand to 12.9 per thousand over the same period; the total fertility rate plunged from 6.14 children per women in the early 1950s to 1.58 children in 2010 (well below the replacement rate); population increased from 20 million in 1950 to about 70 million today; the population growth rate peaked at almost 2.5 percent per year in the 1965–75 period but has since declined to about 0.6 percent; and the elderly (over age 65) have increased from 3.2 percent in 1950 to 9.2 percent of the population now and are expected to reach 25 percent by 2050. This is the demographic transition at warp speed! As discussed below, the acceleration and compression have both positive and negative consequences.

Exceptions

Despite different starting gates, times, and pace, key demographic trends are widespread: reduction of mortality rates, especially for infants and children; increases in longevity; declines in fertility; slower or negative population growth; and aging. Still, there are exceptions. Some are relatively easy to explain, others not. Life expectancy at birth in the Russian Federation *fell* after the collapse of the Soviet Union from 69.1 years in 1985–90 to a low of 65.0 in 2000–2005, before starting to recover. Following the revolution in Iran in 1979, the fertility rate rose modestly to a peak of 6.53 births per woman in 1980–85 before plunging below 1.97 in 2000–2005, despite a public campaign promoting patriotic procreation. Under the threat of depopulation, that campaign has recently resumed. And, of course, there are substantial demographic differences between Western/Northern and Southern/Eastern European countries that are not simple to explain.

The most important exception is mixed trends in fertility in sub-Saharan Africa. This region is important for several reasons. First, the population is now nearly a billion people and it is their well-being that is most directly at stake. Second, the United Nations projects that if, optimistically, fertility, which is now about 5 births per woman, were to converge on a replacement level of 2.1 by the end of this century, sub-Saharan population of world still more than triple, to 3.8 billion people. (This is mainly the result of population momentum, explained later.) Its share of world population will rise from 13 percent to 35 percent. Indeed, 84 percent of world population growth over this time span will occur in sub-Saharan Africa. If, on the other hand, this region is inoculated against the fertility transition that has swept the rest of the world and there is no fertility convergence, then all population bets are off.

Without being overly dramatic, sub-Saharan Africa is the last act of the long-running Malthusian drama of food and population that started in South Asia in the early post–World War II period. If fertility in that region now converges and conforms to the norms of the demographic transition, any future *global* food crisis should be pinned on income and consumption growth (diet) and on pernicious effects of global warming, and not on population. More generally, attention could then be productively focused on the natural resource stress from per capita *economic* growth, and the demographic consequences of population decline and aging. But that convergence of fertility is not assured.

There is no question that until now this region qualifies as an exception. It started out in 1960–65 with a high fertility rate, but one that only modestly exceeded the average for all developing countries at that time (6.53 births per woman vs. 6.08).[4] By 2010–15, however, the average rate in the region had fallen by 23 percent to 5.10 births; whereas, for all developing countries, the rate fell by 57 percent to 2.62 births, not so far above replacement level.[5] Fortunately, however, there is some evidence that this exceptional status need not persist. Some countries in the region have broken away and succeeded in halving their peak fertility rates—Botswana, Lesotho, Namibia, and South Africa. Rwanda went from a peak of 8.4 to 4.6. Ethiopia shaved its rate by 2.8 births per woman and Kenya by 3.7. Equally encouraging is a series of empirical studies in the region that confirm the consensus from other regions—improving female education has a big payoff in decreasing fertility, and politically supported and well-administered family planning works.[6] A downward convergence is not out of reach.

QUIRKS OF MEASUREMENT AND NEW ISSUES

Thus far our treatment of the demographic transition has been descriptive. It will be useful to seek a theoretical explanation. But before doing so we need to clarify two of the somewhat more technical terms: population momentum and tempo. For example, how is it possible that Thailand, whose total fertility rate of 1.6 children is well below the replacement level of 2.1, still shows a positive annual population growth rate of close to 0.6

4. Data from UN (2012).
5. Excluding China does not significantly alter this pattern.
6. Bongaarts (2010); Bongaarts and Casterline (2012); Shapiro (2012); Westoff (2012); Wusu 2012.

percent? More broadly, how is it possible that almost half of the world's countries and territories have sub-replacement fertility rates, yet in only 15 percent is population actually declining? We also need to say something about uncertainty in projections and new issues in what to measure.

Momentum

Setting aside the possibility of inward migration, population momentum can explain population growth despite sub-replacement fertility. In the latter stages of the demographic transition, and as a result of declining birth rates initially lagging declining mortality rates, there is a relatively high concentration of women in their childbearing years. This is especially pronounced if declining mortality had been concentrated in infants and children, as females who survived subsequently entered their reproductive years. It follows that even if the fertility of these women dropped to replacement or sub-replacement levels, their disproportionately high numbers would ensure a large number of births and hence positive population growth. This would in turn create ever-fainter echo effects of additional births in subsequent years. Ultimately, of course, below replacement rates would start to "bite," the baby bulge would shrink, and population growth would turn negative. The momentum phenomenon is quantitatively important. Over the next half century, it is population momentum, not high fertility that will drive most population growth in the South, although fertility and momentum are both at work in sub-Saharan Africa.

Perhaps more important, momentum can work in reverse—negative momentum can accelerate population decline. The mechanism is similar. A declining birth rate today means a smaller cohort of women will enter their reproductive years 20 years hence. Even if their fertility is at replacement levels (now 2.1 births per woman), their declining numbers will mean fewer births, and fewer births will echo a generation later with even fewer births. The contractionary effect will eventually be dampened but the steady state population will be lower. Lutz, O'Neill, and Scherbov (2003), for example, estimate that the European Union started to experience negative momentum in about the year 2000. They estimate that, for 15 EU members, if the current low fertility rate of 1.5 persists for 20 years to 2020, negative momentum would result in 88 million fewer people by the end of this century.[7] This is about 23 percent below its current level.

7. Assuming no change in mortality and no net migration. An (unlikely) immediate return to replacement fertility would moderate, but not eliminate, the population decline.

Tempo

The second technical point is tempo, the spacing of births over a woman's reproductive years. Changes in the average age of childbearing have an effect on what has been the standard measure of fertility, the total fertility rate (TFR). Specifically, if the average age of giving birth is falling, the TFR is bumped up during the period it falls, *even if the number of births per women remains the same.* By advancing the births in time, the TFR rises, but when that advance stops, as it must, the TFR is depressed. The converse occurs when the average age of childbearing is rising, as it has in the United States and in many European countries.[8] As births are postponed, the TFR is depressed during these years, but will rebound if and when postponement comes to an end.

There are several implications. First, delayed childbearing increases the fraction of the elderly in the population, presenting additional challenges for countries with aging and potentially declining populations. Second, the tempo effect undermines the descriptive accuracy of the TFR, the standard measure of fertility. What might appear to be an alarmingly low TFR may be the result of temporary postponement of childbearing.[9] On the other hand, a rise in TFR may be interpreted as an increase in fertility rates when in fact it is merely the tempo effect slowing to a halt. This ambiguity has led to devising "tempo adjusted" measures of fertility. A further important empirical question is whether the postponed births are in fact redeemed with actual births at some later time in the reproductive years. If not, the tempo effect arising from postponement is itself linked to declining fertility.

Tempo and its effect on the total fertility rate have attracted considerable attention in the past few years, especially in European countries. The TFR trend had been downward from the 1960s to the end of the 1990s, resulting in sub-replacement fertility. The trend unexpectedly reversed in the decade 1998–2008 in most of Europe, before falling again in the recession era starting in 2008.[10] One explanation for this pattern appeared to be the tempo effect: the postponement of births that initially depressed the TFR and the partial recovery of TFR after 1998 when the *rate of change* of postponement dropped toward zero. If correct, the explanation is both

8. As an example mean age of giving birth in the Czech Republic rose from below 25 in 1992 to over 28 in 2002.

9. One study in Europe found that when stripped of the tempo effect, the adjusted TFR rose from 1.5 to 1.8. See Goldstein, Sobotka, and Jasilioniene 2009.

10. Sobotka, Skirbekk, and Philipov (2011) investigate the effects of cyclical economic decline on fertility.

good and bad news for those concerned about aging and population decline in Europe. The good news is that the exceptionally low TFR rates recorded in the 1990s were an aberration and substantially underestimated "true" long-term fertility. The bad news is that the uptick in fertility as measured by the TFR in the first decade of this century is also an aberration—there is no relief in sight for sub-replacement fertility levels, although the rate at which population will decline may have been exaggerated.[11] With low mortality and no net immigration, it takes 45 years for a population to be cut in half with a TFR rate of 1.3, but 90 years with TFR at 1.6 (Goldstein, Sobotka, and Jasilioniene 2009). Slowing the *rate* of decline in population may turn out to be more important than the ultimate level. As in many economic situations, spreading out adjustments to a new population equilibrium over long periods reduces the transition cost.

Two other points concerning measurement are less technical. First, crude mortality data expressed as deaths per thousand of population are not very revealing when the age structure is changing. Consequently, age-specific mortality tables are constructed. Additionally, as noted above, a reduction of mortality among the young has lasting effects on population growth; whereas, mortality declines among the old who are past their reproductive stage do not. Data on life expectancy at birth does not indicate whether gains are being made early or late in the life cycle. More specifically, it does not reveal that the massive gains over the past 200 years came mainly by reduction in infant and child mortality rather than extension at the end of life. (This has been reversed in recent years.) Second, as explored in chapter 8, defining who the aged are is not an unambiguous choice. The "threat" of aging looks quite different depending on who is designated as old. Is 75 the new 65?

Uncertainty

Number, age, and sex are fundamental attributes of populations. Estimates for fertility, mortality, and migration are used to project these values into the future. Other attributes that are helpful in projecting population growth, or are of interest in their own right, are education levels, urban/rural residence, labor-force participation rates, and marital status. All of these are subject to uncertainty, and the deeper one looks into the future, the greater the uncertainty.

11. Bongaarts and Sobotka (2012), using new data and new indicators of tempo and parity adjusted total fertility rates, support this interpretation.

Treatment of uncertainty is becoming more sophisticated.[12] Originally a single "most likely" number for population size was projected, with no explicit information about its probability. A second approach has come into widespread use (not only in demographics). It sets out several "plausible" scenarios, usually high, medium, and low scenarios. This provides the user with some information on the range of possible outcomes. And although no explicit probability is assigned to a specific scenario, the common interpretation is that the median is most likely. In projecting population, it has been traditional to make high, medium, and low fertility estimates and combine these with single mortality and migration assumptions to generate three population trajectory projections. The latest advance is to make probabilistic projections of population size that fully reflect the probability distributions and correlations between components of the analysis (e.g., fertility, mortality, migration). This is a form of Monte Carlo analysis. It is done by inputting the probability distributions of the components and their correlations, making a large number of successive computer-generated draws on the data, and building up a probability distribution (expected value and variance) for the output—population projections for the future. Acquiring accurate information on the probability distributions of the inputs can be the weak point of this approach.

Incorporating Education

Size (numbers), sex, and age have been have been at the center of demographic analysis and forecasting since its beginning. Wolfgang Lutz (2010) and others have made a strong argument that education should be elevated to a similar rank. He cleverly anticipated the argument that age and sex are objective variables while educational attainment is subjective by pointing out the growing ambiguity in sex and age assignments.

Indeed educational attainment is already at the center of a great deal of demographic research.[13] The connection between female educational variables and fertility has been well established for half a century, and, as discussed earlier, is currently being reconfirmed in Africa. There is general agreement that the relation is causal and not, for instance, merely covariance between income and education, and furthermore that the relation holds at in both high and low fertility situations. One connection is the

---

12. For a good, nontechnical account, see Lutz and KC (2010).
13. For a current survey, see the 2012 issue of the *Vienna Yearbook of Population Research*.

positive relation of parental education and survival rates for children, which reduces the "demand" for large families. A second is the impact of education on the balance of "quality vs. quality" incentives in family size decisions. James, Skirbekk, and Van Bavel (2012) suggest that historically income and social class was positively associated with high fertility (in the eighteenth century, Empress Maria Theresa had 16 children!). As that association weakened in the modern era, the negative relation between education levels and fertility strengthened and displaced the income/class relation.

The role of education in demographic analysis is not confined to fertility. Both morbidity and mortality prospects, key areas for forecasting future social costs, are closely linked to education. Many studies have found that in the West more education is associated with lower levels of mortality, morbidity and disability. KC and Lentzer (2010) have extended this research to a larger range including countries in Africa, Asia, and Latin America, focusing on the relation between formal education and measures of disability. They reach a similar general conclusion—higher levels of education in these developing regions are associated with better health and fewer disabilities for both younger and older adults. By projecting population forward along with strong improvement in educational attainment, they identify a coming "educational bonus," an increase in health and well-being independent of and additional to savings in social costs.

In the United States, the gaps in life expectancy and mortality rates between more highly and less highly educated persons have been substantial and widened in the period 1981–2000: "With the exception of black males, all recent gains in life expectancy at age 25 have occurred among better educated groups, raising the educational differential in life expectancy by 30 percent" (Meara, Richards, and Cutler 2008, p. 350). Trends in smoking behavior appear to be an important proximate explanation.

In short, adding an education dimension to numbers, age, and sex data enriches demographic forecasting and improves analysis of social policies. Indeed, as discussed in subsequent chapters, the ability to maintain economic productivity with declining population depends in large measure on the stock of human capital, which in turn depends on educational attainment by age and sex.

THEORIES OF THE DEMOGRAPHIC TRANSITION

The DT invites theoretical speculation. We cannot enter this thicket to any great distance but can point out some of the key questions. These come in two flavors. The first centers on the question of how the transition came about, and more specifically how social and economic forces interacted with and propelled the transition forward. Within this, the two principal approaches are the so-called unified theories, and the more pointed investigations of declining fertility, the main driving force in the transition. The second flavor turns the question around and examines the principal social and economic implications of the DT. This leads to the cheerful concept of a demographic bonus but also raises the more problematic issues of aging, fiscal constraints, corrosive intergenerational frictions, economic sclerosis, and so on. The first of these implications, the demographic bonus, is discussed here, but the other problem areas, which are alleged to be the dark side of population aging and decline, are taken up in subsequent chapters.

Unified Growth Theory

This theorizing is ambitious. It attempts to meld a theory of the demographic transition with a theory of economic growth in which the two interact and move from a Malthusian stagnation equilibrium through a phase marked by rapid industrialization and technological progress, and that eventually transmutes into a sustainable, modern economic growth mode. It purports to describe an inevitable process. It puts demographic variables closer to the center of economic growth than any theory since Malthus. It accommodates differential growth among regions and attempts to explain what Oded Galor calls the Great Divergence, the enormous increase in per capita income disparity between rich and poor regions.[14] And it does so by paying attention to the microeconomic foundations of growth and demographic activity. Galor and Weil (2000) and Galor (2005) provide one detailed account and can serve as an illustration.[15]

The two trickiest tasks in unified theory are to engineer an escape from the so-called Malthusian trap, and to explain how and why fertility declined despite sharply rising real incomes. It is also necessary to find a structure sufficiently flexible to accommodate the very different conditions in nineteenth-century Europe and twentieth-century developing countries. Unified growth theory has yet to come up with a compelling account of how the story will end.

14. Galor (2005) states that the ratio of GDP per capita in the world's richest and poorest regions rose from 2.1:1 in 1500 to 3.1:1 in 1800 to 18:1 in 2001.
15. See also models by Becker, Murphy, and Tamura 1990; Ehrlich and Kim 2005.

The first task is especially vexing. Malthusian theory describes a stable equilibrium characterized by high birth and death rates, miniscule technological progress and population growth, and income for the masses stuck close to subsistence level and trapped there by the twin forces of sexual passion and the preventative and positive checks. Moreover, the general belief is that Malthus accurately captured the stagnation of previous centuries and perhaps millennia. How then to escape? In the absence of a fortuitous external event, the explanation boils down to a positive interaction between population size and technological progress.[16] Although in the Malthusian era the modest technological progress was being dissipated by rising births, not rising per capita income, Galor sees a positive and virtuous interaction between population *size*, which was in fact growing, and technological progress. This is very similar to Adam Smith's view that via expansion of the market, division of labor, and faster technological diffusion, population growth begets faster economic growth. At some point the acceleration of technology exceeds the increase in population, real incomes start to rise, and the Malthusian trap is partly sprung.[17] But it is still necessary to explain why, in this phase of rapid industrialization, technological progress and rising real incomes, the initial positive relation between income and population growth weakens and subsequently became negative. That reversal, from income growth first encouraging and then discouraging fertility, sets the stage for the third phase, sustained modern economic growth. This reversal goes to the core of the demographic transition and remains controversial.

Explaining Declining Fertility

To disable the trap and set the stage for modern economic growth, Malthus's assertion that fertility rates increase monotonically with real incomes must be demolished. The empirical evidence from nineteenth-century Europe is clear. Initially, they rose in tandem but after mid- century they

16. Not all analysts are willing to dismiss luck. Becker, Murphy, and Tamura (1990) build a model with multiple stable equilibria including Malthusian stagnation, but then draw attention to the role of accidents and good fortune in determining in which state a country winds up.

17. Interestingly, Galor and Moav (2002) invoke Charles Darwin's evolutionary theory to explain escape from a Malthusian trap; whereas, Darwin used Malthus's theory to help explain evolution. Galor and Moav argue that the lineages of those individuals with characteristics favorable to technological progress had an evolutionary advantage, and their growing number triggered a positive feedback to technology growth.

went in separate directions. Why? Some explanations are freestanding; some are embedded in a more comprehensive unified theory. The lazy and offensive answer is that children are an "inferior good," similar to ramen noodles and jug wine, for which demand falls as income increases. This answer fails to explain the pre-nineteenth-century relation of income and fertility; fails to distinguish the role of children as a consumption *and* investment good; and fails to account for "loading" children with human capital via education.

A more acceptable answer may be found in the almost universal phenomenon of mortality rates initially falling, and a subsequent, lagged fall in birth rates. The logic is uncomplicated. If more infants and children are surviving into adulthood, fewer are needed to work on the farm or provide comfort and security to parents in their old age. The "precautionary demand" for children weakens. But the lag between mortality and fertility rate declines in Europe was 100 or more years, and such sluggish behavioral adaptation is a stretch. It may however have greater explanatory power in twentieth-century demographic transitions in developing countries, where the time lag between mortality and fertility declines has been much shorter.[18]

It is also possible to argue for an indirect link between decreased mortality and fertility working through higher returns to the accumulation of human capital (i.e., education). Lower childhood mortality improves the chances that educating the young will earn a positive return on parental investment. It thus shifts the calculus away from having large families to having fewer but better educated children. In simple terms, the opportunity cost of having large, uneducated families was rising. To put it crassly, additional kids lost their competitive position and became overpriced in the market. "Purchases" by parents fell. Whether they were considered consumption or investment goods made little difference.[19] But decreasing child mortality is only one of several possible reasons why the balance between quantity and quality of children was shifting.[20]

18. Angles (2010) investigates the mortality-fertility link.

19. In technical terms the income elasticity of demand for additional children was trumped by the substitution effect arising from increased opportunity cost of additional children. Birdsall (1988) provides a straightforward explanation of the household demand model of fertility. In Razin and Sadka's (1995) model, an increase in family income can lead to increased spending on quality (e.g., education) but lower numbers of children if the elasticity of substitution between quality and quantity of children is low.

20. The quantity/quality terminology goes back at least to Becker's fundamental work in the 1960s on the microeconomics of family fertility decision-making. Nevertheless, there is something distasteful about designating children who lack a good education or a nest egg provided by Papa as also lacking in quality.

Once again Galor and his colleagues have provided both a story line and evidence of how the initial positive relation between income and fertility was trumped by a preference for quality and thus fewer children, the central feature of the demographic transition.[21] As explained above, slowly increasing population size in the Malthusian era accelerated technological progress. Initially, with quite basic technology, the demand for human capital (education) is weak, and productivity increases are dissipated through population increases. Over time, however, the virtuous circle between population size and technological progress increases the demand for human capital relative to physical capital. The rewards to quality increase relative to quantity, an increasing share of increasing incomes is devoted to building human capital, and the time and monetary costs of having additional children increase. As a result, fertility rates and family size peak and start to decline. More resources are then available to meet the demand for human capital, and the economy is launched into the modern sustainable growth era.

A number of other developments may have supported this transition. Increased life expectancy increases the years available to recoup investment in human capital and hence its rate of return; as the structure of production shifted from agriculture to increasingly sophisticated manufacturing the role of child labor was diminished; a rise in the relative wage of women increased the opportunity cost of raising children and may have contributed by getting them out of the nursery and into the paid labor force; improved contraceptives also played a role in the post–World War II era. The role of children as "status goods" may change in the course of development too. As noted earlier, an evolutionary argument for the ascendency of individuals with strong preference for the quality of their children rather than their quantity has also been made (Galor and Moav 2002). These economic-based explanations tend to absolve us from the harsher view that we have become more selfish when approaching childrearing.

One can have doubts that any particular version of unified theory captures the full complexities of 2,000 years of stagnation and growth. The hurdles include the marked differences between the European experience of the nineteenth century and the radically different conditions surrounding the second wave of the demographic transition that took place a century

21. See especially Galor (2005). This is certainly not the only story that can be told. Recall Becker, Murphy, and Tamura (1990) and the intriguing assumption that the rate of return on investment in human capital *increases* as the stock of such capital increases. Formal education, a vehicle for acquiring human capital, is also closely linked to declining fertility.

later in the South. There are two obvious areas where the theory is sketchy or incomplete. First, the role of natural resources is mostly missing; especially the energy transition from renewables to fossil fuels and most recently a partial shift back toward renewables, as well as the related issue of environmental constraints on growth. How deeply these will bite into the modern era of sustainable economic growth has yet to be integrated into unified growth theory. Second, the theory suggests that the demographic transition is close to completion. But is it? Fertility levels have fallen in many countries to less than replacement levels. What will economic growth look like in an era of declining population? Is the theory robust enough to look forward and make reasoned predictions? Will technological progress, the current driver of economic growth, weaken with an aging population, and reunite economic and population trends in a downward direction? We need to remember Malthus's inadvertent lesson on the danger of looking back rather than forward.

Mortality and Longevity

Although the dramatic fertility transition has drawn much attention, a discussion of trends in mortality and longevity is needed to complete the picture. Whereas declining fertility slows or reverses population growth, declining mortality (increasing life expectancy) acts to maintain or increase it. The net result cannot be understood, however, without considering changing age structure. In the early phase of the DT, mortality declines were concentrated in infancy and childhood, allowing large increases in the reproductive-aged population and laying the foundation for surging population. Mortality declines for the elderly were of lesser importance because there were fewer of them, the declines were smaller, and in any event they were past reproductive age.

The situation has now reversed. Infant and childhood mortality has been squeezed to very low numbers in many countries. Continued declines in aggregate mortality and continued increases in life expectancy must come, if they come at all, in the later years of life—age 60 and up. This shift is the longevity transition and it has profound consequences.[22] While increasing longevity of the elderly may be a benefit to them, and may slow population decline, it cannot stay the *economic and fiscal* problems associated with

---

22. Eggleston and Fuch (2012) estimate that whereas some 20 percent of the increase in US life expectancy was realized by the elderly at the start of the twentieth century, that figure is now 75 percent and increasing.

population aging and decline—indeed it tends to exacerbate them. With low fertility and increasing longevity of the elderly, the age structure continues to tilt away from the working generations. It is longevity that accounts for the surging number of the elderly. These important issues are addressed in chapter 9.

Longevity is not a trap, but its logical consequences cannot be easily dismissed. As it turns out, the severity of the problems hinges in part on whether longevity will continue to advance at its current pace. On a global scale it certainly has scope to do so. Life expectancy at birth stands at 81 years in Europe and 56 years in sub-Saharan Africa, a gap of a quarter century to play catchup. Nor are there clear signs that it is slackening. The global standard bearers are Japanese women (87 years) who as a group have experienced increases in life expectancy of about three months per year for the past 160 years.[23]

Projections of continued steady growth in life expectancy have been challenged however (Olshansky et al. 2005; Couzin-Frankel 2011). One objection is that extrapolation of past gains is misleading when the reason for extension shifts from subduing the infectious diseases of youth to changing lifestyles and confronting the illnesses of old age. The rise of obesity,[24] the prevalence of diabetes and other chronic diseases, and new infectious epidemics, perhaps facilitated by global warming, are often cited. (Dementia is more prevalent and is expensive, but its impact on longevity is unclear.) Moreover, some observers assert there are basic biological limits to longer life.

On another front, Pijnenburg and Leget (2007) have raised ethical objections to extending human lifespans. The issue is closely tied to the question of whether medical research will primarily be directed toward reducing disease and human suffering or merely to gain additional years—which makes better use of scarce resources? If medical advances support healthy lives at advanced ages, the fiscal and economic burden of aging will be eased, permitting later retirement and lower medical care costs (see the concept of compression of morbidity in chapter 9). In the event, the question may become moot. Extending life through technical measures can be very expensive and the binding constraint may turn out to be society's willingness to pay for longer lifespans.

23. Oeppen and Vaupel (2002).
24. For a sobering analysis of the effects of obesity on life expectancy, see Peeters et al. (2003).

ECONOMIC IMPLICATIONS: A DEMOGRAPHIC BONUS AND SUBSEQUENT BURDEN

Age Structure, Dependency, and the Demographic Transition

Before weighing the costs and benefits of a stable or declining population, we should acknowledge a mostly unforeseen boost to economic growth provided by the demographic transition. Ironically, it was in precisely the same decade of the 1970s, when the world population growth rate was near its peak and concern for its negative consequences was greatest, that the DT was starting to deliver "miracle" economic growth rates in parts of Asia. That silver lining results from a favorable age structure. But the growth spurt is flanked by two darker clouds: a rise in the youth dependency ratio that appears at the beginning of the transition, and a rise in the elderly dependency ratio that materializes toward the end.

The crucial question is whether the middle bonus years of the transition are sufficiently productive to launch an economy into high-income status.[25]

The idea of a "burden-bonus-burden" sequence flows from the changing age structure and dependency ratios during the transition. The initial phase exhibits an increasingly young population and a rising youth dependency ratio; the second phase, when the bonus materializes, shows high working-age population and low dependency ratios; and the third shows high and rising dependency ratios driven by an increasingly old population. In short, the bonus appears in those years in which the growth rate of total population falls below the growth rate of the working-age population.[26]

The original empirical work on the growth effects of shifting age and dependency structure trace to the work of Coale and Hoover on India. As described in chapter 4, they were concerned with the first phase, the negative growth effects of a high fraction of young, unproductive children. They saw a dark cloud indeed. Using simulation techniques, they found that a failure to sharply control fertility would result in dramatically lower per capita incomes three decades hence. The explanation was that high

---

25. It may be unduly pessimistic to leave the analysis at two dark clouds and only one silver lining. Mason and Lee (2006) have uncovered another silver lining, a "second demographic bonus" to balance the accounts. It arises "because population aging provides a powerful incentive for capital accumulation." If successfully captured during the halcyon days of the bonus years, it can help fund real incomes in the sunset years. See chapter 8.

26. The traditional UN definition of youth dependency is age 0–14 divided by age 15–64, and elderly dependency as age 65 and up divided by age 15–64. In the early phase of the transition falling mortality rates for infants and children increases the fraction of the young in the population. Falling mortality rates have a smaller impact on the elderly share, as there are fewer of them.

youth dependency diverts resources away from building productive physical capital (e.g., roads, factories) to the feeding, clothing, health, and schooling of infants and children. They did not see these latter activities as building human capital for the future.

The lesson is that the changing age structure should be considered in its three-part totality. It is misleading to concentrate only on the first negative phase, but it would be equally misleading to concentrate solely on the bonus phase. It is the bulge of births that subsequently powers the surging labor force and the bonus. And it is that same earlier bulge of births that is the core of a future aging problem. The changing age structure should be treated as a single phenomenon. It follows that the demographic bonus is not manna floating down from heaven and is not a free lunch. It is best viewed as payment received for expenses incurred earlier in nurturing and raising an educated workforce and as a prepayment for supporting that workforce in its old age.

To take full advantage of the bonus requires sophisticated and far-sighted policy. Otherwise, its promise comes to naught. In the initial stage, this means investment in health, nutrition, and appropriate educational preparation for a productive life. In the next or bonus stage, it means maximizing employment based on comparative advantage (liberal trade policies) and encouraging women to enter the labor force.[27] The bonus may also fall flat if the surge in the workforce is under- or unemployed. Policy in the second stage should also anticipate the inevitable slide into an aging economy and a rising elderly dependency ratio. Short of large-scale and potentially disruptive immigration, this can be done by holding consumption of the "bonus generation" below its output, and using the savings to finance physical and human capital accumulation and boost technological progress or by building up net foreign assets. Effective utilization of the larger workforce and anticipatory savings and investment are the keys, and neither is assured. Note also that potentially large intergenerational transfers may be involved.

Quantifying the Bonus

Due to their different starting times in the demographic transition, dependency ratios vary greatly by region, as well as over time (Bloom and

---

27. David Bloom and his colleagues (2009) found that decreasing fertility during the DT increases female labor supply and can make a significant contribution to economic growth.

Williamson 1998; Bloom, Canning, and Sevilla 2003). For example, in East Asia during the bonus years of 1965–90 working-age population grew 2.4 percent per year and dependent population grew at only 0.6 percent, providing a particularly attractive context for rapid economic growth. But the bonus has tailed off. The authors estimate that in the 2015–40 period the working-age population will *shrink* by 0.36 percent per year and the dependent population will *grow* by 1.24 percent. The bonus generation comes back with a bite! In contrast, in Africa, where the DT was barely started, the 1965–90 growth rates of working and nonworking-age populations were equal at 2.8 percent per year (i.e., no improvement in the dependency ratio). However, Africa is expected to have growth of 2.3 percent for working-age population and only 1.2 percent for dependent population in 2015–40, setting up a potential for bonus growth.[28] Once again, however, to deliver its promise the bonus will need nurturing through a supportive institutional and policy matrix.

The positive effect of the demographic bonus on per capita income growth can be substantial.[29] Bloom, Canning, and Sevilla (2003) conclude between 25 and 40 percent of East Asia's "economic miracle" was the result of the bonus. Feng Wang and Andrew Mason estimate that 15–25 percent of China's torrid economic growth in the 1980s and 1990s was due to the favorable age structure of the population (cited in Wang 2011). The conclusions for Southeast Asia are mixed and somewhat more modest. Navaneetham (2002) divides working-age population into three age brackets based on assumed differences in savings/consumption behavior: 15–24; 25–49; 50–64. He finds statistical evidence of a negative relation between the 25–49 age group share of population and per capita growth for Indonesia, Philippines, and Thailand, which he attributes to low net savings as this group is supporting growing families. The 50–64 age group share however makes a statistically significant contribution to growth for Malaysia, Singapore, and Thailand. The import of this last study should not be exaggerated as the so-called "bonus" window of opportunity had not run its course when the research was conducted.

28. For a relatively sober assessment of African bonus prospects, see Eastwood and Lipton (2011). North America also had a well-known baby boom after World War II. As they hit working age in 1960–90, working-age labor supply was growing by 1.4 percent per year as compared to a dependent population growth rate of only 0.4 percent. Those rates are expected to reverse in the 2015–40 period.

29. Recent research suggests that a substantial fraction of the demographic bonus was in fact due to higher levels of education associated with the changing age structure of the workforce.

Although the demographic bonus has mainly been discussed in the context of developing countries, there is also evidence that changing age structure affects growth in developed countries as well. This becomes increasingly important as the bonus years slip away. The general conclusion from the literature is that a large share of middle-aged workers has a positive impact on growth, and a large share of elderly has a negative effect. This is consistent with the shifting dependency ratios of the bonus theory but can also be reinforced by human capital and life-cycle saving theories. These theories argue that it is not the additional hands at work on the production line that determines output growth, but it is the accumulation of human capital through on-the-job experience that boosts productivity. This suggests that growth due to human capital accumulation would peak with a mature workforce. The theory of life-cycle savings suggests that peak savings occurs in latter middle age, perhaps 50–64, after the major expenses of raising a family have been met. Again a mature workforce with high savings is thought to contribute to economic growth.[30] Bjorn Andersson (2001), for example, uses time series data on four Scandinavian countries to tease out the impact on economic growth of five age groups: youth, young adult, mature adult, middle aged, and retired (ages 0–14, 15–29, 30–49, 50–64, 65+). He finds that, in line with the human capital and life-cycle savings hypotheses, the mature adult and middle-aged groups had the highest positive impact on growth, and that the effect of the retired group was negative.

To summarize, the demographic bonus can, in theory, boost economic growth through two channels. The first is the mechanical nudge of increasing the share of working-age individuals in total population. The second is the potential for higher savings and higher productivity with a maturing of the workforce. Neither occurs without supportive policies, including finding productive jobs for a larger labor pool. As considered in subsequent chapters, the opportunities in the bonus phase become the challenges of the subsequent aging phase.

LOOKING AHEAD: HOW WILL IT END?

The demographic transition was originally thought of as a passage from one semi-stable population size to another; the first state characterized by high birth and mortality rates and the second by low rates. Plunging

---

30. It is remarkable how the Keynesian concern for excess savings has evaporated.

fertility was seen as the main driver. In this view, neither the world as a whole, nor most countries, has completed the transition. Some of the first wave countries have indeed stabilized their fertility rates, but mostly at below replacement level.[31] Barring large-scale migration or dramatic restoration of fertility, their populations are headed for decline. The second wave countries are in the midst of fertility decline, the ultimate low point of which is not yet known. Thus, the final chapter of the transition has yet to be written. We are entering *terra incognito* with respect to population decline.

The demographic transition literature, fortified by unified growth theory, explains how population and economic variables have interacted through three regimes to bring us to the present day. But it has limits as a guide to the future.[32] The following chapters sort through the implications of aging and population decline on economic well-being. However, before addressing this we should consider whether a serious population collapse is conceivable, and more specifically if a low fertility trap lies ahead.

A dramatic, worldwide, long-term decline in population is *feasible* without invoking catastrophic wars, epidemics, or errant asteroids. Indeed, it is feasible in a future that enjoys significant improvements in health and longevity. Basten, Lutz, and Scherbov (2013) and his co-authors, noting that the earlier UN projection of world population to 2300 used a relatively narrow range of fertility assumptions, undertook projections with total fertility rates converging on levels ranging from 0.75 to 2.5, and life expectancy of either 90, 100, or 120 years.[33] Using a 100-year life expectancy and a TFR of 1.5 (just below the current European rate), world population would peak in the middle of this century and be less than one billion in 2300, a level last seen in Malthus's own lifetime. Nudging the TFR rate up marginally to 1.75 would lead to a population of 3.2 billion. (At the current world fertility rate of 2.6, which no one finds likely, total projected world population would be above 80 billion.) See figure 6.3. These results are relatively insensitive to the life expectancy assumption. In short, it is

31. Of the 193 countries and territories tracked by the World Bank over the period 2007–10 or 2011, 164 showed stable or declining fertility rates. Moreover, of the 29 that showed increasing fertility rates, 20 were still well below replacement levels at the end of the period, with an average of 1.6 births per woman. These figures are suggestive but not dispositive due to uncertainty in the underlying data. Lutz et al. (2007), for example, state that published figures for China's fertility rate range from 1.2 to 2.3.

32. The unified theory would suggest that, with population decline, technological progress and hence economic growth would decline, but prognosis is not its *forte*. See Galor 2000.

33. The current low fertility rate is 0.79 for Singapore (Jones, 2012)

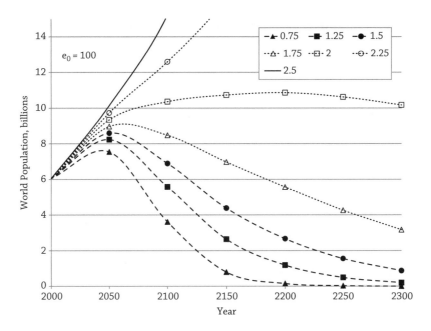

Figure 6.3:
Very long-run global population projections with alternative fertility assumptions
Source: Based on Basten, Lutz, and Scherbov 2013, table S2.
Note: Assumes life expectancy to converge on 100 years.

possible that, despite adequate food, fornication, and fecundity, one can still imagine a future that flirts with population collapse.

We have already identified one mechanism through which population may be caught in a downwards cycle—negative population growth momentum. This trigger does not require that fertility rates continue to decline—only that they come to rest somewhere below replacement level. The logic is straightforward. Fewer births this year means fewer women enter their reproductive years two decades hence and therefore, even with constant fertility rates, there are fewer births and smaller population in the following cycle. Sufficient increases in life expectancy could, in theory, stave off this result, but would imply implausibly long lifetimes. Of course, continued decline in fertility rates would simply hasten the population decline.

Beyond this mechanistic explanation of a trap, we can only speculate as there is little to guide us from the past. Populations have certainly crashed before. The ravages of the Black Death in the Middle Ages, the decimation of native populations in the New World following European colonization, and the oft-told story of the decline of Easter Island society come to mind.[34] But in these and many other cases, the crash was the result of plague and infectious disease, climatic change and unsustainable stress on natural resources, or deprivations from war and political reversals.[35] While these threats are not fully banished, they are not *necessary* to envision a crash. In present circumstances, population decline, if it materializes on a global scale, could be the result of voluntary, willful decisions concerning family size made at the individual and family level. Oswald Spengler, the controversial prophet of doom for the West a century ago, wrote, "Children do not happen, not because children have become impossible, but principally because intelligence at the peak of intensity can no longer find any reason for their existence" ([1918] 1928).

Beyond the mechanistic momentum factor, which will operate in any event, three forces will drive the outcome: sociocultural pressures, about which we know relatively little; economic pressures, for which a speculative case can be made that economic growth slowdown due to aging will make large families increasingly unattractive; and vigorous new government programs to boost birth rates and reverse population decline.[36] Some observers suggest that the first, sociocultural pressures or social norms, can lead a downward spiral and be difficult to exit (Zemac, Hallberg, and Lindh 2010). The operative assumption in this theory is that the desire to acquire children is influenced by the number of children around us—the fewer the children, the weaker the desire.[37] The prospective relaxation of the one-child policy in China will test this view. The second force may contain the elements of a low fertility trap—a growth slowdown due to aging undercuts the financial foundations of the welfare state and endangers the generational bargain described in chapter 9. Shifting a greater share of the burden of support for the old *and* the young is likely to discourage prospective parents. Whether government should take on a more active and effective role in pro-natalist policy is discussed in chapter 10.

34. Population crash has a suitably ominous sound. Europe lost an estimated one-third of its population to the plague in the Middle Ages. The native peoples of the Americas were reduced by 70 percent after colonization. But not all declines are as dramatic and calamitous. Despite having lost over 17 percent of its population in the century following World War I, Vienna recently tied with Vancouver as being chosen the world's most livable city.

35. Cellarier and Day (2011) have attempted to model the population response in structurally unstable variations of the Solow growth model.

36. Lutz, Basten, and Striessnig (2013) discuss a somewhat longer list. They also engage the interesting question of what *ought* to be the low fertility goal.

37. It seems equally likely that "only" children, bowed down by the expectations heaped upon them by their parents and bereft of siblings, may, when fecundity permits, overturn these projections and upon reaching maturity, deliver enough children to confound the more dire projections.

Note that conflicts can arise among these forces. Confronted with low fertility and the prospect of a declining workforce, countries such as Singapore and South Korea seek economic growth through education and accumulation of human capital. Delayed marriage to complete education and the conflicts between career and family tend to depress fertility further, especially in cultures without full gender equality. Government incentives for childrearing must contend with the long hours and commitment of the modern workplace (James, Skirbekk, and Van Bavel 2012). Aspirations for income growth can lead to lower birth rates and, over time, a shrinking of the workforce.

To summarize, at one point it appeared that the demographic transition framework, with suitable adjustments for the first (Western) wave and the second (developing country) wave, offered a plausible and comprehensive narrative for two centuries of economic and demographic change. But its weakness was ultimately exposed. It foresaw a new equilibrium, with fertility close to replacement levels and a stabilizing population. As it turned out, there was little theoretical basis and even less empirical support for this assumption. The end point of the transition has evaporated, undermining its foretold conclusion.

One response has been to stay with the basic DT framework, acknowledge that it is incomplete with respect to the endpoint, and scramble to fill in the missing pieces. A second response, not totally different, is to discern two distinct transitions, the traditional DT that brought the West to the mid-twentieth century and which is, at different stages, ongoing in many developing countries, and a *second* demographic transition with roots in Europe in the last half of that century (Lesthaeghe 2010). According to proponents of a second demographic transition, sociocultural changes are now mainly responsible for fertility decisions. More specifically, whereas the first transition was anchored in a culture of realizing basic material needs, the second is focused on nonmaterial aspirations—independence, self-realization, social mobility, and so forth. For our purposes, the implication of the second demographic transition concept is that sub-replacement fertility rates could become an intrinsic feature of the demographic regime. This tends to confirm that the assumption of stable population endpoint has to be scrapped.[38] None of this is much help in forecasting global population in the long run.

---

38. Van Bavel (2010) makes an interesting case that sub-replacement fertility levels in the interwar period (1920–40), currently thought to be an aberration due to war and economic crisis, were at the time attributable to the same features that characterize the second democratic transition in the post–World War II era. If so, one can point to almost a century of "modernization" forces that act to depress fertility rates.

CHAPTER 7

⌗

The Upside of Downsizing

. . . depopulation can often be a highly beneficial and necessary thing.
—Knut Wicksell, 1914 on the benefits population decline

In this and subsequent chapters, we refocus from the past to the future. The defining *demographic* feature in the future appears to be decline—both decline of population *growth*, already well underway, and prospective decline in world population itself. Decline is not unprecedented, but in the past it has been either short-lived or local, and in only a few cases has it been the consequence of deliberate decisions to limit family size below replacement levels. The notable exception is the twentieth-century inter-war period when, as discussed in the previous chapter, fertility was below replacement levels in a number of European countries.

Decline has a morbid connotation, in part, because it implies aging. And, as the economist Lionel Robbins put it almost a century ago, aging means "fewer toys, more foot-warmers." Decline does indeed have a downside that we will examine. But in the spirit of Dr. Pangloss we will first seek the positive effects. The logical place to look is relief from environmental and natural resource stresses. The exploding population in the last half of the twentieth century revitalized interest in curbing its growth. Environmentalists were at the forefront. For example, Lester Brown and his colleagues at Worldwatch Institute, writing in 1998, discussed 16 challenges posed by population expansion. Of these, 12 directly concerned environmental resources, including food supplies (Brown et al. 1998).[1] Now that the fevered view of continuous global population upsurge is past and declines are in prospect, it is time to assess what has been gained. The main question is whether decelerating and reversing population growth will significantly relieve stress and arrest environmental degradation.

It would be tedious to discuss each of Brown's challenges individually. We limit ourselves to two issues—global warming and adequate food supplies.[2] Global warming is *the* environmental threat of the current century, and food has been a favorite candidate for population pessimists since Malthus. As it turns out, the prospects for global warming and food supplies are closely intertwined. Before examining food and climate directly, however, it is useful to disentangle demographic variables (mainly population growth) from economic variables (mainly per capita income, or affluence) as environmental drivers. We will use global warming as our example.

POPULATION, AFFLUENCE, AND GLOBAL WARMING

In the 200 years between 1800 and 2000 world population rose sixfold, affluence measured by per capita GDP increased twelvefold, and CO_2 emissions, the principal greenhouse gas, surged twentyfold. A driving force for affluence and CO_2 growth was fossil-fuel energy, which increased by a factor of 35.[3] What are the links between these forces, and how will they play out in the context of a slowing or declining population? Answers are needed to allocate responsibilities in international climate negotiations and to fashion efficient climate policies.

The outlook is guardedly hopeful. Until now population and economic growth trends have reinforced each other in driving carbon emissions upward. From now forward, however, with the slowdown and ultimate reversal of world population growth, they will tend to work in opposite directions. The direct effect of lower population growth and depopulation will be reduced CO_2 emissions, a plus in limiting global warming. This will offset some of the deleterious effects of rising living standards and higher energy consumption. But we must be cautious before celebrating, and we

1. The other four were jobs, housing, urbanization, and income.
2. The current term of art is "food security," which includes physical adequacy and economic access. For a broader review of population and ecological interactions, see de Sherbinin et al. 2007.
3. Jiang and Harrdee (2009). The twentyfold increase in carbon emissions comes in spite of a declining trend in energy use per unit output and a declining trend in carbon per unit energy over much of the past 200 years.

need to investigate the links between population slowdown (depopulation) and economic growth. It may be that depopulation will also slow per
capita economic growth and thereby reinforce the reduction of emissions.
But, instead, it may be that with a declining world population, natural resources and physical productive capital per person are higher, allowing an
increase in per capita production and consumption (affluence).[4] If so, some
of the direct gains in lower emissions from a smaller population will be
erased by increasing output and energy use per capita.[5] And the task is not
just to stabilize emissions but to drastically reduce them. We return to
these questions later.

Quantification: IPAT and Kaya and Their Limitations

There is no simple way to link demographic changes and greenhouse gas
emissions. This is unfortunate as emissions scenarios are at the foundation of integrated assessment models (IAMs), the principal tool for climate policy analysis. A misjudgment concerning the emissions trajectories
affects estimated atmospheric concentration levels, temperature increases, physical impacts (e.g., sea level rise, loss of genetic diversity), the
monetization of those impacts, and their discounted present value, the
last of which is fed into a cost-benefit model for policy evaluation. In short,
a misjudgment in the demographic-emissions linkage leads to policy recommendations that are either too severe or too lenient. More broadly, the
climate benefits of demographic declines are uncertain.

Early attempts to quantify population-environmental linkage relied on
the IPAT formula, a staple of environmental economics for four decades.
The formula states that environmental impact (I) equals population size
(P) times the level of affluence or income per capita (A) times the technology (T) employed in producing and consuming goods and services, or $I =
(P)(A)(T)$. The Kaya formulation is an improvement on IPAT specific to the
problem of climate change. It states that CO_2 emissions are equal to population size (P) times affluence, as measured by per capita income or output,
times energy use per unit output, times the carbon intensity of energy:

$$CO_2 = (P)(Q/P)(E/Q)(CO_2/E),$$

---

4. Recall from the Solow model that a smaller population leads to capital deepening and higher per capita output and income.
5. Despite several decades of restrictive population policies, China's affluence and
emissions have both soared.

where P is population, Q is output of goods and services, and E is units of energy (e.g., BTUs).

Note that the left-hand side measures emissions, not physical environmental and ecological impacts, which requires converting emissions to atmospheric concentrations and then to temperature change before arriving at environmental impacts.

IPAT, as conventionally used, and Kaya are identities, elaborate definitions.[6] They do not imply causality. However, they are helpful in drawing attention to the principal drivers of environmental effects. For projecting emissions trajectories, Kaya identifies population growth, increasing affluence, trends in energy efficiency, and the carbon intensity of energy, which in turn depends on the mix of fossil fuels and renewables and the mix of fossil fuels themselves. These projections can then be adjusted for land-use changes (deforestation), an important additional source of CO_2, and other greenhouse gases (methane, nitrous oxides, etc.).

While potentially helpful, IPAT and Kaya have serious limits and can be misleading. One problem is that as identities they are definitionally true but do not reveal causal relations and cannot be used to test hypotheses linking the variables. In its multiplicative form, an identity requires strict proportionality between, say, population and emissions. Holding other variables constant, a 10 percent increase in population must lead to a 10 percent increase in emissions. The *assumption* is proportionality.[7]

This leads to a second problem, as examined by Alcott (2010). Interactions among the right-hand side variables are not revealed. For example, as discussed in earlier, there are reasons to believe that rapid growth of total population can depress per capita income growth: P and A are jointly determined (as in the simple Solow model). If so, some of the emission reduction gains from lowering population growth could be erased by accelerating the growth of affluence. Alternatively, following the "new growth" theory, P and A may have a positive relation and could reinforce one another in curbing emissions. Slowing population may slow affluence and slow emissions. Finally, an improvement in energy efficiency reduces costs and encourages greater energy use, an example of Jevons's Paradox, now referred to as the rebound effect. The additional use would be associated with an *increase* in emissions, not captured in Kaya.

Another limitation of the IPAT and Kaya formulations is that they allow for only one demographic variable, population size, to affect emissions.

---

6. Technology (T) in IPAT has to be defined in terms of environmental impact per unit GDP.
7. Technically, unitary elasticity.

Other relevant attributes such as the average age of the population, rural/urban ratios, and average household size that are neglected. And, of course, IPAT and Kaya are incomplete as they do not include social, political, and institutional variables that may affect emissions. Indeed, they do not consider any feedback from emissions and climate change to population variables. While the morbidity and mortality consequences of global warming have been extensively studied, they are rarely part of the initial population projections. Population growth is treated as exogenous.

Quantification: STIRPAT

The Stochastic Impacts by Regression on Population, Affluence, and Technology (STIRPAT) approach attempts to improve on the two identities. As Dietz, Rosa, and York (2007) explain, STIRPAT is a nonlinear regression equation in which coefficients are hypotheses to be tested and which can include additional demographic variables such as age, urbanization, and household size.[8] The newer research shows more complicated relations between emissions and population than were first assumed and used as inputs to IAMs. Anqing Shi (2003), for example, uses a modified STIRPAT model to estimate the elasticity of emissions with respect to both total population and per capita income. He finds that a 1 percent increase in population leads to a 1.4 percent increase in CO_2 emissions, whereas a 1 percent increase in per capita income (affluence) leads to only 0.8 percent increase in emissions. These are substantially different than the unitary elasticities assumed in the IPAT and Kaya frameworks. Moreover, the responsiveness of emissions to total population is itself different at different income levels, with the highest elasticity estimated at almost 2 for lower-middle-income countries and the lowest estimate at 0.8 for high-income countries.

Finally, it should be emphasized that the IPAT approach cannot be used to directly investigate the effects of environmental impacts (e.g., CO_2 levels) on population and other demographic variables.

These findings have important implications for climate policy. First, early analysis based on a fixed elasticity of one for population growth *underestimates* greenhouse gas emissions trajectories and the severity of the climate problem. The impact is more than proportional. Remember also

---

8. In this particular study, STIRPAT had the general form $I = aP^bA^ce$, where I is environmental impact measured in "ecological footprint" units (not emissions), a is a scale factor, b and c are the elasticities (i.e., responsiveness) of impact with respect to total population and to affluence, and e serves as an index of technology.

that the climate change time horizon is hundreds of years, and a small error in estimating emissions compounds over the years. Second, the study shows that *where* the population increases occur matters. All else equal, the emissions elasticity of population increase is highest in lower income countries, exactly where most of population growth is expected to be. Rich countries are not off the hook however. Although their elasticity is lower, their base level of emissions per person is higher.

These refinements should be reflected in climate policy, but the general conclusion remains: the slowing and reversal of population growth will help ease the threat of global warming—an upside to population decline.

Quantification: Aging, Household Size, and Urbanization

How important are other demographic variables, apart from population size, in determining greenhouse gas emissions? We can reasonably assume that the trends—aging, shrinking household size, and urbanization—will continue for most of this century and perhaps longer. Each has the potential to alter emissions trajectories, although IAM modeling has been slow to incorporate them (O'Neill et al. 2010).

A slowdown and ultimate decline in population means an aging population. As documented elsewhere, the aging can be substantial and rapid, and indeed is already underway in most countries. An aging population can affect greenhouse gas emissions through three channels. First, the composition of consumption changes. For example, in the United States, the percent of household expenditures spent on utilities is 3.7 for age group 25–35; whereas, it is almost double at 6.7 percent for age group 75–85 (Dalton et al. 2008, table 1). Transportation is 8.3 percent for the younger group but is only 6.8 percent for the elder group. As expected, shares spent on health rises from 3.8 for the young to 16.3 percent for the old. The consumption shifts can be linked to energy use and hence emissions. If the consumption pattern is less energy-intensive, the presumption is that emissions would be lower than they otherwise would be.[9] In fact, Dalton finds the energy intensity of older households' expenditures is *greater* than younger households, but this is in proportion to their incomes and not absolute levels.

---

9. This is a bit facile. CO_2 emissions occur during production as well as consumption. International trade drives a wedge between where a product is made and where it is consumed. Currently the country of production is tagged with emissions regardless of where the product is consumed. This inflates the role of China and other net exporters of manufactures in attributing emissions. See Pearson (2011).

Second, if retirement age is relatively fixed, an aging population implies the ratio of retired persons to workers increases. As examined in the following chapter, shrinking the relative size of the active workforce tends to depress output, energy use in production, and ultimately emissions.

Third, the life-cycle savings hypothesis suggests that savings are largest during working years and lowest (or negative) during retirement. In that event, an aging population would reduce aggregate savings and investment and tend to reduce aggregate economic growth and greenhouse gas emissions. The second and third channels just listed suggest an involuntary and not necessarily welcome start to a declining or "de-growth" economy.

Dalton and his colleagues (2008) have attempted to sort out the implication of aging for CO_2 emissions for the United States by using an energy-economic growth model that incorporates changing age structure. They find that the compositional changes in consumption associated with aging have negligible effect on emissions, but the effect on labor income working through aging and a reduction in labor supply is potentially large. Specifically, by 2100 US CO_2 emissions are 11 percent, 18 percent, and 37 percent lower as a result of aging in, respectively, high, medium, and low population growth scenarios. The lower the population growth, the greater the aging, and the lower the emissions. This result leaves a bittersweet taste however. The lower emissions are "purchased" by decreased labor supply and lower levels of economic output.[10]

Another demographic feature that may affect greenhouse gas emissions is the changing size of households. The worldwide trend is strongly toward smaller households. It can be hypothesized that smaller households use greater energy per person for heating, cooking, appliances, and perhaps transportation, but it is difficult to disentangle household size from urbanization and per capita income data. There is some evidence of economies of scale in energy use in larger households that may be lost as the shrinking trend continues, but the effect may be different in developing and post-industrial countries. It is also difficult to disentangle the effects on emissions due to the correlation between aging and smaller households. O'Neill et al. (2010), for example, found that in China smaller households lead to *lower* emissions. However, it appears the reason is that small, older households have seen their working age children depart and the remaining old folks have withdrawn from the labor market. As a result, labor output and emissions per household decline.

---

10. The model assumes labor-force participation rates by age group remain unchanged. This may be unduly pessimistic. With better health and longer life spans, the age of retirement may rise.

Urbanization has the potential to increase emissions via a labor productivity effect. The reasoning is straightforward. Urban productivity, measured as output per worker, is generally a multiple of productivity in rural areas. Output is related to energy and thus related to CO_2 emissions. But a more complicated link may be at work in the opposite direction. There is considerable evidence that in many countries, rural population growth in the context of poverty leads to deforestation, a major source of CO_2 emissions. Urbanization may moderate deforestation pressures. Also, if correctly planned and equipped with efficient public transport, urban development can be energy efficient. More generally, one weakness in the literature linking demographic variables and greenhouse gas emissions is that it has not extended to non-CO_2 gases such as methane and nitrous oxides, both of which are strongly associated with agriculture.

Results

Brian O'Neill and his colleagues (2010) have provided a comprehensive analysis of the emissions consequences of a slowdown in world population growth. The results are mixed: abstracting from population size, aging can reduce emissions by up to 20 percent in the long term; urbanization may increase emissions by 25 percent due to higher productivity of urban labor, especially in developing countries;[11] and (where data were available) smaller households apparently lead to lower emissions, again working through reduced labor supply in small, elderly households.

These effects can be aggregated to reveal the difference that population slowdown can make. Using the IPCC's B2 scenario for emissions and a population-energy-emissions growth model, the study estimates that moving from a medium to a "low" population growth rate reduces emissions by 1.4 gigatons of carbon per year by 2050.[12] This represents about 16 percent of the reductions needed to obtain the 2° C temperature change target that has been established. By the end of the century slower population growth could reduce emissions from fossil fuels by about 40 percent. These optimistic conclusions must be treated cautiously. They reflect an assumption that labor supply rates by age group remain unchanged. If, instead, retirement is postponed, some of the emissions gains from aging will be wiped out. Moreover, and as noted previously, these gains arise from decreasing aggregate productivity, as the elderly withdraw from the

---

11. Some other studies have shown that urban living tends to be energy efficient.
12. One gigaton is one billion tons.

labor force. This is not an attractive swap for those with economic growth aspirations. Nor is the timing ideal. The bulk of the emissions reduction from population decline will come in the second half of the century, but it is emissions in the next few decades that are critical for long-term global warming. Finally, this analysis considers population projections to be exogenous. No attempt is made to estimate changes in mortality due to climate change, nor changes in fertility working through climate-related changes in economic growth rates.

POPULATION AND CLIMATE: POLICY MATTERS

The Politics of Population vs. Affluence

There is a political overlay to the population-affluence-climate discourse. In its crudest form it pits numbers (population) against per capita greenhouse gas emissions (affluence) in dissecting the roots of the problem and in crafting climate policy. There are many studies that document the disproportionate use (and often abuse) of natural and environmental resources by the rich North as compared to the poor South. Even today, despite the stunning economic growth in China over the past four decades, and despite being far less efficient in its energy use, its *per capita* CO_2 emissions are less than one-third the level of the United States. This creates a large stumbling block in climate negotiations. China, and even more so India and other poor countries, point out their modest per capita contribution and insist that they need energy to grow. Their conclusion is that a disproportionate share of emissions reductions should be done by affluent countries.

In general, the North has accepted the principle of differential obligations. But it points out complications. The sheer size of the South's population and its cumulative output are such that it must participate in a serious fashion if global emissions are to fall to "safe" levels.[13] And because of inefficiencies in the use of energy, the South has much lower cost emission abatement opportunities. A least-cost global climate strategy requires that much of the abatement activity be undertaken in the South. (This does not mean however that the financing burden need be mainly shouldered by the South. Transfers from North to South can separate abatement actions from their financing.) In short, because of its population

---

13. "Safe" has been politically (but not scientifically) determined to permit a 2° C global average temperature increase. Temperature change targets can be converted to "safe" emissions levels, although that conversion is subject to considerable uncertainty.

size, rapid drive toward affluence, and relatively low abatement cost opportunities, participation by the South in controlling greenhouse gas emissions is necessary. Declining population growth, or indeed depopulation, may reduce global abatement costs, but will do little to solve this blockage to effective international action on climate change.

Population Policy as Climate Policy

Given population's central role in greenhouse gas emissions, one might expect population policy would have an equally central role in abatement strategies. This has not been the case. The Intergovernmental Panel on Climate Change, the principal international effort at analyzing climate change, did not mention population policy in its 2007 summary for policymakers of ways to mitigate climate change (Working Group III). The 2009 Copenhagen Accord invited members of the UN Framework Convention on Climate Change (UNFCCC) to submit lists of mitigation actions they planned to implement, but a perusal does not reveal any population commitments. The 2014 IPCC working group draft report on mitigation acknowledged that economic and population growth will continue to be the most important drivers of CO_2 emissions. But they presented no analysis or recommendations, confining themselves to the technical variables in Kaya. By and large, the thrust of climate policy analysis and efforts has been on technological solutions and market-friendly abatement tools such as carbon taxes and cap and trade schemes.

One reason for this inattention may be that population policy has a highly contentious and divisive history in international negotiations and to import these disputes into the North–South global warming discussions could be provocative and unwise. A second reason is that population is not a policy knob for emissions control that can be tuned up or down at will. Specifically, some argue that the pre-condition for declining fertility (and ultimately for reducing emissions) is increasing living standards. If so, greater affluence and slower population growth will tend to cancel one another out. Finally, and most importantly, overall population trends are already working in a favorable direction. Rates of growth are declining; depopulation is in prospect. The population urgency that was felt in the 1980s has dissipated.

Having said this, the contribution of population and population policy to climate policy has not been completely neglected. Three perspectives— externalities, ethics, and efficiency—have received attention.

Externalities

Reproductive externalities were discussed earlier, and empirical studies suggest that the size of the (negative) global warming externality ranges from significant to dramatic. The implication is that limiting population growth could have substantial benefits in coping with climate change by reducing emissions and emissions abatement costs. Several researchers have picked up on this point and argue convincingly that closing the gap between wanted and unwanted births through more funding for family planning would support climate objectives. O'Neill et al. (2010), for example, argue that if unmet family planning needs were met, fertility could drop substantially in the United States and in developing countries, leading to significant emissions reductions. Alcott (2012) states that unwanted pregnancies may account for perhaps 75 percent of global population increase. Still, calls for more coercive measures such as a tax on childbearing set at its externality cost are rare.[14]

Because serious coercive measures justified by climate concern are highly unlikely, attention shifts to voluntary reproduction decisions based on personal ethics. This fits into a much larger discussion of personal actions to limit "carbon footprints." Calculating one's footprint has become a popular activity, if not an exact science. For example, the World Wildlife Fund offers an online calculator based on two dozen lifestyle questions. None of the questions however touch on one's procreative life. This is unfortunate as the decision to have or not have a child is of great significance for future carbon emissions.

Ethics

That brings us to a tricky problem in ethics. To what extent should prospective parents with an ethical bent be concerned not only their own carbon emissions, but the emissions of their offspring, and indeed the emissions attributable to the descendants of those offspring? To sharpen the point, is there a valid distinction between the carbon emissions emanating from one's own children, and the carbon emissions emanating from decisions by one's children themselves to have children? Does an ethically based responsibility carry past that first generation, for which

14. Recall that in the Bohn and Stuart study, a Pigouvian tax would lead to a long-term, steady state population about 75 percent below what households would otherwise choose. Alcott (2012) attempts to reintroduce population concerns into the global ecological debate.

the parents are quite clearly responsible at least during their child's child-hood, to the second, third, and subsequent generations?

For those inclined to answer yes, Paul Murtaugh and Michael Schlax (2009) have provided a cleverly constructed analytical framework for as-sessing responsibility. The basic premise is that "a person is responsible for the carbon emissions of his descendants, weighted by their relatedness to him." For example a grandfather is one-fourth responsible for the emis-sions of his grandchild and one-eighth for his great-grandchild whether or not he survives to know the child. With data on projected fertility rates by country, a survival function, and assumptions concerning future per capita emission rates, an individual's "carbon legacy" can be calculated.[15]

The results are quite remarkable. The lifetime carbon emissions of an individual in the United States are 1,644 tons and, if that individual has a child, that child and his or her (ever attenuating) descendants will add an additional 9,441 tons over their lifetimes.[16] As might be expected the life-time carbon emissions of an individual in India are far less, at 70 tons, and a single child and its descendants will add an additional 171 tons. (The calculations do not take into account a possible surge in Indian economic growth rates over this century.) A more optimistic assumption on future emission rates dramatically lowers the carbon legacy estimates, especially for the United States. The carbon legacy results of an additional child can also be compared to other personal decisions motivated by climate con-cerns. For example, in the United States switching from a 20 mpg auto to a 30 mpg model or cutting yearly miles by one-third from 13,500 to 8,000 would avert about 150 tons of emissions over a person's lifetime—small change compared to becoming a parent.

However, the ethical foundation for carbon legacy analysis remains murky. We do have responsibility for the consequences of our actions—cars purchased, miles driven. Reproduction decisions have consequences, and it is reasonable to expect our children to generate emissions. That ex-pectation may well enter our decision. But to go a generation beyond this is to hold ourselves responsible for decisions taken by others, our children and their partners. It has an air of infinite paternalism. Responsibility is reasonably tied to our decisions, not theirs, and is not bestowed through genetic links. Just as we cannot devolve responsibility for our own carbon emissions back in time on our ancestors, we should not assume it for our progeny. If we did include our grandchildren's emissions should we not

15. Not all the lineages will die out and it appears the calculations in this exercise are terminated in 2400.

16. Using medium variant fertility projections and constant 2005 emission rates.

also include their contributions to pensions in support of their parents, who are our children?

Efficiency

The final perspective is efficiency. How does population policy stack up against other abatement alternatives on a least-cost or cost-effective basis? If it is shown to be competitive, international funds pledged for climate change activities could be partially allocated to family planning and female education budgets, and the resulting declines in fertility and births averted could contribute to emission abatement and climate objectives. At the same time, the funds would contribute to broader sustainable development objectives where family planning and female education is underfunded and underserved. The basic analysis requires estimating the monetary costs of a birth averted through improved family planning services (and perhaps augmented by improvements in female educational opportunities), estimating average or marginal carbon emissions per individual and from this calculating the cost per ton of carbon abated through population policy. This can then be compared to the cost per ton of alternative abatement strategies such as renewable energy—nuclear, solar, second-generation biofuels and so forth, the costs of which have been estimated elsewhere in the literature.

David Wheeler and Dan Hammer (2010) have indeed done the analysis. They find that for a large number of developing countries, family planning or family planning together with support for female education can be cost-effective in comparison to abatement opportunities such as curbing deforestation and promoting low carbon energy. While encouraging, we need to keep in mind that the large sums of money pledged for abatement and adaptation activities have not yet materialized. The funding of a global public good—a stable climate—in a system of sovereign states is a stumbling block, whether the policy tool is carbon taxes or support for family planning programs.

Climate Policy as Population Policy

We now turn the question around. Do climate policies have population *policy* implications? It is possible in theory to show that they do. A novel argument can be made that pollution control generally, including greenhouse gas abatement, has a pro-natalist bias. More specifically, controlling the carbon emission externality may encourage procreation and, on that account, perhaps population should be subject to some capping policy as well (de la Croix and Gosseries 2012).

The logic is as follows. Consider an economy consisting of three activities: production of goods and services, leisure, and procreation. As used in this study, procreation means the rearing of children, not their conception. The first activity, production, pollutes, and by assumption leisure and procreation do not. As a result of either a carbon tax or a cap and trade pollution control scheme net wages fall and, for households, time spent at production (work) becomes relatively less rewarding. The untaxed activities of leisure and procreation become relatively less expensive more rewarding. "Reproduction" is substituted for production; population tends to increase, and output per worker falls. The bump up in population growth tends to reduce future income as conventionally measured and a cap on population may be indicated. The broader point is that with multiple externalities—carbon emissions and reproductive externalities—correcting one through say a carbon tax may exacerbate the other and require a second policy measure. In principle and at a high level of abstraction, optimal resource policy and optimal population policy should be jointly determined. This is a counsel for perfection that is unlikely to happen.

FOOD PROSPECTS

Diet

We are looking for the upside of population slowdown and decline. It is obvious that Malthus's old nemesis, inadequate food supplies and the resulting checks of famine and starvation, will receive some relief by the slowdown.[17] Had the world's population continued to grow at over 2 percent annually, the rate of the 1980s, by 2050 population would be 17.8 billion rather than the projected 9.6 billion.

Whether the prospect of fewer stomachs to fill will fully alleviate pressure on world food supplies is another matter. If considered in isolation from other forces, it does not appear unduly daunting. Current medium UN population projections are for a 3.1 billion increase from 2012 to a peak population of 10.1 billion sometime about 2100. This

17. It is sometimes useful to distinguish between the adequacy of supplies in a physical sense and the adequacy of income needed to buy food at prevailing prices. Sufficient physical supplies do not guarantee the latter.

suggests a growth rate of about 0.4 percent per year. Looking back over the period 1961 to 2010, FAO data show world production of four basic crops—maize, wheat, rice, soybeans, which together contribute 75 percent of the calories humans directly or indirectly consume—had increased by a much higher rate, 2.6 percent per year.[18] Most of the gains came from higher cropping intensity and higher yields. With sufficient research and investment these gains may be expected to continue through this century. Advances in agricultural biotechnology still hold great promise.

To simply extrapolate population and productivity trends is not sufficient, however. The experience of Malthus and Jevons suggests caution in looking back to see what the future will bring. There are known and unknown uncertainties. The known uncertainty centers on predicting human fertility 50 and 100 years out. If fertility rates fail to decline as rapidly as projected, population in 2100 could reach 16 billion, an increase that more than doubles current population and an absolute increase that is far in excess of what we faced in the past. The unanticipated baby boom following World War II is a useful caution when projecting fertility. On the other hand, the extraordinary decline in fertility in developing countries in the same period was also unforeseen.

Two other developments, one affecting food demand, the other affecting food supply, may undermine the positive effects of population slowdown. They are dietary trends associated with higher incomes and global warming. Dietary changes pose the lesser threat and are not new. Over the past 50 years, while population increased by about 124 percent, worldwide meat consumption increased over 300 percent. IFPRI projects per capita meat consumption to rise from 90 to 100 kg per year in high-income countries and from 25 to nearly 45 kg in low-income countries by 2050.

Food, feed for livestock, and grazing are all in competition for agricultural land. Increased meat consumption is a land-intensive method to acquire protein and calories for human consumption. Stehfest Bouwman, van Vuuren, Elxen, Eickhout (2009) estimate that it takes 2.4 times as much land area to produce a kilogram of protein from ruminant meat (cattle, sheep, goats) as it does from pulses (beans, peas, lentils). With utilization of grazing land close to capacity, additional meat supplies will come from feedlots and

18. For maize, 2.9 percent; 2.2 percent for rice and wheat; 3.6 percent for soybeans. In a balanced assessment two decades ago, Vaclav Smil (1994) concluded that a population of 10–11 billion could be fed this century, but the task should not be approached with complacency.

the conversion of grains to meat is unfavorable. Brown, Gardner, and Halwell (1998) place it at seven kg grain to one kg meat for beef, four to one for pork, and two to one for poultry.

The key concern for the future is not meat consumption per se, but the energy, land, and water inefficiencies of a meat-based diet as compared to a cereals- and legumes-based diet, and the prominent role livestock plays in greenhouse gas emissions. Pimental and Pimental (2003) calculates that it takes 25 Kcal of fossil fuel to produce 1 Kcal of animal protein but only 2.2 Kcal of fossil fuel to produce 1 Kcal of corn protein, an efficiency ratio of 1 to 11. The world will not run out of meat, but the diversion of basic agricultural inputs to meat production will erode food supply improvements resulting from population slowdown. It will also increase the relative price of all foods and limit the ability of the poor to buy food. While rising prices will tend to increase supplies, income distribution is a central concern.

Food and Global Warming

Ironically, it is not Malthus's fixation on land, but the capacity of the earth's *atmosphere* to absorb CO_2 without triggering runaway temperature increases that has emerged as the latest limit to growth candidate. And it is here, under the threat of global warming, that the Malthusian race between food and resources is again being run. The preceding paragraphs identified two possible pitfalls even before that race has begun—an uptick in fertility rates and the adoption of affluent diets. Both have substantial uncertainty. But global warming displays cascading uncertainty, making categorical dismissal of Malthus impossible.

In thinking through the food–climate nexus it is helpful to distinguish between agriculture's contribution to global warming and the effects of global warming on food production. The first is substantial. The second could bring severe problems.

Food → Warming

Population growth, rising incomes, and dietary changes will increase food demand over the next century. This will spill over into increased greenhouse gas emissions unless a serious climate change policy is established. Livestock alone accounts for 18 percent of total greenhouse gas emissions (Stehfest Bouwman, van Vuuren, Elxen, Eickhout 2009). Paddy rice culture is also significant. To be efficient and effective, climate policy will require a tax or cap and trade system to put a price on greenhouse gas emissions, including CO_2 and methane. Conventional agriculture and food distribution are fossil-fuel intensive and the real costs of food production will go up. Expansion of cultivation to currently forested areas is not a solution, as deforestation releases stored carbon. Sufficient food may be produced despite rising costs, but food prices will increase and access by the poor will be impaired. The bottom line is that global warming policy measures themselves will increase food prices. While this need not reflect physical scarcity, it will affect diets of the poor.

Alternatively, as discussed below, a weak or nonexistent climate policy would almost surely lead to higher temperatures, depressed world food production, and higher real prices. The horns of this dilemma can be blunted with nuanced policies—for example, new technologies to reduce emissions from livestock and wet rice cultivation, limiting food waste from storage and so forth. But the dilemma is real and will persist. In this sense, a low population growth rate over this century is desirable, and the lower the better. It will reduce emissions directly and reduce climate policy related increases in food production costs.

Warming → Food

We turn to the effects of global warming on food supplies. There are multiple uncertainties. We do not know how much warming will take place in the absence of effective climate policy. Sokolov and his colleagues (2009) use MIT's integrated climate-economic assessment model to put a bound on the uncertainty. They conclude that with no deliberate climate policy there is a 95 percent probability that average world temperature would rise by 3.5–7.4° C by the end of this century. For the metrically challenged this is 6.3–13.3° F. These are world averages and there will be wide variations by location and season. One estimate is that summertime temperatures in California's agriculturally rich Central Valley could rise by 2.5 times the world average (Hanemann 2008). Moreover, we do not know what climate policies will be put in place. An international consensus reached in Cancun Mexico in 2010 set an aspirational target of limiting global average increase to 2° C, but that target does not rest on firm scientific or economic analysis, nor is there a binding international agreement and financing to back it up.

Even if the extent of warming was known the effects on food supplies are uncertain. There is some prospect that increases in atmospheric CO_2 will act as a fertilizer and increase yields for some crops. Additional land may also be opened for cultivation at higher latitudes. But the consensus in the research literature is that the effect will be negative, falling particularly harshly on poor countries in the tropics.[19] We quote a recent survey:

> Few global-scale assessments have been carried out, and these are limited in their ability to capture uncertainty in climate change projections and omit potential aspects such as extreme events and changes in pests and diseases. . . . The dependence of some regional agriculture on remote rainfall, snow melt and glaciers adds to the complexity. Indirect impacts via sea level rise, storms and diseases have not been quantified. Perhaps most seriously, there is high uncertainty in the extent to which the direct effects of CO_2 rise on plant physiology will interact with climate change in affecting productivity. At present, the aggregate impacts of climate change on global-scale agricultural productivity cannot be reliably quantified.[20]

The International Food Policy Research Institute (Nelson et al. 2010) has attempted to estimate real price increases for basic crops over the 2010–50 period using the three variables we have discussed: population, income and diet, and climate change. Their baseline case is an average of four climate scenarios and they distinguish between two drivers, population and income change working on increased demand, and adverse effects of climate change working on productivity and supply. For the 40-year period, they find a 100 percent increase in the real price of maize (corn), the cause of which is split 50–50 between population plus income growth and the negative effects of climate change; about a 58 percent increase in wheat price, again split 50–50 between the two factors; and a 55 percent increase in rice prices in which a somewhat smaller fraction is due to climate change. As expected, they conclude that the world's poorest people will bear the brunt of the effects of climate change on food prices. More broadly and unlike the falling world food prices in the twentieth century, we may see rising food prices that bring Malthusian style miseries to the poor in their wake.

19. Ackerman and Stanton (2013) argue that very recent work on agriculture and global warming is more negative than earlier research, but has not yet found its way into policy modeling exercises. Lobell, Schlenker, and Costa-Roberts (2011) find evidence that recent temperature changes have already had significant negative effects on maize and wheat yields. For pessimistic projections of US maize and soybean yields, see Schlenker and Roberts (2009).

20. Gornall et al. (2010). See also Schmidhuber and Tubiello (2007).

Biofuels: Another Dilemma

Finally consider the interesting case of biofuels. Biofuels come in three flavors depending on feedstock: ethanol made from sugar and starches (sugarcane, corn); biodiesel made from fats and oils (palm oil, rapeseed, soy); and cellulosic ethanol made from cellulose (woody material, grasses). The technology for the first two is well established but costs are generally higher than fossil-fuel-based energy and large subsidies are needed.[21]

Biofuels have two possible advantages. First, they are liquid fuels suitable for transportation needs. Second, in principle, they can reduce carbon emissions. Unlike fossil fuels, which extract carbon that is safely stored underground, burn it, and release carbon to the atmosphere where it is damaging, biofuels *withdraw* carbon from the atmosphere as the feedstocks are growing and release it when burned, potentially reducing net carbon emissions. These two features make them attractive for an aggressive climate strategy and, if successful, might contribute to reducing global warming and easing the strain put on the world food system.

But biofuels have disadvantages as well (Chakravorty, Hubert, and Nostbakken 2009). First, it is not clear that switching from fossil to biofuels actually reduces carbon emissions within a relevant time frame. Land has to be converted to biofuel feedstock. The large-scale conversion of, say, tropical rainforest to palm oil plantations releases a pulse of carbon during the conversion by the burning of vegetation cover and disturbance of soils. One study (Fargione et al. 2008) concluded that the carbon "debt" created by the conversion of a hectare of Amazon forest to growing soy for biodiesel would take 319 years to be paid off—in other words, the annual reduction of carbon from switching from fossil fuel to biodiesel would need to be cumulated for over three centuries to equal the release of carbon from the land conversion activity.

A second disadvantage is directly relevant to our concerns. Some biofuel feedstock is diverted from the food chain and food supplies, and some diverts the underlying land resources from food to fuel. In 2012 the United States produced about 39 percent of world corn output, and about 35 percent went to ethanol production. Thus, biofuels can play conflicting roles: potentially strengthening climate policies by providing a renewable source of transportation fuel and thereby reducing climate change as a limit on food growth but also competing with food production for crops and scarce land. Once again the interconnectedness of energy, food, and climate must be considered. A major push to convert from fossil to biofuels will

21. Ethanol from sugarcane in Brazil is an exception.

intensify irrigation and fertilizer uses to maintain food production, but both are themselves greenhouse gas intensive inputs. An ill-designed biofuels policy can undermine both food supply and climate objectives. These complications have a distinctly Malthusian ring to them.

CONCLUSIONS

The decline in human fertility that started in the industrial countries in the second half of the nineteenth century, and that surfaced in most developing countries in the second half of the twentieth century, will deliver much welcomed dividends in the second half of this century. The dividends will materialize as relief in the oldest and the newest constraints on human well-being; food supplies and climate change.[22] Had population growth continued at rates typical of the 1980s, globally adequate food supplies and ambitious climate stabilization targets most likely would be out of reach. As it has turned out, population trends offer some respite, a window of opportunity. But population stabilization and decline are not enough. To take full advantage of the respite will require major technological advances in both mitigation and adaptation to climate change, and sustained efforts at agricultural productivity increases. Agriculture, which is primarily market-based and which can look back on a long and successful history of innovation, is reasonably placed to meet the challenge, but it is hostage to runaway climate change. To date the global response to the challenge of global warming can only be described as flabby. Moreover, as analyzed in chapter 8, the beneficial effects of slower population growth on greenhouse gas emissions appears to work through aging and its depressing effect on economic growth. This is not an attractive trade-off for many.

---

22. Those who treasure solitude and wilderness are also beneficiaries.

CHAPTER 8

༺∿༻

Downsizing

The Pessimist's Case

Four centuries of negative views on population decline

A seventeenth-century mercantilist's view: "People are the real Strength and Riches of a Country. . . . When Countries are thinly inhabited, the People always grow Proud, Poor, Lazy and Effeminate."
> —Charles Davenant, quoted by Overbeek (1973)

The stationary [state] is dull; the declining, melancholy.
> —Adam Smith, *The Wealth of Nations*, 1776

. . . the first result to prosperity of a change-over from an increasing to a declining population may be very disastrous.
> —Keynes (1937)

Population growth is the mother of necessity. Without it why bother to innovate?
> —Longman (2004)

The prospect of population decline excites almost as much febrile discussion as did the population explosion four decades ago (and, indeed, as did the collapse of population growth in the West before World War II). Notwithstanding the large number of environmentalists and others who see gains, the preponderant view is that troubles, especially economic troubles, are coming. The bonus years are slipping away.

A loss of economic vitality is in the offing. Some comments focus on the decline in births and the emotive terms "baby bust," "empty cradle," and "demographic winter" are employed. We are reminded that, without a surge in births or immigration, Japan and some European countries are on track to lose nearly half their population by the end of the century. More often, the connection between population decline and aging is the basis for concern. Our own personal aging and societal aging are easily conflated, and contemplating one's own inevitable aging may color one's view of societal aging. The term "grey tsunami" has appeared and gray is a gloomy color.

This chapter addresses the key economic question at the root of impending challenges: the impact of decline and depopulation on per capita economic growth—broadly speaking, economic well-being or the standard of living.[1] If the impact is modest, the challenges are less daunting; if the impact is substantial, the pessimists may have it right. The following chapter considers financing problems associated with aging and population decline—retirement, health, and long-term care—with an emphasis on intergenerational transfers. This is an imperfect separation, as the *economic* milieu will condition the financing needs, options, and policies, and financing policies themselves have economic consequences. For example, labor-market reforms can moderate a decline in economic growth *and* help close financing gaps in public and private pension schemes. Nevertheless, some structural distinction between economic growth and financial challenges is helpful.

It bears repeating that the key issue for us is per capita income and its growth, not aggregate economic income and growth. The two are often confused. If Quebec chooses to part ways with Canada, Canadian population shrinks by 23 percent but *ceteris paribus* its per capita income remains constant. In general, only if depopulation retards per capita income growth does it deserve serious attention.

MINING THE PAST

As a first cut, it is tempting to go back to our earlier chapters that investigated the joint effects of economic and population growth, and simply run the population analysis in reverse—substituting decline for growth, and thus unspooling the narrative. While tempting, this approach to population

1. For thoughtful speculation on the social and cultural implications of population decline, see Reher (2007).

decline is not satisfactory for two reasons. First there was no consensus. Smith saw harmony between population and economic growth via expansion of the market, specialization of labor, and technological progress. He would have found depopulation deplorable. Malthus found the opposite, with excessive breeding the source of misery and subsistence level wages. He would have found long-term depopulation incredible but, recovering from his shock, might have been cheered. Neither had anything to say about the modern problem—a shrinking workforce in an aging society. Ricardo and Mill had their long-term eyes fixed on the stationary state and did not have sustained growth uppermost in their minds. Fast-forward to Keynes and Hansen in the 1930s, who faulted a declining population for not providing sufficient incentives for full-employment investment. They might feel vindicated in their pessimism but disturbed by current population trends.[2] The (inconclusive) debate about population and economic development that took place between 1960 and 1990, in which a central issue was alleged runaway population growth in poor countries, was a detour and has little to contribute to the modern problem of population decline. The single exception was the concept of surplus labor as developed by Lewis and by Fei and Ranis, which foreshadowed the concept of a demographic bonus. That bonus is now withering in many countries, to be replaced by a demographic burden, and *is* relevant for today. In fact, the burden and bonus years are yoked together.

Postwar growth theory based on the Solow-Swan model does not give us much insight into depopulation. In its simple form it suggests that in the long term a smaller population may enjoy a higher but stable per capita income. It places the burden for any economic growth on technological change, but leaves that unexplained and unconnected to population size, large or small.[3] Nor does it consider the age structure of the population. In the "new growth" literature, (exogenous) population growth and size

2. It is not altogether obvious that we can dismiss the Keynes-Hansen concern for insufficient aggregate investment in a stationary or declining population. World War II inflated demand and the postwar baby boom saved the thesis from being put to the test. Currently the internationalization of capital markets and trade liberalization plus international differences in rates of aging and decline reduce the force of their argument. But the current Eurozone crisis may segue into long-term disinclination to invest.

3. A number of studies do meld population and neoclassical growth theory. For example, Accinelli and Brida (2007) use a Solow-style framework but assume population growth is positive and declining toward zero. They find that declining population growth improves long-run economic growth as compared to a constant rate of population growth. They do not consider depopulation. Cellarier and Day (2011) modify the Solow framework to introduce structural instability and study demographic responses to disaster with a population survival growth rate.

make cautious reappearances as positive forces for growth, and if taken seriously, suggests that depopulation is indeed trouble down the road.

This history is a mixed bag of views on population decline with Smith, Keynes, and the New Growth theorists most likely to be concerned; Malthus and more recently the environmental community to be pleased; the development community, savoring a win over the population explosion, and often with decades to go before depopulation engages, on the sidelines; and the neoclassical growth crowd with little to say about present population trends.

A second reason for not simply winding the population-economic growth literature counterclockwise to deduce the effects of decline is that our understanding of the importance of age structure has changed. While Coale and Hoover recognized the drag imposed by a high youth dependency ratio as early as 1958, they did not fully anticipate the subsequent productivity gains from the demographic bonus and certainly did not anticipate the even more distant demographic burden of an aging population. Today the focus is on the increasing old-age dependency ratio.

A FRAMEWORK FOR DATA AND ANALYSIS

Population aging and decline will affect economic growth directly through labor markets and indirectly through capital and product markets. In sorting out the channels through which they are connected, it is useful to consider the *age structure* of population separately from the *size* of the population. The first concentrates on the impact of an aging population on economic output. Changes in population *size* involve economies and diseconomies of scale. Both structure and size can affect productivity. Moreover, the connections between structure, size, and productivity take place in internationalized labor, capital, and product markets among countries that are at very different stages of the demographic transition. This diversity will, in general, moderate the severity of the effects. We consider age structure first and then turn to the economics of shrinking populations.

Demographic Structure: Aging

The first point to make is that while population decline and aging may go together they need not. Historically, there have been cases in which population declines due to famine or epidemics but average age does not increase. Setting aside migration, population declines only when birth rates fall below death rates. This, of course, *does* describe the *prospective* situation in many countries.[4]

The second point, which is relevant for this century, is that declining fertility rates and stable or increasing longevity *do* result in population aging. This occurs even if total population is increasing due to momentum. Despite major differences among countries in *levels*, declining fertility is widespread and increasing longevity is almost universal today.[5] As a result, aging is a global phenomenon. All countries save one (Zambia) will see the share of elderly rise between 2012 and 2050. For the world as a whole, the share of those over 60 is expected to double. While they start from a much lower base, the percentage increase of the elderly in the less developed countries exceeds that of the more developed countries. For these countries, it is a race to get rich(er) before they get old. This involves capturing whatever is left of the demographic bonus and preparing for an unprecedented increase in the ratio of old to young. Any slackening of economic growth due to aging is of concern, especially for the poor. The already rich, starting from a higher income base, wind up with unprecedented numbers of elderly whose needs will multiply. This implies meeting the needs of the elderly without unduly burdening working generations. Societal graying will be the norm, but the challenges differ for the rich and the poor.

Table 8.1 provides some details. Over a 40-year span, the projections should be quite reliable. Measured as a share of their population, the so-called more developed regions have the highest number of elderly today and will maintain that position in 2050, with the share increasing from 22 to 32 percent. The less developed countries are not off the hook and will see their elderly share more than double from 9 to 20 percent. In absolute numbers, the over-60 population living in less developed countries will be almost four times the number living in more developed regions. At the country level, Japan, which currently leads in aging with a 32 percent share, will continue to lead in 2050 at 41 percent. Italy at 38 percent will not be far behind. Even the once young and vigorous Brazil will almost triple its ratio from 11 to 29 percent. The United States is spared these dramatic numbers, moving from 19 to 27 percent, five percentage points

4. In part due to immigration, the US population is both growing and aging. More generally, the very long-run effects of sub-replacement level fertility on population size and age structure differ. Holding mortality constant and assuming no migration after a few generations, age structure stabilizes at an older average age but population heads steadily toward extinction (Coleman and Rowthorn 2011).

5. Increasing longevity is not certain. It is possible that obesity, diabetes, cardiovascular disease, cancer, and other diseases may cut short progress.

Table 8.1. GROWING OLDER

Country or area	Proportion of total population 60+		Share of 60+ 80 years or over		Old-age support ratio[a]		Proportion 65+ in labor force	
	(%)		(%)				(%)	
	2012	2050	2012	2050	2012	2050	Men	Women
World	11	22	14	20	8	4	42	20
More developed regions	22	32	20	29	4	2	26	15
Less developed regions	9	20	11	17	11	4	50	22
Least developed countries	5	11	8	10	16	9	68	43
United States	19	27	20	30	5	3	35	25
Italy	27	38	23	34	3	2	12	4
Japan	32	41	22	35	3	1	42	23
Brazil	11	29	15	23	9	3	44	21

Source: UN 2012.

[a] Population age 15 to 64 over population 65+.

below the average for the advanced countries, and indeed below the ratio expected in Brazil.

One might reasonably object to these numbers on the grounds that the aging outlook is exaggerated by using age 60 as the cutoff for defining the elderly. Instead, one could argue that 60 is the new 40 or, more realistically, the new 50.[6] As discussed elsewhere, there is more than a kernel of truth to this, but it does not fully reverse the aging problem to come. First, labor participation ratios often drop sharply in the 60–65 age bracket, and if one is interested in the burden of aging on the working population, 60 is a pivotal age. Second, table 8.1 shows support ratios (workers per elder) using age 65 and up as perhaps a more realistic definition of the elderly. But there is little comfort in these data either. The general pattern is sharp declines in the support ratio between now and 2050. For the world as a whole, the support ratio falls in half from 8 to 4 and for Japan from 3 to 1. If still not convinced, one need only look in table 8.1 at the "old elderly"—those aged 80 and up. The old elderly are now 1.5 percent of

6. Recall from mid-twentieth-century US pop culture, the songs, movies, and TV shows proclaiming "life begins at 40."

world population and this will climb to 4.4 percent by 2050. Individual countries will confront more dramatic numbers. Italy's old elderly ratio will jump from 6.2 percent to 12.9 percent. In short, these projections show quite dramatic increases in aging over the next four decades although particular features will differ from country to country. The projections also suggest that the aging issue will confront us before the population decline issue hits full force.

Sharpening the Measuring Tools

The preceding paragraphs paint aging in a dark hue. And, indeed, many consider aging to be the crux of the population problem. But there is another way to conceptualize, define, and measure aging that uses a lighter palette and leads to less harsh conclusions. The basic measure of the burden of the elderly now in use is the old-age dependency ratio—the ratio of those over 65 to the working age population age 15 or 20 through 64. Alternatively, the inverse, the old age support ratio (the number of working age persons per elderly person) is presented. These measures are grounded on chronological age. But over time there have been large gains in health and life expectancy and further gains are expected. (The United Nations projects world average life expectancy at birth to rise from 70 years today to 82 by the end of the century.) As a result, it may be misleading to compare people of a particular age today, say 65, with someone age 65 who lived a hundred years ago, or someone who will be age 65 a hundred years in the future. Their health status and life expectancy would be very different—better today than in the past and better in the future than today. Accounting for these improvements has major implications for retirement and health spending, and for economic growth prospects.

Wolfgang Lutz, Warren Sanderson, and Sergei Scherbov (2008) have developed an alternative measure of aging that accommodates and adjusts for advances in health and longevity.[7] The basic idea is that rather than measuring age as years since birth, one measures the expected years to death—life expectancy—and uses that as the benchmark for delineating the elderly. In their initial work, the researchers use a life expectancy of 15 years or less as the boundary for entering old age. In this fashion increases in life expectancy will, *ceteris paribus*, reduce the number of those designated as elderly. It also calls into question the assumption that mortality declines in upper age brackets ("longevity increases") will

7. See also Sanderson and Scherbov (2008, 2010, 2013).

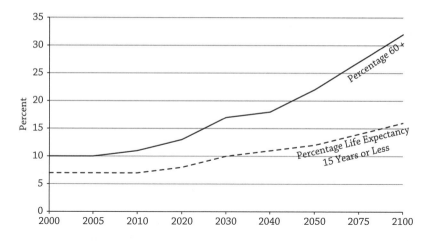

Figure 8.1:
Two measures of aging: Percent world population age 60+, percent with life expectancy 15 years or less
Source: Based on Lutz, Sanderson, and Scherbov 2008, table 1.

necessarily require ever larger intergenerational transfers to the elderly (Eggleston and Fuchs 2012).

This new measure has a powerful impact on how we view the aging problem. Figure 8.1 displays a conventional measure of aging, the percent of world population 60 and older and a second measure, the percent of world population with remaining life expectancy of 15 years or less, the new definition of the elderly. The conventional measure shows the elderly share rising from 10 percent to 32 percent over this century. The new measure shows a slower increase from a lower base: from 7 percent to 16 percent. Table 8.2 provides additional detail with the same general pattern—the new measure (Prop RLE 15 –) rises at a slower rate from a lower base than the conventional measure (Prop 60+). Moreover, in the regions with the largest initial share of elderly (Japan/Oceania, Western and Eastern Europe) aging tapers off sharply in the second half of the century. Note that the new measure captures regional differences in life expectancy and its prospective growth.

The new metric does not eliminate the prospect of aging. Consider the China Region. The new measure suggests the proportion of the elderly in the population will triple, surpass Western Europe, and reach the level of Japan and Eastern Europe. Still, the Chinese increase is less than the projected quadrupling under the standard measure from 10 to over 40 percent. North America is particularly well placed. Whereas the conventional measure shows the elderly ratio will more than double from 16 to 39

Table 8.2. INDICATORS OF AGING

Region	Indicator	2000	2050	2100
World	Prop 60+	0.10	0.22	0.32
	Prop. RLE 15–	0.07	0.12	0.16
North America	Prop 60+	0.16	0.3	0.39
	Prop. RLE 15–	0.11	0.14	0.15
Middle East	Prop 60+	0.06	0.19	0.34
	Prop. RLE 15–	0.04	0.09	0.16
South Asia	Prop 60+	0.07	0.17	0.35
	Prop. RLE 15–	0.06	0.11	0.19
China Region	Prop 60+	0.10	0.35	0.42
	Prop. RLE 15–	0.07	0.21	0.22
Pacific Asia	Prop 60+	0.08	0.23	0.36
	Prop. RLE 15–	0.06	0.14	0.17
Japan/Oceania	Prop 60+	0.22	0.42	0.51
	Prop. RLE 15–	0.13	0.20	0.21
Western Europe	Prop 60+	0.20	0.37	0.46
	Prop. RLE 15–	0.13	0.19	0.19
Eastern Europe	Prop 60+	0.18	0.42	0.44
	Prop. RLE 15–	0.13	0.22	0.21

Source: Lutz, Sanderson, and Scherbov 2008, table 1.

percent, the new measure shows the ratio to rise from 11 to 14 percent by 2050 and holding steady over the remainder of the century.

Adjusting for improved health and longer life expectancy also casts a new and more optimistic light on calculating an old age dependency ratio. Table 8.3 displays the traditional old age dependency ratio (OADR) and a new measure, prospective old age dependency ratio (POADR). The latter is simply the ratio of those over the old age threshold (life expectancy less than 15 years) to the working age population, defined as those between 20 years and the old age threshold. Note that because life expectancy varies not only over time but from region to region, someone age 65 may be "old" in Kenya but not "old" in Canada.

Using the traditional measure, the world OADR is expected to double from 13 to 26 percent from 2005 to 2045. Using POADR, the rate moves more modestly from 12 to 18 percent. This pattern reappears in all regions except Africa. Again the problem of an increasing dependency rate (declining support ratio) does not disappear but appears more tractable. This new view of aging is important when considering the economic and fiscal challenges of funding retirement and rising health-care costs.

Table 8.3. CONVENTIONAL AND PROSPECTIVE MEASURES OF POPULATION
AGING FOR MAJOR WORLD REGIONS, 2005 AND 2045

	Conventional age dependency ratio (OADR) x 100		Prospective age dependency ratio (POADR) X 100	
	2005	2045	2005	2045
World	13.3	26.5	11.9	17.7
More Developed	25.1	47.0	18.2	25.7
Less Developed	10.3	23.4	10.5	16.8
Africa	7.7	10.7	10.1	9.8
Asia	11.4	27.7	11.1	19.5
Europe	25.9	49.7	20.9	29.0
Latin America and Caribbean	11.2	28.7	8.2	15.5
North America	20.7	37.1	14.3	21.0

Source: Sanderson and Scherbov 2008, table 2.

LINKING AGING AND PRODUCTIVITY

How does aging affect productivity as measured by income and output per
capita? There are four possible channels.

Shrinking the Labor Force

First, if aging leaves the employed labor force a smaller fraction of the
population, aggregate productivity will decline. This is sometimes called
the "accounting effect." If, for example, more people leave the workforce
for retirement than enter it as youths coming of age, the ratio of the
workforce to the population tends to decline, and output per capita also
declines, even if there were no loss of productivity per worker. For instance, if over a period of years the share of the non-working elderly increases from 15 to 30 percent of population and the share of youth falls
from 30 to 25 percent, the ratio of workers (those who by assumption
are neither youth nor elderly) to population will fall from 55 to 45 percent. With no change in age-specific labor participation rates, no immigration, and no change in individual productivity, this represents an
approximately 18 percent decline in per capita income and output for
the economy.

Many consider this to be the guts of the population decline/aging problem: fewer workers to support more old folks. But putting it this crudely also points toward possible solutions as well as complications. In this example, the assumed decline in the youth dependency ratio from 30 to 25 percent, perhaps due to fertility decline, helped cushion the aggregate productivity shock. If the youth share had remained at 30 percent, the decline in aggregate per capita income would have been about 27 percent. On a worldwide basis, the United Nations projects that the youth dependency ratio will decline from 47 percent in 2000 to 31 percent in 2050, offering some relief in some countries from aging trends.

However, the youth and old-age ratios should not be simply added together to obtain a total dependency ratio and then use that to infer public expenditure trends. Public expenditures per individual vary widely by age. Moreover expenditures on youth can be justified as an investment, not consumption. Finally, must one must be careful in interpreting productivity effects from old-age and youth dependency ratios. Both are purely age-based statistics and do not measure who is actually working and producing. For that, labor-market participation rates need to be measured and projected. The key point is that the negative productivity effect of an increase in the old-age dependency ratio can be neutralized with an increase in labor-market participation rates by youth, by the elderly, and by the working age population.

The United States shows a mixed picture in recent years. Between 1990 and 2010 the labor-market participation for individuals 16 and older declined modestly from 66.6 percent to 64.3 percent, but there were dramatic differences by age group. The rate for those 16 to 24 fell sharply from 67.3 percent to 55.2 percent. In contrast, the participation rate for those 60–64 rose from 44.8 to 55.3, and from age 65 and up rose from 11.8 to 17.4. While some portion of the youth decline is no doubt due to lengthier education and will boost subsequent productivity, it appears there is some slack at the front end of the labor force.[8] One also wonders if there isn't some slack still left at the tail end.[9] We return to the issue of the elderly in

---

8. Theory suggests that, due to discounting, there may be a net utility gain by trading off leisure in retirement years for greater leisure in youth, if it can be financed.

9. For labor participation details for the United States, see Maestra and Zissimopoulos (2010). The US Bureau of Labor Statistics estimates the participation rates to jump another 5.7 percentage points for 60- to 64-year-olds and 5.2 percentage points for those 65 and over between 2010 and 2020. At the same time, we should remember that labor productivity (GDP per capita) is a very imperfect measure of well-being. Gains made through increasing labor-force participation can carry substantial real costs.

the labor force when we discuss social security issues. In any event, simply using a change in the old-age dependency ratio to measure per capita output change is not meaningful.

It is also important to remember that an increasing old-age dependency ratio is the logical sequel to an earlier demographic bonus (Weil 1999). If it turns out that living standards are depressed, it suggests that the bonus was a "prepayment" that was not wisely used.

Individual Productivity

The second way in which aging can affect productivity is at the individual level, output per worker. Neither theory nor empirical evidence gives a clear-cut answer as to whether older workers are more or less productive than younger workers. In thinking about the question, it is useful to distinguish among several factors at work: physical stamina, sectorial shifts, human capital, and innovative capacity.

There can be little question that the ability to perform physically demanding work diminishes with age. But manual work, while not totally abolished, represents a diminishing role in production in advanced countries. The effects on total output attributable to aging by loss of physical strength and endurance are likely to be minimal and replaceable by mechanization.

A plausible case can be made that aging shifts the composition of demand and production toward lower productivity and productivity growth sectors. For example, Hashimoto and Tabata (2010) construct a model in which aging causes a shift in labor from high productivity, non-health-care sectors to lower productivity health and long-term care, thus lowering the per capita income growth rate. But this is not inevitable. A shrinking youth cohort will also release labor from the education sector, which is notorious for low productivity growth. The net result may be ambiguous. Reliable productivity measures in services sectors are difficult to construct, and sectorial shifts in labor were occurring long before aging became a concern. In any event, some outsourcing of elder care might weaken the negative productivity implications.

The connections between aging, human capital, and individual productivity are complex. On the one hand, human capital, like physical capital, depreciates. Hopefully, what we learned in graduate school is not identical to what we teach as we move toward emeritus status. Early vintages of human capital can deteriorate and new skills must be learned. But the notion of learning by doing suggests that, unlike physical capital, human capital may also expand with experience. For some types of work activities, we may become more productive as we age.[10] The ambiguity surrounding aging and productivity is captured in a study by Thomas Lindh and Bo Malmberg (1999), who examined the issue in OECD countries over the period 1950–90. They conclude that growth patterns of labor productivity are, to a large extent, explained by changes in age structure. The study found that the 50–64 age group had a positive influence on productivity growth, the 65 and over group had a negative impact, and younger age groups had an ambiguous influence, but they were unable to resolve the mechanisms behind these results.

Finally note that the productivity effects of a shifting workforce age structure depend on the degree of substitutability among workers of different age. In a series of simulations based on projected demographic changes, Prskawetz et al. (2008) found that in selected industrial countries the age mix will shift to a more productive structure in the next few decades, an encouraging result.

Indirect Effects on Productivity: Induced Savings and Investment

The third way in which aging can affect labor productivity is indirect, working through increases in physical and human capital that boosts the productivity of labor. If indirect effects are accounted for, it is possible to construct a more benign view of aging. Depending on how the parts are assembled, one can build a model in which the negative effects of an increase in the dependency ratio (non-workers to workers) is trumped by aging-related increased savings and investment, which increases productivity. This is the basis for Mason and Lee's (2006; Lee and Mason 2010) concept of a second demographic dividend arising from enhanced savings and capital deepening. The idea is that, confronted with the prospects of longer life and an increasing dependency ratio, a rational response is to accumulate larger assets during one's working years. This may include greater investment in physical capital but also in education and human capital, which can then be amortized over a longer life. Fewer children may also increase parental investment in youth education. Fewer future taxpayers but earning higher taxable incomes! In short, simple dependency ratio

---

10. Skirbekk (2004) in a literature review finds that by some measures productivity peaks relatively early (before 50) and before earnings peak. The later finding may reflect seniority-based compensation schemes. See also Skirbekk (2008) for sensible policy options. Malmberg et al. (2008), in a plant-level study in Sweden, found support for the hypothesis that there is a positive relation between workforce aging and productivity growth.

analysis may be too crude to capture sustained improvements in human capital due to greater expenditures on youth education and health.

To capture this second bonus, however, requires foresight and anticipatory actions. It also requires that private savings incentives be maintained and not dissipated through the promise of overly generous public pension schemes. The authors estimate that in several world regions the second demographic bonus provides a stronger bump to growth rates than did the first. It is worth noting that neither the first nor the second bonus is a free lunch—the first is "paid" for by the costs of raising and educating the bonus generation and the second is "paid" for by the generation that forgoes consumption to acquire more assets for old age. The *amount* that the working generation is expected to pay is not settled.[11]

The second demographic bonus hypothesis is part of a larger inquiry into life-cycle savings behavior. The initial view by Modigliani and others was that individuals attempted to smooth consumption over their lifetime by acquiring assets in their younger working years (saving), and then divesting those assets (dis-saving) in old age. If, indeed, this were the case, current population aging following the post–World War II population boom might have led to an asset price meltdown and rising interest rates in the early decades of the twenty-first century. This scenario has proven too simplistic. In fact, dis-saving by the elderly has not (yet) materialized (Lee and Mason 2011), in part because precautionary and bequest motives intervene, and in part due to reliance on public transfers. Equally important, the internationalization of capital markets allows older economies to buffer the effects of aging by investing internationally in regions with younger age profiles.[12] More generally, the appropriate amount of forgone

11. Writing in 1990, when the United States was contemplating two more decades of declining dependency ratios due to declining birth rates, but steeply rising rates thereafter, Cutler et al. (1990) concluded that "recent and prospective demographic changes do not appear to warrant increasing national savings rates" (p. 53) in the United States. If anything, demographic changes suggested a *reduction* in the optimal savings rate. In other words, the tail end of the demographic bonus could be enjoyed through current consumption even though productivity was projected to decline in the long run. This remarkable conclusion appears to result from the dependency burden being remote and discounted to a low present value; that additional savings at the time would lead to rapidly diminishing returns; and that with slower population growth, less savings and investment was needed to equip new workers. The 1990 conclusion was reaffirmed a decade later by two high officials in the Treasury Department and the Federal Reserve who, in a quite remarkable lack of intergenerational solidarity, argued against any increase in US savings, writing "the optimal response to the aging of the U.S. population is to allow future cohorts to bear much or all of the burden" (Elmendorf and Sheiner 2000, p. 58).

12. International capital flows resulting from differential rates of aging are investigated by Tyers and Shi (2007).

consumption (i.e., increased savings) to expect current workers to bear remains a contentious issue and is further complicated by weak employment growth.

Creativity and the Gray Tsunami

The fourth and final facet of the aging-productivity puzzle involves the links between aging, creativity, innovative capacity, and productivity increases. This chain may well be the most important determinant of economic growth in the coming era of population decline but is the most speculative. Since Adam Smith and especially since the resurgence of economic growth studies in the last decades of the twentieth century, the wellspring of long-term growth has been thought to be technological progress. That progress is related to creativity and innovative capacity, not only in the production of goods but in the organization of markets and the creation of new wants and new products. Will the old folks of the future be up to the challenge? Will creativity flower in developed countries in 2050 when one-third of the population will be over 60, and almost one-third of those will be over 80?

There is a widespread belief that entrepreneurship, risk-taking, creativity, and innovation are the hallmarks of youth, not middle and old age. But there is little solid evidence to support that. The eminent French demographer Alfred Sauvy spoke in favor of youth and cautioned against a state in which "old men lived in old houses pondering old ideas" (cited by Coleman and Rowthorn 2011). But Sauvy himself continued high-level writing and scholarship up to the time of his death at age 92. At the moment we may speculate that creativity and innovation-driven technological progress will slacken in rapidly aging countries, but it remains just speculation.[13]

DOES SIZE MATTER?

The preceding analysis deals with the age structure of the population. Setting aside the question of age structure, does population *size* matter?

13. It is interesting, but hardly conclusive, that patent applications from Japan, the world's most rapidly aging country, surged by 52 percent between 2008 and 2012, whereas applications from the United States, a much younger country, fell by 1 percent. Patent applications per capita in Japan are twice what they are in the United States.

More specifically does a shrinking population matter for per capita economic growth? Empirical work is limited. There is a great deal of analysis of population *growth* and economic growth (much of which is inconclusive), but the universe of shrinking countries is still relatively small.[14] Population growth and decline may not be symmetrical. Depopulation is, at the moment, incipient for most. One source lists 42 out of a total 231 countries and territories shrank in 2012 including net migration, but most were small or subject to minor declines (CIA Factbook). The major shrinking countries were Russia, Poland, Japan, Germany, and South Africa, where the annual rate of decline ranged from 0.01 to 0.41 percent. Germany's population peaked in 2004, declined by less than 1 percent, and has started to rise. Japan's population peaked in 2008 and has declined by only 0.2 percent until now. These countries are on the cusp, and we have not yet had enough experience with prolonged, major population declines to make confident predictions concerning economic growth.[15] There is greater confidence in the population projections however. The current modest levels of population decline are not likely to last. Countries comprising over 80 percent of current world population, including China and India, are projected to experience declining population sometime this century. Germany and Japan are projected to shrink by about one-third by 2100.

Economies of Scale

The standard approach to the shrinkage problem would be to look through the prism of economies of scale—efficiencies that might be forgone as population stabilizes or efficiencies previously captured and which must be forfeited as numbers dwindle. There undoubtedly are such efficiencies, but they are not so obvious. First, many economies of scale derive from the scale of production and the market, not the size of population. With continued per capita economic growth the domestic market and production can continue to grow, albeit perhaps at a slower pace. Second, unless liberal trade is reversed, the relevant market and opportunity for

14. Sub-replacement fertility rates are not new. They were common in the interwar period in the twentieth century in Europe. But population momentum kept growth in positive territory.

15. Ireland is an exception, losing population over an entire century, from the mid-1800s to the mid-1900s. Despite this, it recovered and became known as the Celtic Tiger in the latter part of the twentieth century, before hitting the wall in the Euro crisis.

capturing economies of scale in production is no longer the national level but the international level. It is precisely this opportunity that allows small countries with high trade ratios to enjoy efficient scale production and high levels of income. Switzerland and Singapore are good examples. The moderating effect of international trade is reinforced by the differential rate at which population decline will strike internationally. Even as the leading edge countries face declining population, the world as a whole will have up to a century more of population growth.

There are, of course, true economies of scale that cannot be captured by international trade in goods and services. Transportation and distribution costs fall with population density and will tend to rise with depopulation. Congestion costs, however, will be lower. Falling transportation costs were a major force for efficiency and growth in Adam Smith's world and remain important. The bleak results of depopulation in many rural areas in the United States, especially during the Great Depression, are well documented and similar forces are now at work in rural Japan. The worldwide trend to urbanization may be sufficient to maintain or increase transportation scale economies in urban areas but will contribute to rural decline.

Still, the old notion that low population density retards efficiency in transportation and communication, and the spread of new ideas, sounds increasingly quaint. The expansion of electronic communication and most notably the Internet (whose success is built on network externalities) may soften the social and economic effects of rural depopulation. While the size of network externalities (efficiencies) depends on the number of users, there is no serious prospect that population decline will impede their growth. Finally we note that there may be significant economies of scale in the provision of public goods, for example, national defense (the geopolitical consequences of which are discussed further in chapter 10), judicial systems, and some, but not all, public education activities. The ability to finance these at optimal scale may be frayed and, as a consequence, productivity may suffer if population declines too fast or too far.[16] But one should also keep in mind the *dis-economies* of scale arising from coordination and supervision difficulties that may be avoided with smaller populations. These dis-economies occur in the production of both public and private goods but in principle are more vexing in public goods, which depend on a single supplier. And, of course, environmental assets in fixed supply should benefit from reduced population pressure.

---

16. The optimal supply of public goods may also decline with smaller populations. But very rapid population decline may cause premature scrapping of sunk capital such as public schools and hospitals.

Endogenous Growth Theory and Population Decline

Population size and growth made a modest positive reappearance in the endogenous growth literature reviewed in chapter 4. Can endogenous growth survive and thrive in an era of population decline? That literature identifies two threads that link the size and growth of population to economic growth. Both suggest some pessimism for the future when population peaks and declines. The first thread, with roots in Adam Smith's connection of market size to productivity enhancing investments, emphasizes the role of new investments embodying new knowledge. These investments are the vehicle for introducing new and more productive capital, and population is a driver for these investments. This thread runs through the contributions made by Svennilson, Arrow (learning by doing), and Scott. The implication is that stagnant or declining population slows new investment and hence productivity growth slackens. This may moderate if production for the international market is expanding but still the tilt is toward slower economic growth.

A second, complementary thread relies heavily on the public goods nature of knowledge to overcome conventional diminishing marginal returns and achieve sustained economic growth. Examples include Romer (1986, 1990) and Aghion and Howitt (1992). Romer (1986) considers "knowledge" an intangible capital good with public good qualities (non-rivalry and partial excludability), and exhibiting increasing rather than diminishing returns. As knowledge grows in one firm, it boosts the productivity of others, allowing for sustained economic growth without any increase in conventional capital or labor inputs. While per capita economic growth does not depend on a growing labor force, he does suggest that it may be faster in countries with large rather than small populations, as the spillover effects benefit a larger number of producers. In this fashion a permanently smaller population may experience slower growth. In a subsequent model (Romer 1990), he continues the assumption that knowledge (technology) is non-rivalrous and only partially excludable and makes the stock of human capital engaged in research and development the driving force for economic growth. In this model an increase in the labor force may divert educated workers with high human capital away from research into the production of final goods, dragging down productivity and growth. Conversely, a decline in population and the labor force might have the opposite effect. Educated workers with high human capital might be drawn away from production of final goods as those markets slow, and divert them to research, thus boosting boost growth rates. The two models leave us with no clear message connecting economic growth and population decline.

These models shift the focus from the labor force per se to human capital accumulation in an era of declining population. One line of argument is that an increase in population lifts the supply of potential R and D workers. Suppose, as in Aghion and Howitt (1992), innovations generated by competitive research are the driving force behind economic growth. Suppose also that the demand for such research is motivated by temporary rents that can be earned from innovations, and suppose further the size of the rents themselves increase with the size of population. In that case, one has the elements of a theory linking population and growth. An increasing population provides both the supply and demand for the inputs to research, the end result of which is sustained economic growth. The implication of this string of suppositions is that population decline may depress economic growth. Becker et al. (1999) build a model in which population density, arising from population growth and urbanization, leads to greater and more productive human capital. They warn that a *declining* population could have negative effects on economic productivity and growth.

Jones and Romer (2010) leave the question open. They see "ideas" and the sharing of those ideas as the wellspring of economic growth and propose that more people lead to more ideas. The implication in an era of shrinking population is that the growth of the stock of ideas will no longer be supported by growth in the world's population. But they concede that the *sharing* of ideas may intensify via urbanization and integration, postponing the negative growth impact.

To summarize, with the effects of population size on economic growth ambiguous, the centerpiece of the pessimists' argument rests on the "burdens" of aging. As discussed earlier, their chief concerns are a smaller relative workforce, which can be relieved in part by higher participation rates, and a potential loss of individual level productivity, which may be relieved by sufficient investment in physical and human capital. Chapter 9 examines public and private financing problems associated with aging from the perspective of generational transfers.

CHAPTER 9

✧

Aging

Retirement, Health, and the Generational Bargain

First the young, like vines, climb up the dull supports of their elders who feel their fingers on them, soft and tender; then the old climb down the lovely supporting bodies of the young into their proper deaths.

—Lawrence Durrell, *The Alexandria Quartet*

It is still her use [Fortune's custom]

To let the wretched man outlive his wealth,

To view with hollow eye and wrinkled brow,

An age of poverty.

—Shakespeare, *The Merchant of Venice*

The previous chapter established that the principal challenge posed by population downsizing will be aging, and a major challenge posed by aging will be deterioration in the support ratio for the elderly: the ratio of the working age population to the non-working elderly. The concern is for both the well-being of the elderly and for the additional burden it places on working adults. The challenge manifests itself as fiscal strains on government pensions, and health and long-term care schemes. It also strains intra-familial relations and can be a source of generational conflicts. This chapter approaches aging from three perspectives: intergenerational transfers, retirement and pensions, and health care.

INTERGENERATIONAL TRANSFERS: A VISUAL METAPHOR

To understand the challenges of aging requires a generational perspective.[1] It also requires paying attention to both age and time. At an abstract level goods and services are being continually reallocated from one generation to another. Furthermore, over time cohorts are moving through the traditional life stages of youth, maturity, and old age, each with different expectations and obligations. Intergenerational transfers become increasingly important in a modern economy. A greater share of the social product is being transferred down to children as childhood has been prolonged by educational demands, and a greater share goes up to the elderly as old age has been extended. The intergenerational bargain is stressed.

As a mental image, it may be useful to visualize a three-carriage train moving through time. The first carriage boards newborns and consists of children below working age. The second carriage consists of the working age population, and this is where economic production takes place. The third carriage is for the old folks after their productive life, and before they depart into the void. At all times consumption takes place in in all three carriages. This means there is an excess of production over consumption in carriage two and part of this excess is transferred up to children in the first carriage and part transferred back to the elderly in the third carriage. This is the movement of economic goods and services among generations.

Two other movements should be kept in mind. Setting aside migration and premature death, over time all individuals will move from carriage one to carriage two and then to carriage three, through the normal life stages of youth, maturity, and old age. Finally the train itself moves through time. Thus, the individuals who boarded as newborns at the 1950 station—the immediate postwar baby boom cohort—were finishing their sojourn in carriage two and starting to crowd into carriage three as the train passed station 2012. Virtually all will be gone to their final rewards when the train reaches station 2050.

Not only will the total number of passengers on the train change over time but so too will the relative number in each carriage. The number of passengers and their seating in the three carriages are the result of fertility and mortality trends. In our mental model train and based on current

1. The National Transfer Accounts (NTA) project has collected and organized cross-sectional information in some 23 countries on age-specific economic flows. These data include labor income by age, public and private consumption, intergenerational transfers, asset income, and savings. The research provides the raw material for analyzing the intergenerational effects of aging. Mason et al. (2009) explain how the NTA system is linked with the standard National Income and Products accounts.

demographic trends, the first carriage takes aboard fewer newborns each year, the third carriage holds their passengers longer and is projected to be increasingly overloaded as it reaches future stations. Modern-day pessimists see the overloading and scramble for seats in carriage three, and the pressure that places on carriage two producers, as a cause for alarm.

The train metaphor could be pushed a little further. We can introduce the government as a conductor who collects taxes in carriage two and dispenses benefits in all three carriages (public intergenerational transfers). Shortfalls between collections and handouts set up the potential for a fiscal crisis. Collapsing pension schemes have been a major concern in the aging literature. We can also allow family members in carriage two to wander forward and take care of their children, or wander back and take care of their aging parents (private intergenerational transfers). Note that the public and private transfers are substitutes, and an overly generous public transfer system may discourage private transfers. Generous public transfers to children may also increase birth rates. Conversely the deterioration of intra-familial transfer systems can increase the urgency of creating public schemes. We can add further flexibility to the metaphor by allowing workers in carriage two to save, acquire productive assets and carry those assets or titles to these assets with them as they enter old age in carriage three, thus funding part or all their own consumption during retirement. We can accommodate bequests from the elderly in carriage three back to their children and grandchildren in the first two carriages. More broadly, we can think of a fleet of trains, one for each national economy, all with the same basic three-car structure but differing in their position in the demographic transition. Comparative analysis of the fleet's characteristics and demographic trends can hint at problems down the track.

We are interested in reallocations and intergenerational transfers and the effects of fertility decline and aging on the system. While the makeup of the trains will differ, all societies, rich and poor, young and old, growing, stable, or declining, will confront similar choices: the size of transfers, the form they take (public or private), the direction (down to youth, up to the elderly), their financing, and how robust the decisions are in the face of rapid aging, falling support ratios, and sluggish economic growth.

THE GENERATIONAL BARGAIN

The generational bargain is an informal or quasi-formal arrangement between generations concerning the direction, size, and composition of transfers and access to goods and services. It is a bargain or compact in that different generations interact within a commonly accepted set of rights and obligations. The obligation of the working generation is to support the rearing and appropriate education of youth. It may also be their obligation to see to the well-being of the elderly. In return, the working generation presumably derives satisfaction from rearing productive children and may also view it as the quid pro quo for the education and other transfers they themselves received in their youth. This is indirect reciprocity. On a more pragmatic level they may view the transfers to youth as an investment in the productive capacity of those who will hopefully support them in their declining years. This is self-interest.

The working generation's support for the elderly is a mixed bag. Unlike investment in youth, which increases productivity down the line, transfers to the old are mostly for consumption and have little or no productivity payoff. The motivation for voluntary transfers from carriage two to carriage three may be gratitude to, and affection for, one's parents and grandparents, or the self-interested expectation that generous transfers today set a persuasive example for today's youth to follow suit a generation down the line. Not all transfers to the elderly are voluntary, of course. Public pension benefits are set by politics and law, and the elderly are well known for defending their interests at the polls. And in countries where legal property rights carry weight, assets owned by the elderly represent claims for goods and services made in the second carriage but consumed in the third. Transfers in both directions are, of course, greatly influenced by customs, traditions, and prevailing ethics.

The stripped-down role of the state is to tax parents (indeed all workers) to help fund their children's education; subsequently, the children (now workers) are taxed by the state to pay the now-elderly parents (and others) a pension in their retirement years.[2]

The basic concept can be captured in a stylized diagram. As an example, figure 9.1 displays age-specific per capita labor income and consumption of a developed country.[3] Per capita labor income is miniscule under the age of 15, rises to a peak during working years and then declines to low levels after age 70. Per capita consumption, which consists of private and publicly funded goods and services, rises through all three stages of life. Note the uptick in consumption near the end of life. This is mainly for health and long-term care and is largely publicly funded.

2. Market defects such as the inability of children to make contracts and the inability of parents to lay claim to the returns on their children's education support a public role in funding education.

3. Note that the data are on a per capita basis and do not measure total national consumption by age, as they do not account for the total population at various ages.

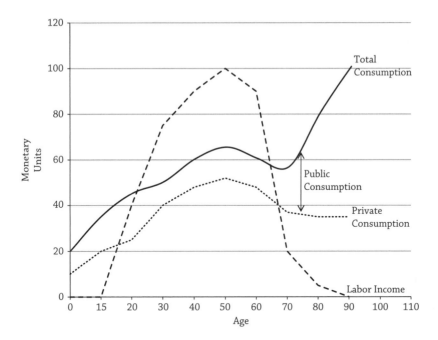

Figure 9.1:
Stylized consumption and labor income per capita

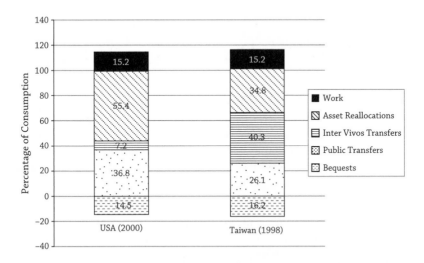

Figure 9.2:
Financing the consumption of the elderly: The United States and Taiwan
Source: Mason et al. 2009, figure 3.8. With permission.

The gap between labor income and consumption in childhood and in old age must be filled. Public transfers upward to the elderly for retirement and health expenses and public transfers downward to children for health and education are important in filling the gap and are essential elements of the generational bargain. But they do not tell the whole story. Figure 9.2 displays the financing of consumption of the elderly in the United States and Taiwan in 2000 and 1998, respectively. For the United States, income from work continued to cover 15 percent of consumption, income from the ownership of assets 55 percent, and public transfers including health care 37 percent. (The excess over 100 percent represents bequests made by the elderly.) Private transfers to the elderly were a modest 7 percent. In contrast, in Taiwan, private transfers from young to old played a more important role than either assets or public transfers.[4]

FRAGILITY AND FAIRNESS

All generational bargains require a modicum of fairness and trust. Transfers to the elderly are the weakest point. Arrangements that rely heavily on intra-family transfers are vulnerable to ingrate children who baulk at taking in elderly parents when the time arrives. The bargain is also vulnerable to elders who are cared for by their children out of love but also in the expectation of an inheritance that never materializes. The ability to renege on implicit commitments—bequests as well as end-of-life care—weakens intra-family transfer systems. Moreover, societies undergoing rapid social change including urbanization (as, e.g., in East and Southeast Asia) can be severely tested even with the best intentions by young and old.

Systems that rely mainly on private pensions may encounter fraud, inflation, or market crash. If these failures remain the exception, they are not fatal and indeed some may be insured against. But if they are frequent, the bargain is compromised. Public transfers are not immune to issues of trust and fairness. Unfunded public pensions and health-care schemes, known as "pay-as-you-go," or "pay-go" arrangements, are especially vulnerable as the temptation is always to promise more generosity than can be delivered. Weak spots are revealed during major downturns, such as the recession starting in 2008, but may trigger needed fiscal reform. Even schemes that appear backed by productive assets such as fully funded

---

4. The authors label the difference between consumption and labor income as reallocations, which consist of transfers (no direct quid pro quo) and asset-based reallocations.

public pension systems are subject to plunder in wartime or with a change in government.[5]

The advent of rapid and sustained aging simply adds to the fragility. Trailing generations in pay-go schemes look ahead, see an age bulge and ask themselves if the bargain will hold through their own retirement. If they think not, their own commitment to their elders weakens and the bargain can unravel. At the same time, if a government is hard pressed between a shrinking workforce and an expanding, selfish, and politically active retired population, the temptation is to cut education transfers to youth. This may prove to be very costly in the long run because, as explained previously, education fosters improvement in labor productivity and may be essential to blunting the economic effects of aging.

It is not enough to have reasonable assurance that the system of transfers embedded in the generational bargain is stable. It should also be seen as fair to different generations. Who gains and who loses? There are two levels at which fairness can be addressed. The first is the macroeconomic level in which the balance of all generational transfers, public and private, is considered. This cannot be done without information on age-specific, asset-based income, as well as transfers. The second, narrower, question is the fiscal balance within specific unfunded public pension or health schemes. Fairness also has a time dimension—is the transfer to youth or to the elderly "fair" to all generations at a particular point in time and is a particular cohort treated "fairly" over its life cycle? The NTA research casts some light on fairness at a point in time, but because it is based on cross-sectional data, it does not track cohort transfers over time.[6]

There is no absolute standard for fairness, but the NTA project contains information on 23 diverse, advanced and developing countries, allowing for comparisons. One suggestive statistic is the ratio of per capita consumption of the elderly to per capita consumption of the working-age population. Defining consumption to include private and publicly produced goods and services, the study finds that the United States, Japan, Sweden, and Brazil have the highest ratios, clustering around 1.3 (Lee and Mason 2011). This tends to undercut the view that the elderly in the United States

5. Global warming also exhibits major intergenerational transfers but is not comparable. The time scale is such that, unlike aging, the generations most seriously affected are not yet here to defend their interests. Moreover, addressing global warming will involve international, as well as intergenerational transfers, immensely complicating the problem. Thus far, the international community has been unable to come up with any viable generational bargain in abatement strategy. See Pearson (2011).

6. By including countries at different stages of the demographic transition and aging, some insight into intergenerational equity can be gained.

are impoverished relative to younger generations. It would be an error, however, to infer lavish living. The data are age-specific averages and say nothing about distributional equity among individuals of that age. Asset distribution is likely to be highly unequal among the elderly. Moreover, on closer inspection, the US ratio reflects high health-care consumption, which rises sharply with age. The publicly provided share of these costs is much higher in Japan and Sweden than in the United States, where health-care costs are famously high and individuals pick up a larger share of the tab. For the United States, the important questions raised by this study center less on intergenerational equity and more on why health costs are so high and health outcomes so unimpressive, and whether costs can be controlled before the baby boom generation fully settles in as the elderly bulge. In that regard the NTA exercise plays a helpful role in highlighting the importance of health spending in assessing the effects of aging.

QUANTIFYING "FAIRNESS" BY BIRTH COHORT

Data to track fairness among generations are not generally available but Antoine Bommier and his colleagues (2010) have made an interesting start by focusing on the three main government (public) generational transfer programs in the United States: public education, Social Security, and Medicare. They have collected, assembled, and projected age-specific data on benefits received and taxes paid for the three programs for all birth cohorts from 1850 to 2200. This allows them to calculate the benefits and tax costs for each program for each year and for each of the 240 annual cohorts from 1850 to 2090. The difference between benefits and taxes can be cumulate over a life cycle and expressed as the present value at birth or it can be expressed as a fraction of that cohort's lifetime earnings.[7] This analysis offers information on which generations gained the most from each program and which lost most heavily.

Figure 9.3 illustrates. For individuals born before 1870 Social Security was irrelevant. But for an individual born in 1914 the value (in 1914) of the benefits he was to receive from Social Security, expressed as a fraction of his lifetime earnings, was about 9 percent, whereas the present value of the taxes he was to pay was about 4 percent. In other words, he enjoyed a

---

7. Important assumptions include interest rate set at 3 percent, rate of growth of productivity at 1.6 percent, total fertility rate at 1.95, and net annual immigration of 900,000. This figure does not measure sustainability of Social Security. The baseline assumption of the analysis is that solvency is achieved by equal cuts in benefits and increases in taxes.

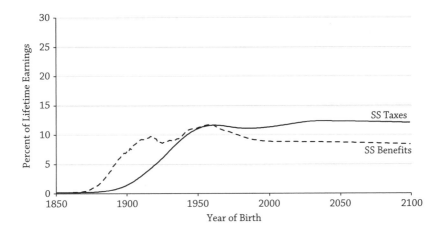

Figure 9.3:
Percent of lifetime earnings of present value at birth of Social Security benefits and taxes by cohort year, 1850–2100
Source: Bommier et al. 2010, figure 1. With permission.
Note: See original source for baseline assumptions.

windfall gain from Social Security of about 5 percent of his total earnings. Indeed, on average, everyone born before mid-century enjoyed a net intergenerational transfer via Social Security. (More accurately, this measures the gains or losses to an age cohort. Individuals within a cohort who die young do not share the cohort's gains.) But the lines cross about 1950 and, on average, everyone born after then would have a net loss. The implication is that Social Security has not been generationally neutral. Cohorts born before 1950 are winners; those born after are losers.[8] In this particular study, net losses tend to stabilize for those born after 2000 at about 4 percent of lifetime earnings.

This is not the whole story. Medicare and education transfers also have strong intergenerational effects. Consider Figure 9.4. One line represents the total net benefits (benefits minus taxes) for Social Security and Medicare combined. Again these are expressed as a percent of lifetime earnings. Notice that whereas the net loss on Social Security had stabilized for generations born after 2000 as shown in figure 9.3, the combined loss of Social Security and Medicare plunges steadily for all those born in this century. The fundamental reasons are the increased number of the elderly, their high-level use of health care, and the rising relative cost of health care itself. According to this model, toward the end of this century, a

8. Early cohorts paid little in taxes but received large benefits. Ida May Fuller may have been the biggest winner. She paid $49 in Social Security tax and collected $22,888 in benefits (Aaron 2011).

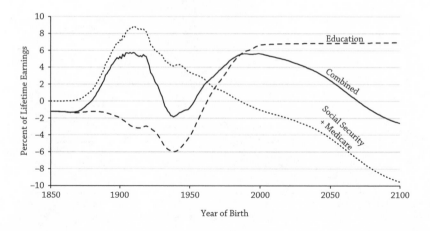

Figure 9.4:
Present value at birth of education, Social Security, and Medicare net benefits as percent of lifetime earnings by age cohort, 1850–2100
Source: Bommier et al. 2010, figure 7. With permission.

newborn can expect to lose 10 percent of his or her lifetime income via net transfers to Social Security and Medicare.

All is not lost. Public sector educational transfers, which send benefits downward to younger generations in the form of human capital rather than upwards to the elderly as does Social Security and Medicare, are a key component of the generational bargain. Originating in the United States in the second half of the nineteenth century, education is the largest component of public transfers, amounting to over 5 percent of GNP. Moreover, because it moves funds from older to younger generations, it is less affected by discounting than the old-age benefits of Social Security and Medicare. As shown in figure 9.4, net educational transfers were negative for every generation born between 1850 and 1958 and reached a low of minus 6 percent of lifetime earnings for those who were born in the mid-1930s. The underlying reason for the long run of negative transfers was the gradual increase in public-sector funding. Taxpayers paid for a higher level of education than they themselves received. This was particularly evident for those cohorts born in the 1930s who were subsequently taxed in their working years to fund the education of the baby boomers. It is only for generations born in this century that net benefits from educational transfers stabilize at a significant positive level.

Figure 9.4 also combines all three transfer programs. To summarize, if generational equity is restricted to Social Security and Medicare, there is considerable truth to the widely held view that older generations, born before the mid-1980s, are sticking it to their children and (yet unborn) grandchildren. Aging of the population is implicated, as both programs are transfers upwards to the elderly. Adding education transfers changes the picture sharply. The net gains to the older generations are diminished by net losses from educational transfers and, for some cohorts, born in the mid-twentieth century, were sufficient to yield net losses. At the same time though, the postwar baby boom generation and all subsequent generations will realize gains from educational transfers. These gains are projected to be enough to keep the combined net transfer of benefits positive for most of this century, despite the age-related drag of Social Security and Medicare.

FINANCING AGING: RETIREMENT

Publicly funded pensions are a central feature of generational transfers.[9] Most countries have variations on pay-go systems. Current taxes fund current retirees and are based on promises made earlier. Currently working generations are promised that their retirement will be funded by future taxes. This requires a balancing of inflows and outflows over long periods of time and the issue of aging and fiscal sustainability immediately arises.

A Positive View

An argument could be made that concern for aging, like the earlier concern for population growth, can be easily exaggerated. That argument makes three points but they are thin. First, from a global perspective, the increase in the elderly dependency ratio is more or less offset by a decline in youth dependency ratio and this moderates any budget implications. The primary fallacy with this observation is that it compares apples and oranges. From a narrow accounting perspective, shifting a dollar away from youth and spending it on the elderly may appear to be a budget wash, but they are not the same. The first is an investment in future productive capacity; the second is consumption expenditure.[10] A secondary fallacy is the appeal to global data. The aging/retirement problem is almost universal but differs

---

9. Pension schemes are rife with risk: uncertainties about life expectancy, future purchasing power, insolvency, policy changes, and so forth. Whitehouse (2007) investigates how these risks are shared in public and private schemes.

10. This may be too harsh. As explained below, many health care expenses can be viewed as investments to maintain the productivity of human capital and reduce future disability cost.

among three groups of countries: those already old and rich; the aging middle-income countries that aspire to get rich before they get truly old; and the diminishing number of countries that need to capture their demographic bonus for investment and growth, yet confront a doubling or tripling of their elderly population in the next few decades. Global dependency trend data conceal important differences in the common problem of aging. Countries with already low fertility rates will find little relief.[11]

A second argument is that, as individuals and countries grow richer and enjoy extended life expectancy, they will naturally wish to "purchase" more leisure via longer retirement. A rebalancing toward fewer working years and longer retirements thus reflects successful economic growth and improved health conditions, not a calamity. There is a kernel of truth here, but to accomplish this without putting great strain on the younger working generations requires that anticipatory savings and pension contributions be made throughout the retiree's earlier working life. The alternative is to shift the cost burden of funding longer retirements to current workers, causing intergenerational conflict. Pay-go public pension schemes are especially vulnerable.

A third argument is that the fiscal problems arising from an aging population are transitory. If fertility rates stabilize at replacement levels, population size will tend to stabilize and after some time the age structure will also stabilize. Current and prospective fiscal strains on public pensions will moderate. While this too has a kernel of truth, there are weaknesses. Stabilization of age structure will be slow in coming, and aging will almost surely continue to occur throughout this century. Moreover, fertility rates may continue to fall, prolonging the aging phenomenon. At some (extreme) point, declining fertility would shift the focus of concern from the burdens of an aging population to the contemplation of extinction. To summarize, fiscal issues associated with aging cannot be easily wished away.

A Realistic View

A two-way squeeze on public pensions is possible. First, as discussed earlier, the support ratio—the ratio of those age 15 to 64 to those 65 and older—will decrease. The numerator is depressed by low fertility. The denominator is increased by longevity. Second, retirement may start at an *earlier*

---

11. Meier and Werding (2010) confirm this with OECD country data for total and old-age dependency ratios through 2050.

age, increasing the time span in which benefits must be paid. Even with an unchanged retirement age, as life expectancy gradually increases, the period over which benefits are paid will increase. It is worthwhile thinking through the pressures that these place on the sustainability of public pensions.

Support Ratio

Consider first the deterioration in the support ratio for Western Europe. Currently (2012) it is 3:1. The United Nations projects that this will fall to 2:1 by 2050. If there is no change in retirement age or benefits the average worker in 2050 will bear a 50 percent higher pension contribution burden. The real burden may be less, however, if worker productivity rises over the next decades. A 1.1 percent per year increase in worker productivity would effectively stabilize the support burden at its current level. But 1.1 percent is a very large fraction of anticipated economic growth and to devote it to supporting the aging means sacrificing other aspirations. Moreover, retirement benefits are often tied to *current* wages and productivity, and thus would fail to solve the problem.

Retirement Age

Trends in retirement age may also exert pressure on pension financing. One needs to distinguish between two concepts: a trend toward earlier (or later) retirement, and a change in the legal age for collecting full pension. The former has no effect on total benefits paid if individual benefits are adjusted down (or up) for the longer (or shorter) payout period. But in practice benefits are not actuarially adjusted and are sometimes manipulated upward in periods of high unemployment, or downward, to delay retirements and maintain contributions. D'Addio, Keese, and Whitehouse (2010) document the extent to which the average age of exit from the labor market falls short of standard pensionable age in a number of OECD (Organization for Economic Co-operation and Development) countries.[12] Voluntary early retirement withdraws workers from the workforce and represents an economic trade-off between lower output and greater leisure. Heijdra and Romp (2009) argue that overly generous early retirement provisions can act as a "trap" and induce workers into premature retirement.

The more dubious action is legislated reduction in the age at which full benefits can be claimed. Rafel Chomsik and Edward Whitehouse (2010)

---

12. The OECD consists of 34 advanced countries.

have collected interesting information on pension eligibility ages in 30 OECD countries since 1950 and as scheduled to 2050. They found that the average for men fell from 64.3 years in 1950 to 62.5 years in 1993, a decline of almost two years. The average for women also fell in the same period, from 62.9 to 61.1. Since then the average age for men has inched up to 63 years (2010) but, based on current and announced changes, will remain below its 1949 level until 2040.[13]

Life Expectancy

The task of financing public pensions becomes more daunting when longer life expectancies and hence longer retirements are considered. Between 1960 and 2010 OECD life expectancy at age 65 increased by 3.9 years for men and 5.4 years for women. The United Nations projects further increases of 3.1 years for men and 3.6 years for women by 2050. Using data on official retirement age and life expectancy, one can calculate trends in the number of years that pension benefits can be expected to be paid. The numbers are sobering. The average OECD increase from 1958 to 2050 is from 13.4 years to 20.3 years for men and from 12.8 years to 17.7 years for women. In other words, pensions are to be paid for an additional seven years for men and five years for women. In some cases, the length of benefits payments effectively doubles—for France from 12 to 24 years. The current upward trend in official retirement age is moving in the right direction but failing to catch up with rising life expectancy.[14]

The point is not that the aging/retirement problem is unsolvable; reforms are discussed in the next chapter. Rather, it is that the fiscal problem of public pensions is more than just an artifact of aging. The understandable desire to purchase greater leisure in one's "silver" years, unwise manipulation when setting full benefits retirement age, and failure to confront the cost implications of extended lifetimes, all play a role.

It is worth pointing out that even fully funded pension systems, completely backed by real assets, face an *economic* challenge from the convergence of these factors, even if there is no fiscal crisis. Earlier retirement, and longer lifetimes depress support ratios and mean lower total and per capita economic

---

13. The United States was ahead of the curve. In 1983, it legislated a phased-in increase of full retirement age from 65 to 67, starting in 2002.

14. Adjusting pensionable age can also be used to increase or decrease the benefits while maintaining fiscal sustainability. OECD models conclude that an increase from age 65 to age 70 would allow the pension replacement rate (i.e., pension benefit as percent average wage) to rise from 60 percent to 72 percent and remain sustainable. A decline in pensionable age from 65 to 60 would require a decline of the replacement rate from 60 percent to 52 percent.

output, unless offset by strong increase in worker productivity. Either total consumption falls and the current generations (old and young) bear the burden, or total investment falls and future generations are less well-educated, equipped, and compensated. If these forces were correctly anticipated, a fully funded pension scheme would remain solvent, but the economic pressures would remain.

Sustainability

In pay-go and other pension systems, shortfalls between inflows and outflows may be predictable decades before they materialize.[15] Projections of mortality, fertility, immigration, real wage growth, and retirement age will indicate the size and time path of surpluses and deficits. There are two responses. One is to initially devise a system that automatically adjusts receipts and payments to demographic and economic changes, including aging. This could be done through automatic adjustments in contributions, benefits, or both, and could be structured to spread the risk of shocks over several generations.[16] The alternative is to have periodic substantial legislative adjustments that attempt to reset inflow and outflow balances for a substantial period of time. These (politically difficult) adjustments could include phasing in higher full benefit retirement age, increasing the contributions tax, fiddling with the target replacement ratio, and others. All lead to some uncertainty for participants, but advance announcements and phase-in rules can soften this.

Reforms to avoid insolvency can take a number of forms but on inspection reduce to two—increased contributions and/or decreased benefits. Both have indirect effects through the labor markets and via savings and investment, and both can have important distributional (equity) effects. Increased contributions can be obtained by extending the pension scheme to new groups, and by raising contribution rates. The former is limited when 100 percent domestic participation is approached but can be augmented with a vigorous immigration policy. However, signing up new groups and pumping up immigration builds future pension liabilities for governments. Extracting higher contributions also has limits. Like any labor tax, "excessive" contribution rates discourage the employment of labor and send the labor market underground to untaxed activities. Moreover high and rising taxes may discourage private savings. Specifically, if

---

15. The US Social Security system has a 75-year time horizon.
16. Auerbach and Lee (2011).

workers have a fixed consumption target, they may react to the increased public pension taxes by reducing private savings. If the lost private savings would have been invested in productive assets, economic growth slows. The bottom line is clear—the direct calculation of increased revenues must be accompanied by calculating the indirect effects working through labor and capital market responses.

Benefit reduction can take a number of forms, including modifying the target replacement rate and the age at which full benefits become available.[17] Both can have labor and capital market effects. Some increase in average effective retirement age is no doubt part of a sensible response to aging and its fiscal pressures, and can be supported on the basis of increased life expectancy and, as examined below, the prospect of improved health. But reform must be sensitive to a number of aspects. Ideally raising the retirement age "crowds in" private savings as individuals see the need to accumulate more assets if they persist in a fixed retirement date. This behavior reinforces the notion of a second demographic dividend discussed earlier. None of the indirect effects of reform are fatal, but sensible measures need thoughtful analysis.[18]

The US Public Pension Situation

The United States is unique among industrial countries in its reliance on private spending in total social spending (mainly pensions and health).[19]

17. The replacement rate is the ratio of post-retirement benefits to pre-retirement earnings. It can be relatively easily manipulated by redefining the measurement of pre-retirement earnings. Workers can also manipulate the time profile of their earnings to increase benefits. For comparative data on OECD members social spending, see Adema, Fron, and Ladaique (2011).

18. For example, moving from a pay-go to a fully funded system is sometimes touted as a way to increase the savings rate and hence productivity. But a public fully funded pension scheme might crowd out private savings, with no net gain. Martin and Whitehouse (2008) review retirement reforms in the OECD through 2005.

19. The US Social Security system is widely misunderstood and needs a word of explanation. First, it is social security insurance not only for old age but for disability and incapacity to work, and for dependents of a deceased wage earner. Because of its multiple roles, it cannot be evaluated solely on its rate of return for pensioners. Second, it operates through a trust fund that receives money from payroll taxes and other sources. When inflows exceed outflows the excess is invested in special non-tradable US government bonds, backed by the faith and credit of the government, but not backed by any specific economic assets. The bonds are considered an asset of the Social Security system and a liability of the US Treasury. For a discussion of distributional inequities, see Aaron (2011).

Whereas, the OECD average social spending shares are 11 percent private and 89 percent public, the US split is 39 percent private and 61 percent public. *Private* social spending in the United States is about 10 percent of its GDP, more than three times the OECD average. Despite the early establishment of Social Security in the 1930s, US expenditures on public pensions in 2007 were 6 percent of GDP, less than the OECD average and far less than in Italy (14 percent) and France and Austria (12 percent).

Nevertheless, the United States does not fully escape the triple public pension squeeze described above. As in many other countries, an aging population and a pensionable age that lags life-expectancy gains undermines Social Security solvency. By most indicators, however, the strain is relatively modest. From 2012 to 2050, the share of US population age 60 and above is projected to climb 8 percentage points to 27 percent; whereas, Europe will experience an increase of 12 percentage points, to 34 percent. The old elderly (those over age 80) are expected to reach 8.1 percent of population in the United States and 9.5 percent in Europe by 2050. The old age support ratio for those over 65 will fall from 5 to 3 for the United States and more sharply from 4 to 2 in Europe. The full pensionable retirement age in the United States never dipped below 65 and is on track to reach 67. In contrast, the OECD average age started lower and is projected to reach only 64.6 by 2050. Finally, life expectancy at full pensionable age—a measure of how long an individual will collect benefits—is currently lower in the United States than the OECD average (16.8 years vs. 18.5 years) and is expected to grow by only 0.9 years by 2050; whereas, the OECD average is expected to grow by 1.8 years.[20] The expert consensus seems to be that, for the United States, relatively minor adjustments to benefits and financing are sufficient to close the prospective funding gap.[21]

HEALTH AND LONG-TERM CARE

Concepts

Aging and health intersect at two important points. The first concerns the health and long-term care costs of an older population and how they

---

20. Remember this is a measure of the increasing gap between full pensionable age and life expectancy at that age and not a measure of increase in life expectancy.

21. The Congressional Budget Office estimates that the actuarial shortfall in the Social Security system over the next 75 years is equal to 0.7 percent of GDP over that period. It could be covered by an immediate increase in the payroll tax rate of 1.9 percent from its current 12.4 percent, or an equivalent reduction in benefits spending, or some combination.

should be apportioned between the public purse and the private sector. The question becomes more urgent in countries such as the United States, which already incur high and rising health-care costs independent of aging. The second nexus is whether the health status of older workers will allow further increases in pensionable age, a favorite proposal for relieving financially strapped public pensions. An optimistic view of improving health of the elderly would moderate the health costs of aging and also, by allowing for longer working lives, would ease pressure on pension budgets. A pessimistic view would undermine both.

Conflicting Views

Two apparently conflicting views on the health of the elderly have been labeled the "compression of morbidity" hypothesis and the "failures of success" paradigm. In its simplest form the first argues that, with appropriate medical strategies, "the age of onset of chronic illness may be postponed more than the age of death, squeezing most of the morbidity in life into a shorter period with less lifetime disability" (Fries, Bruce, and Chakravarty 2011; Manton, Corder, and Stallard 1997; Manton, Gu, and Lamb 2006). Shorter periods of morbidity would have the double advantage of reducing health and long-term care costs and supporting increases in pensionable age. If this hypothesis is correct, the reduction in health costs will occur whether or not life expectancy was increasing—all that would be required is the delay in onset of disabilities to be longer than the change in life expectancy. A weaker version of this hypothesis—the healthy aging concept—proposes that an age-specific health-care expenditure curve shifts rightward as life expectancy increases. For example, the expenditures for a 70-year-old man would be the spending previously recorded for a 67-year-old and so forth. In this weaker version, disabilities and spending are postponed, allowing for longer working lives, but there is no necessary reduction in total spending over one's lifetime.

The second view is darker and traces back to the 1970s. Ernest Gruenberg (1977), a Professor and Department Chair at the Johns Hopkins School of Hygiene and Public Health, began by observing that anti-infectious drugs, starting with sulfonamides in the 1930s, had been postponing the death of persons suffering from chronic disease. The patients receive an extension of life but also an extension of disease and disability. He concludes that modern medicine has "produced tools which prolong diseased, diminished lives and so increases the proportion of people who have a disabling or chronic disease." He does not investigate the monetary costs of these changes but does conclude with a strong call for greater research on mitigating chronic diseases.

The modern version of this unintended consequence is increasing prevalence of Alzheimer's disease.[22] Michael Hurd and his colleagues (2013) have estimated the current and prospective cost to society of dementia in the United States. They calculate that prevalence is about 15 percent in age 70 and above. Total costs including care and treatment in 2010 were estimated to be between $157 and $215 billion dollars, of which Medicare paid $11 billion. The financial burden ranks with cancer and heart disease. As a result of aging, the cost by 2040 is expected to more than double. The point is not only that modern medicine prolongs the period of morbidity, but that advances elsewhere in medicine result in an increasing share of the population becoming subject to this lengthy and expensive disease. That said, some recent studies find that better general health can lower age-specific dementia rates.

The two views can be partially reconciled. Following Gruenberg's earlier plea for research on chronic diseases, progress has been made in prevention (reduction in risk factors), slowing progression, and mitigating the effects of morbidity for many (not all) diseases. In their recent review article, Fries, Bruce, and Chakravarty (2011) compile empirical support for the compression of morbidity hypothesis, a positive finding. Manton, Gu, and Lamb (2006) found a significant and accelerating decline in the prevalence of chronic disability from 1982 to 2004. Specifically, during these years, disability in the 65–74 age group fell from 14.2 to 8.9 percent; for age group 75–84 from 30.7 to 21.9 percent; and for the 85+ age group fell from 50.3 to 37.9 percent. The evidence is not conclusive, however, and past success does not guarantee the future. The declines may have been associated with better medications, not a reduction in disease. Also recent studies suggest that earlier reductions in disabilities among the elderly may have stagnated or reversed (National Research Council 2012). And, as discussed below, a reduced incidence of morbidity and disability among the elderly does not necessarily translate into reduced health expenditures. Increasing obesity can also upset positive trends. The American Heart Association warns that increasing rates of obesity, unhealthy diets, and inactivity may cause life expectancy to start to fall.

One further point needs to be made. The empirical link between aging and increasing health-care expenditures is weaker than expected (Breyer, Costa-Font, and Felder 2010). We have already noted that it may shift according to the compression of morbidity and healthy aging hypotheses. A further confounding twist in this conceptual tale is the so-called "red

---

22. Gruenberg does consider increasing senility.

herring" challenge thrown out by Peter Zweibel and his colleagues (1999). The essence of this argument is that the size of health-care expenditures for the elderly depends on remaining life time (proximity to death) and not age per se. As Fuchs (1984) foresaw, the reason expenditures rise with age is the fraction of people near death increases. Because everyone ultimately dies, the implication is that population *aging* contributes less to projected *per capita* health expenditures than is generally claimed. This is consistent with the compression of morbidity view. A consensus view appears to be emerging that accounting for the proximity to death reduces but does not fully remove the direct impact of aging on expenditures. Breyer, Costa-Font, and Felder (2010) review various studies generally supporting the red herring challenge and make the sensible suggestion that separating long-term care from other health-care expenditures is a useful step.

Forecasting Health-Care Expenditures

Projecting future health-care expenditures and identifying those that are due to demographic changes—population growth and aging—is not for the faint-hearted. Total expenditures will be the net result of numerous factors in addition to demographic variables: advances in medical technology, which may lead to increased or decreased treatment costs; the increased demand for health care arising from increased per capita income;[23] the extent of insurance coverage, which tends to increase demand; reliance on competition vs. regulatory pricing of medical services; the split between public and private funding, which also affects demand and may be influenced by demographic variables, especially the voting strength of the elderly; success of prevention campaigns for smoking, obesity, and other risk factors (with lags); the relative cost of health input costs, especially labor costs; and other factors.

Despite weaknesses, researchers have been tempted to use information on age-specific health expenditures. These data are often available, show striking increases in expenditures as people age, and utilize available projection of demographic variables. Fogel (2009), for example, citing earlier data, puts the annual per capita financial burden of health care tripling from age 52 to age 75 and doubling again to a sixfold increase by age 85.[24]

---

23. For income elasticity estimates, see Fogel (2009); Hall and Jones (2007); and Baicker and Skinner (2010).

24. Fogel correctly considers shifts in the age-expenditure curve in his assessment of future health care costs.

Using data from Blue Cross, Blue Shield, and Medicare, Alemayehu and Warner (2004) estimated that annual per capita medical expenditures increased almost fourfold from age 40 to age 65, and more than sixfold from age 40 to age 85.[25] The reasons behind these and similar studies seem obvious. Our health tends to deteriorate with age, and we require increasing expenditures to stay the consequences.

Using age-specific health expenditure data and data on changes in the age distribution of the population over the next decades one can estimate the incremental health costs of aging. Christian Hagist and Laurence Kotlikoff (2009) follow this approach by decomposing the growth of government expenditures on health care in 10 OECD countries into those accounted for by aging of the population and those accounted for by increases in benefits levels. (The benefit level should be thought of as government spending per beneficiary at a given age rather than beneficial in a medical sense.) Looking back over a three-decade period, they find that about 80 percent of the growth in government health-care spending has been for increasing benefits levels and only about 20 percent from demographic changes. Looking forward, the rate of growth of benefits remains the key variable but, because the elderly are an increasing share of population and because health expenditures rise steeply with increasing age, demographic change (aging) becomes increasingly important. The authors express the budgetary implications of allowing benefit levels to grow at current rates in the context of aging in a rather dramatic fashion. For example, if the United States maintained its current level of benefits growth for the next 40 years (highly unlikely), government health-care spending would rise from its 2002 level of 6.6 percent of GDP to 19 percent of future GDP, when cumulative future spending and GDP are both discounted at 3 percent and expressed in present value terms. These projections are restricted to government health-care spending and do not include private spending.

One shortcoming of this analysis is that it assumes that the profile of age-specific health-care spending remains constant over time. It thus rejects the "compression of morbidity" thesis described above and the related "healthy aging" literature. In doing so, it most likely exaggerates the budgetary effects of aging. By holding the age-specific spending constant, an increase in life expectancy increases the duration of disability and illness, and thus increases total health spending. An alternative would be to

---

25. See also US National Health Expenditure data, which breaks down spending by age and medical services.

use proximity to death as the metric. As death recedes (life expectancy increases), health expenditures at specific ages decline.

The OECD has made a sophisticated attempt to project public health and long-term care spending increases among its members and in selected other countries between 2010 and 2060 (De la Maisonneuve and Martins 2013).[26] The study identifies the drivers for health spending as demographic changes (aging), income growth (as reflected in income elasticity estimates), and a residual which reflects changing medical technology, policies, and relative prices. Long-term care spending is driven by demographics, the availability of informal care, and low productivity growth in this sector. Two scenarios are considered: one in which the residual in health spending continues to grow at 1.7 percent annually for the entire period (the cost-pressure scenario), and one in which the residual is forced to zero by 2060 (the cost-constraint scenario).

The overall result is that average public spending in the OECD for health and long-term care may rise from about 6 percent of GDP to almost 14 percent of GDP in the cost-pressure case, and to almost 10 percent in the cost-constrained case. Long-term care will increase the fastest, rising from its 2005 level of 1.1 percent GDP to 2.4–3.3 percent, depending on the scenario but health-care costs will continue to dominate in absolute terms. The BRIICS countries are also estimated to face large percentage point increases in these costs. These results confirm that increasing health and long-term care spending is a serious fiscal and economic issue throughout the OECD and beyond.

When health-care spending in the OECD is considered separately from long-term care, the role of demographics is surprisingly modest. Under the healthy aging hypothesis discussed earlier, "On average the demographic effect accounts for only a small increase in [public health care] expenditures" (less than one percentage point of GDP). That spending is expected to rise from 5.7 percent of GDP to 7.7 percent of GDP in the cost-constrained case. The apparent reason for the modest demographic impact is that the pure aging effect is largely offset by the healthy aging assumption discussed earlier. If that assumption proves unrealistic, population aging emerges as a stronger driver of health spending.

Keep in mind that the OECD study dealt exclusively with *public* health and long-term spending.

26. They also examine six large industrializing countries—Brazil, Russia, India, Indonesia, China, and South Africa—the "BRIICS."

The US Situation

The United States does not start from a strong position in confronting the economic and fiscal impacts of future health-care spending. Total spending, public and private, on health-care services and supplies rose from 4.7 percent of GDP in 1960 to 17.4 percent in 2009, before dipping to 17.2 percent in 2012. Some of the slowdown in growth reflects the recent recession (Martin et al. 2014). This is by far the highest percentage in the OECD, but the corresponding health statistics are not impressive. The title of a recent (2013) report by a panel convened by the National Research Council and the Institute of Medicine is blunt: "Health in International Perspective: Shorter Lives, Poorer Health." Compared to the average of a peer group of countries the United States scored worse in nine health categories including life expectancy, infant mortality, HIV and AIDs, obesity and diabetics, heart disease, chronic lung disease, and disability. Whether the Affordable Care Act recently enacted can improve this record and maintain some discipline of costs remains to be seen. Looking at the bright side, the US demographics with respect to aging are relatively favorable, but the consistent, if surprising, research conclusion is that demographic factors, and in particular aging, are a relatively minor driver of health-care costs. The income elasticity of demand for spending on health and the cost-increasing bias of new medical technology appear to be the dominant forces. Chandra, Holmes, and Skinner (2013) conclude that new and expensive technology is a major driver of US long-term health-care costs and that total expenditures are likely to rise by the GDP growth rate plus 1.2 percent over the next few decades.

The US Congressional Budget Office (CBO 2012) has wrestled with projecting US health-care costs. It is refreshing, if a bit disturbing, to learn that they have no satisfactory analytical basis for projecting the long-term effects of the 2010 Affordable Care Act. For the very long term, they make do with a more formulistic approach centered on an assumption of declining excess cost growth. Nevertheless, the numbers remain interesting. Two scenarios for federal spending on Medicare, Medicaid, and the Children's Health Insurance Program are analyzed: an extended baseline reflecting current law and regulations and an extended alternative in which some of the current constraints on spending are dropped. The latter results in higher spending. Current spending (as of 2012) on these programs is 5.4 percent of GDP and that is projected to rise to 9.6 percent in 2037 under the first scenario, and 10.4 percent under the second scenario. Aging is expected to play a significant role, accounting for three-fifths of the spending growth. Note that these numbers do not include all public health-care spending, for example, by the Department of Veterans Affairs. Note also that *private* spending on health care equals public spending so that aggregate health-care spending in 2012 is estimated 17 percent of GDP and is expected to rise to 25 percent by 2037.

Financing expenditures of this magnitude will be a challenge and can have macroeconomic consequences. The public share of health-care spending is increasing in the United States. The principal financing sources are payroll taxes, general government funds derived mainly from income taxes, and premiums. Taxes create inefficiencies in the economic system, and a common measure of the extent is the efficiency cost (deadweight loss) per dollar of tax revenue.

Baicker and Skinner (2011) attempt to measure these efficiency costs if US public health expenditures continue to rise between now and 2060. The simulation is carried out under the assumption that the government will have to raise additional funds equivalent to 8 percent of GDP by 2060 to pay for higher health-care spending. How the spending is financed becomes important. In this model, if funding is primarily financed by raising marginal tax rates on high income families, the efficiency costs are highest, amounting to $1.48 per dollar of taxes raised. If financed by a flat payroll tax, the efficiency costs are lowest at $0.41 per dollar raised, but the share of the tax burden borne by low-income taxpayers more than doubles. This represents a clear trade-off between efficiency and equity principles.

Health Spending Redeemed

Health-care spending projections make dreary reading. Costs are high and rising, and having an aging population does not help. But it is deeply misleading to dwell exclusively on past and prospective spending without considering the benefits. They include major extensions of life expectancy and reduced morbidity among the elderly. Indeed one can make a strong argument that health spending has led to a triple bonus (Manton 2009): improvements in labor productivity; reduction in future disability costs; and greater utility and well-being of the elderly. No valid conclusions as to whether spending has been "too much" or "too little" can be made without attempting to quantify these great accomplishments.

One approach is to estimate the "value of a [statistical] life year"—the amount of additional utility derived from increased life expectancy and decreased morbidity (improvement in the quality of life) as a result of improvements in health.[27] This is not a question of aging per se, although demographic variables will enter the analysis. Kevin Murphy and Robert Topel (2006) have constructed a sophisticated analysis of the valuation that may be attributed to health improvements in the United States over the past century. The results are very large gains indeed. For the most part, the gains are excluded from national income and output accounts, which therefore understate real welfare gains. The authors estimate that the life expectancy increases achieved in the period 1970–2000 had a summed value for those alive in 2000 and for subsequent birth cohorts of $95 trillion. This would be equivalent to a flow of about $3.2 trillion per year. The capitalized value of medical expenditures during this period grew by $34 billion, giving a favorable ratio of value to cost of almost three to one.[28] One demographic implication of this model is that the closer the population's age is to the onset of disease, the greater the social value of health improvements. The aging of the baby boomers has justified greater expenditures. A second implication is that the larger the population, the greater the social value of health spending. A growing population benefits from past health expenditures. Population decline is not imminent for the United States but is for a number of other countries and may cut into projected benefits. The internationalization of medical knowledge tempers this conclusion however.

Hall and Jones (2007) add to this literature with a model that attempts to estimate the optimal share of US GDP to devote to health expenditures. The analysis is based on a clever insight. The marginal utility of additional consumption of conventional goods and services declines with additional income, but the marginal utility of extending life does not. The intuitive logic is that the satisfaction (utility) derived from the third glass of wine is positive but less than the second glass. In contrast and all else equal, the satisfaction from extending life by yet another year does not decline. It follows that, as countries grow richer, the share of spending to extend life (health spending) will optimally rise so long as life expectancy responds to additional spending. In economic jargon, health improvement is a superior good with an income elasticity well above one. They suggest that by 2050 the optimal share for health spending in the United States might be about 30 percent of GDP.

27. Estimating the monetary value of statistical lives saved (or lost) may sound odd, but is widely practiced by economists and government officials.

28. Not all categories of expenditures had a favorable ratio. There is evidence that expenditures for men over 85 and for women over 65 the ratio is value to cost less than one. In these cases the expenditures on health tended to be larger than the monetized benefits.

Studies in this vein do not resolve either the fiscal or the economic issues of health-care spending in an aging economy (and do not consider rising income inequality). But they do cast a less menacing light on spending projections. Shifts in the composition of expenditures can be rationalized, and a mental balancing of benefits and costs is helpful in lightening the gloom. Attention can be refocused on the yet unresolved problems of supplying health care efficiently, humane long-term care, and allocating the cost equitably.

MORE DOWNSIDES?

Asset Collapse

Anemic economic growth, economic and fiscal challenges to pensions, and ballooning health-care costs appear to be the principal economic concerns associated with aging and depopulation. Others have been suggested but appear either too speculative or too inconsequential to rise to the same level. One concerns financial markets and rates of returns on assets. Some have argued that population aging will be associated with dis-saving, and as assets are put on the market, their prices will fall. Living standards for the elderly will be depressed. This line of reasoning resonates in the United States, as it is exceptionally dependent on private financial assets to fund retirement, and because of the recent movement from defined benefit to defined contribution type pension plans.[29] The latter puts the risk of declining returns more squarely on the individual than the entity offering the retirement plan.

Depressed prices for financial assets may well materialize, but the effect is likely to be mitigated by a number of factors (Tyers and Qun Shi 2007). Aging is proceeding at different rates in different countries. We live in a globalized capital market in which rates of return, adjusted to risk, tend to equalize. Financial capital flows from low to high return countries can take some of the sting out of dis-saving in the most rapidly aging countries. Cross-border flows of goods, human capital, and labor will also tend to equalize capital returns internationally. Moreover, the recognition of aging and the frailty of public pensions may galvanize the savings of the current working generation to compensate for declining yields. The amount and timing of dis-saving may be moderated by bequest and precautionary motives among the elderly. Finally, from the perspective of

---

29. For discussion of these two types of pension plans, see Barr and Diamond (2006).

capital markets, demographic variables move rather slowly providing generous lead time for adjustment. In short, the effects of depopulation and aging are likely to be modest, with one exception. Rapid depopulation in a specific region may have substantial effects on a major asset of the elderly, housing prices. That could seriously affect the economic well-being of those who, by choice or necessity, remain. But even then the use value of the housing remains.

Who Will Empty the Bedpans?

Finally, there will be labor-market consequences to depopulation and aging. The main adjustment in the composition of the labor force will be toward skills and professions that serve the elderly. There is little mystery here and an expectation that labor markets can adjust.[30] Increased immigration of health-care workers may be part of that adjustment in some countries but the centerpiece for most will be increasing standards, training, working conditions, prestige, and wages for workers in this sector. The relative cost of long-term care is likely to rise but that is part of the adjustment. The plaintive cry sometimes heard, that there will be no one here to take care of us when we are old, strikes a receptive cord, but it is flawed. If care of the elderly is properly valued, and labor markets are not hobbled by calcified regulations, they will respond. The more difficult problem is the transition from family-centered care for the old, to societal care. What has for millennia been traditionally private, personal, and non-commercialized is changing to a marketed service, and that change is emotionally costly for young and old.

The broader complaint, so often heard, of an impending labor shortage has little merit. A labor shortage is the normal state of affairs—it is economic scarcity that gives labor its value. And it is international trade based on comparative advantage that tends to even out this scarcity internationally. Labor may become scarcer relative to capital, but in general this is a good thing and provides the basis for high wages.

---

30. This may be optimistic in cases of persistent high un- and underemployment, rigid labor market regulations and persistent mismatches between supply and demand for specific skills.

CHAPTER 10

✧

Coping Strategies

Fertility: Be fruitful and multiply.
> —Genesis 1:28

Work: By the sweat of your brow you will eat your food until you return to the ground.
> —Genesis 3:19

De-growth: Every Increased possession loads us with new weariness.
> —John Ruskin

If, as appears likely, aging and population decline will bring slower economic growth, what responses are available and appropriate? The quotes point to three possibilities. First, crank up the fertility and immigration numbers for repopulation; second, notch up productivity and work harder, longer, and smarter; third, accept the slowdown and pursue other objectives of social value such as scotching inequality, increasing economic security, and expanding choices—the de-growth alternative.

PRELIMINARIES

Before sorting through and assessing coping strategies, it is helpful to review some preliminary insights.

Economic vs. Fiscal Challenges

For advanced and some developing countries, the *economic* challenge arises from low fertility and longer life expectancy, a shrinking labor force, an aging population, and prospective depopulation. The challenge is to meet expectations for continued economic growth. The *public finance* challenge for the advanced countries arises from the welfare state structures built in the halcyon years following World War II. These include public education, health care, and pensions. The structures were established when the demographic profile was favorable—a large workforce and a still modest elderly cohort. That configuration has now reversed and financing the welfare state structures is itself a serious challenge. We are not as wealthy as we thought we were when the bonus years prevailed.

Responses to the two challenges overlap, but it is helpful to keep the distinction in mind. Of the two challenges—economic and financial—the first is of greater importance. The latter could be "resolved" by increasing taxes or dismantling benefits, but this would merely shift the burden of supporting an aging population from the public sector to the private sector and would likely create new inefficiencies and inequalities. The demographic facts would remain unchanged and reneging on benefits would not address the fundamental economic challenge. Some measures, however, such as increasing labor-force participation and productivity would respond to the economic challenge and also help relieve financial strains on public health and retirement programs. Removing unintended incentives for early retirement can serve both objectives. In contrast, limiting access to, say, publicly funded health care addresses the financial challenge but does not increase the output of medical services or economic activity generally. Similarly, increasing social security taxes eases the drain on public funds, but does not boost productivity and economic output.

As suggested in chapter 8, the economic challenge can be further refined by distinguishing between per capita income growth and aggregate growth (GDP), and focusing on the former. Per capita income, with suitable adjustments for income distributional attributes, is preferred over GDP as a measure of economic well-being. The chapter also suggests that changes in per capita income can be decomposed into those associated with changes in population size (e.g., depopulation) and those associated with changing demographic structure (aging). Finally, it connects population *size* to the concept of economies of scale and connects *aging* to productivity changes. This last depends on labor participation rates and productivity per worker, both of which are related to aging. This taxonomy offers a framework for analyzing coping strategies. It bears repeating that the main problem is with aging, not population decline itself. As noted in chapter 6 and as Basten, Lutz, and Scherbov (2013) have shown, aging and population do not hang together forever. In the long run, they become unhooked, and population can continue to decline without further aging.

One Size Does Not Fit All

It is also helpful to remember that a "one size" coping strategy will not fit all. Countries are at diverse points in their demographic transition and are moving at different speeds. The pace of aging and depopulation partly determine the costs of adjustment. Countries confronting rapid aging and depopulation may wish to use a more aggressive blend of strategies. A seemingly small increase in the total fertility rate, perhaps from 1.6 to 1.8 births per woman, can greatly slow the pace of aging and depopulation, giving time for economic and fiscal adjustments. Economic circumstances, customs, cultures, and governance also differ. For example, the United States and Nigeria are projected to have roughly the same population in 2050 (422 and 402 million, respectively), and between now and then the ratio of their population over 60 will increase by about the same percent (40 percent), but they start from very different positions and will travel different roads. Current per capita income is about $48,000 in the United States and $2, 533 in Nigeria; the fertility rate (births per woman) is below replacement at 1.9 in the United States and is 5.5 but falling in Nigeria; the ratio of working age to the elderly (old age support ratio) in 2050 will be 3 in the United States and 12 in Nigeria; 27 percent of the population will be over 60 in the United States and 7 percent in Nigeria. While both countries are growing and aging, the challenges they face are not commensurate and susceptible to the same response.

As a very rough guide, it may be useful to distinguish between the three groups mentioned earlier: Group 1, the rich, aging countries, with Japan as an exemplar[1] in Asia and Italy in Europe; Group 2, the middle-income countries with sub-replacement fertility rates, which confront rapid aging and possible population decline by 2050, and for whom economic growth remains a priority, exemplified by China and Thailand; and Group 3, poor countries for whom the demographic transition is at an early stage, mainly

1. Japan is atypical, however, in its high male labor market participation rates and low rates of immigration.

in sub-Saharan Africa.[2] Within these categories, there are wide variations in social, political, and economic conditions that will influence coping responses.

Little need be said here concerning Group 3 countries. A stabilized population is still far off. The main tasks are to bring fertility rates down and to seize the demographic bonus as it appears (Sinding 2009). In a simulation model, Ashraf and his colleagues (2013) find that by accelerating already declining fertility in high fertility countries, per capita incomes may be 6 percent higher at a 20-year horizon and 12 percent higher at a 50-year horizon, a modest but positive improvement. There will be increased aging in these countries, but the absolute numbers will remain relatively small for decades. At some point, decisions will have to be made concerning the public and private roles in intergenerational transfers to the elderly, but this is not yet urgent. Group 3 countries will also stand to benefit through trade and capital flows linked to demographics, and migration to group 1 and 2 countries.

Group 2 countries may face the greatest difficulties. They are not yet rich; their demographic bonus is fading; the rapidity with which their fertility rates fell increases the rapidity and burden of their aging; and public social security networks to replace informal family support structures for the ill and the aged remain patchy and incomplete. Social costs will be high.[3]

Group 1 countries have the special problem of financing their extensive social welfare commitments, but, of course, have greater monetary and real resources at their disposal.

It follows that an appropriate coping strategy will vary greatly depending on economic and demographic differences among countries. The differences themselves are helpful. Some relief from aging problems will be found through international migration, international capital flows, and trade. The greater the differences among countries, the greater the opportunity for mutually beneficial intercourse. Using an inter-temporal demographic model for 2005–50, Warrick McKibben (2006) showed that international spillover effects of demographic changes, operating through international trade and capital flows, would increase GDP growth in all of the 10 countries/regions examined.

---

2. Eighteen of 20 countries with the world's highest fertility rates are in sub-Saharan Africa.

3. Extended family support systems are vulnerable to low birth rates. Wang (2011) estimates that partly because of state policy, one-third of households in China may wind up with only one child. A marriage of two only children may have four parents over 60, with long life expectancy ahead of them.

A Life Cycle Approach

Finally, it is useful to take a life cycle approach to coping measures. While the stages of personal life are obvious to all—childhood, maturity and work, old age—the stages of societal aging are not always acknowledged. The postwar baby boom in poor countries was considered a drag on growth, although it was a great triumph for human health. The subsequent demographic bonus of an expanding workforce came as something of a surprise and was not recognized until decades later. In similar fashion, the roots of tomorrow's aging problem go back decades to earlier fertility declines, but public awareness is only now catching up.

Coping measures should be assessed for both their immediate and longer term impacts. For example, a liberal immigration policy can relieve current labor shortages, but immigrants also age and will require health, retirement, and long-term care. Easing the current fiscal problem may not solve the longer term economic problem. Another example is a decline in the youth dependency ratio, which may be considered a plus in the near term, but it signals a declining workforce and problems a generation from now. Measures to increase fertility may be desirable to stabilize long-run population, but reduce female labor-market participation in the short run, with depressing effects on current economic growth and social spending budgets.[4] On the other hand, measures to maintain female labor-market participation may depress fertility, accelerating population decline in the future through the (negative) momentum effect. In short, both the immediate and longer term effects of coping measures need to be thought through.

A TROUBLING COMPLICATION

While our focus is on the fiscal and economic consequences of aging and population decline, geopolitical considerations intrude. Absent such considerations, one could make a strong economic case that the *size* of a country's population and GDP do not greatly matter, but *per capita* income does. It is easy to think of small population, high-income countries where life is more comfortable than in large, poor countries. If economic well-being were the sole objective, one could concentrate on coping measures to maintain and increase per capita output and income rather than focusing on a declining population. In effect this would mean a focus on blunting

---

4. Bloom et al. (2009) estimate that there is a loss of 1.9 years of female labor market participation for each additional child born.

the effects of aging. Chapter 8 suggests that population size per se is of second-order importance for productivity, as small countries can capture some economies of scale through international trade, and other scale economies in, say, transportation may be offset by diseconomies of scale such as congestion. And in a world open to human capital and technology flows, the new growth theory support for large national populations to capture positive externalities loses force. In sum, it is tempting to dismiss depopulation and concentrate on coping with aging.

Introducing national security objectives throws a clinker into this argument. National security is a classic *public* good (service) meaning that if provided to one, it must be provided to all. If population is growing, the cost per person of providing this service is declining; if population is declining the cost per person rises. Thus, in a country with declining population, either the cost per person goes up or the amount of national security "purchased" falls. This is the heart of an argument that, as global population trends tilt further against the West, its willingness and ability to engage in international activities to maintain global security are compromised.[5] In this sense population *size* continues to be relevant. Aging is the central concern and is almost universal, but population decline acting through geopolitical channels cannot be completely ignored. How much weight does this argument deserve?

The idea that a large population confers power and influence in international relations is ancient and need not be reviewed in depth. It is ultimately based on the conflation of population and military power, and held greatest sway when weapons were relatively primitive and manpower dominant.[6] The losses inflicted on France by Germany in the nineteenth and early twentieth century have been attributed to the earlier pernicious results of French fertility decline. Looking ahead to war in the 1930s, both Germany and Japan exhorted their citizens to make babies. Popular reporting on the Korean War emphasized the wave after wave of Chinese soldiers who entered the war on the side of the North and who initially turned the tide of that war.

Remnants of the view that population matters for national security persist. Jackson and Howe (2008) and Howe and Jackson (2011) argue that demographic decline of the West reduces its ability and willingness to maintain global security. The channels are both direct, shortage of manpower to

5. The activities are not merely military. Distributing money is also a tool for national security objectives. Moreover, relative population and GDP size plays a role in many regional security issues.
6. Fact and perception can become blurred. The success of the Mongol "hordes" in the thirteenth century was precisely because they were *not* a horde, a disorganized mob, but because they were a disciplined force consisting exclusively of cavalry.

deploy and maintain security forces on a worldwide basis, and indirect, working through reduced economic willingness and capacity due to population decline and aging. At the same time, as the global population balance shifts, the authors see a rising risk of social and political upheaval in the developing world in the decade of the 2020s. That risk is tied to demographic variables. In their analysis, the United States stands apart in the West due to relatively favorable demographic trends, including immigration. In their view, the reemergence of its dominance *in the West* (not globally) adds to the US's obligation to maintain global security. The analysts recommend a multipronged US demographic policy—pro-natal policies including cash payments for births, inducements for greater female labor-force participation, and measures allowing an increase of immigration.

Although well sprinkled with conditional words such as "may" and "could," the analysis has an alarmist ring to it and its central message should not be dismissed out of hand. The most telling argument is that *if* demographic changes trigger serious and sustained economic slowdown in the West, the public's appetite for active international involvement, including the use of force, is diminished and new structures for security are needed. This brings the geopolitical concern with demographics back to the central concern of this book, the implications of demographic change for economic activity. But it should be borne in mind that the core concern is for a sapping of economic vitality, not the sheer numbers of people. A distinction between economic clout and population clout remains relevant. Recall also that the BRIICSs, the new economic powerhouses, are also aging. Brazil, Russia, India, and China will, on average, have a larger fraction of their population over age 60 in 2050 than will the United States. On closer examination, the proposition that national security considerations should drive population policy is weak.

EXAMINING THE TOOLBOX

A rapidly aging country, on the verge of or experiencing population decline and committed to maintaining positive economic growth, has four compartments in its toolbox: (1) boosting fertility; (2) increasing productivity, including labor-force participation rates; (3) immigration; and (4) building international assets to obtain rentier state status as explained later.[7] An alternative to deploying these tools is to embrace a de-growth option. A brief discussion of the tools and the alternative, de-growth, follows.

7. It also has tools specific to easing public financing pressures.

Boosting Fertility

There are numerous suggestions for increasing the birth rate, many of which date to the 1930s and sometimes earlier. Cash for babies, tax relief for (parents of) babies, free health care for babies, subsidized day care for infants, paid paternity leave, free education, preferential access to housing, policies to better combine work and family, general family support policies, setting Social Security benefits to reward parenting, public match-making services, and more. The expectation is that by reducing the costs and sacrifices of childbearing and rearing, prospective parents will respond with larger families. This prompts three questions. Do these policies work? Which are most cost-effective? Would they pass a rigorous cost–benefit analysis?

There is mixed evidence on the first two questions, beyond our ability to review. France and the Scandinavian counties are generally considered relatively successful, Japan and Singapore as relative failures, but distinguishing between general pro-family policies and those with specific pronatal objectives is difficult. Culture also appears important. What has worked in country A may not work in country B. Norway has been successful in maintaining fertility and female labor-market participation. Available, affordable child care is often mentioned (along with a culture of gender egalitarianism). But Norwegian oil confers special status and allows generous government subsidies not readily available elsewhere. Moreover, difficult economic conditions and labor-market uncertainties, as experienced in Europe since 2008, can depress fertility and undermine pro-natal policies (Goldstein et al. 2013). In a comprehensive survey of fertility research, Balbo, Billari, and Mills (2013, p. 19) cautiously conclude that "there is mixed evidence regarding the effectiveness of social policies on fertility."

The cost–benefit question is especially interesting. One can in principle measure the financial costs: expenditures by firms for extended paternity leave, the costs of day-care centers picked up by governments, and so forth. With some juggling, these financial costs may be a reasonable approximation of the social (economic) costs incurred, and careful econometric work may tease out an estimate for incremental births. The *benefit* analysis would have to deal with the tricky ethical question of accounting for the well-being of a potential person, as discussed in chapter 5. If that person's lifetime utility, as measured by his or her consumption, were not included as a benefit, it is unlikely that an additional birth would have positive social value even in a shrinking and aging economy. Moreover, if the purposes of the policy are to reverse a declining workforce and replenish the tax base so as to support the sick and the aged, the time lag between an additional birth and that person entering the work world, and his or her consumption and educational costs over that period, would need to be considered. If children are viewed and valued as capital goods,[8] proper valuation techniques should be followed. Delayed benefits waiting for children to mature and become productive are costly in present value terms due to the principles of discounting.

Note also the intergenerational implications. The real costs of child-rearing are current and cannot be passed forward in time. To burden the current working generation with the cost of bearing and rearing *additional* children for the purpose of increasing future supply of workers available to fund their retirement sounds quixotic. One reason for being skeptical is that a similar sized investment in human or physical capital (or technology) might have a higher return. A more straightforward approach might be to invest more in the productivity (human capital) of the children that we have (Striessnig and Lutz 2013). Second, because pay-go pension systems do not set benefit levels on the basis of number of children reared, a fiscal externality that discourages parenting remains. Finally, a credible cost–benefit analysis of measures to increase fertility would have to balance potentially large, but as of yet unquantified, negative environmental externalities. The full array of difficulties in determining optimal population discussed in chapter 5 would be involved.

To summarize, in the short run (25 years), there is little to be gained from increasing births in terms of greater economic output or relief in financing public social services. On the contrary, output and financing may suffer by diverting resources to the rearing and education of children. Per capita incomes would, of course, be depressed in this period as the denominator "capita" in per capita is inflated. As noted earlier, pumping up birth rates today to build a tax base for future public health and pension costs sounds a bit like an inter-temporal Ponzi scheme.

To dismiss pro-natal policies as a tool for solving near term public finance problems does not mean they cannot be justified. Nudging up the birth rate should properly be considered a medium- and long-term investment, and at that point the calculus of a pro-natal policy becomes unclear. In principle, higher fertility could stabilize population, hold aging at bay, and infuse the workforce with youth, vigor, and creativity. Even modest increases in fertility can significantly slow the population aging process and moderate adjustment costs. Moreover, some current policies subvert

---

8. Capital goods, sometimes called "producers goods," are distinguished from consumption goods.

family size objectives and should be removed. Chapple (2004), for example, notes that in Japan doctor visits during pregnancy are not covered by health insurance, as they are not payments for illness or injury. This hardly seems family-friendly. And certain pro-natal policies, such as securing gender equality in the workplace, making work and family more compatible, and research on infertility, have independent merit. In any event, it is unlikely that purely economic considerations will dominate fertility debates.

Increasing Productivity via Labor-Force Participation Rates

Efforts to increase productivity, measured as output divided by population, will be a central pillar in coping with a declining support ratio for the elderly and an aging workforce. Productivity increase addresses both the public-sector fiscal challenges of pensions and health care, and the economic challenge of meeting economic growth aspirations. When appropriately tailored, productivity enhancing tools are relevant for countries at all stages of the demographic transition.

There is no need to wait for babies to be born and mature or workers to be imported. Productivity gains can be secured in two other ways: by increasing labor-force participation rates and by increasing the productivity of individual workers. Participation rates, measured by gender and age bracket, are generally defined as those employed or actively seeking employment as a percent of the relevant population. In general, the rates can be increased by starting work earlier (younger), working longer (older), and working harder (more hours per week)—not always an attractive package.

Trends in Labor-Force Participation Rates

Table 10.1 provides participation data over the period 2000–2012 broken down by age group (15–24, 25–64, 65–69), gender, and various country and regional groupings. With OECD labor-force participation rates for males in the traditional work years of 25–64 high and relatively stable (Italy an exception), it is clear that large gains would have to come, if at all, from youth, females, and the upper age brackets such as age 65–69.

Male youth participation in the labor market is low and has fallen substantially for the OECD as a whole, from 57 to 51 percent over the 12-year period. Female youth rates declined from 47 to 43 percent. There are large variations by country. Italy is well below OECD and European averages

Table 10.1. LABOR PARTICIPATION RATES BY AGE AND GENDER, 2000–2012

Country	OECD and Selected Countries					
	Age Brackets					
	15–24		25–64		65–69	
	2000	2012	2000	2012	2000	2012
Male						
OECD	57.0	51.5	87.2	86.5	23.8	29.8
Europe	52.9	48.7	84.2	85.1	13.8	13.3
United States	68.6	56.5	87.6	84.3	30.3	37.1
Japan	47.7	41.5	94.2	92.2	48.4	49.0
Italy	44.6	36.5	80.8	81.5	10.6	12.8
Female						
OECD	46.5	43.2	62.4	66.7	12.8	17.8
Europe	41.3	39.4	60.2	66.7	6.1	6.8
United States	63.0	53.2	72.5	70.9	19.5	27.6
Japan	46.6	42.0	62.5	67.2	24.0	28.3
Italy	34.3	26.5	48.8	58.6	2.8	4.0

Source: www.stats.oecd./Index.aspx?DataSetCode=LFS_SEXAGE_I_R

and the United States well above. Some of the decline can be explained by increasingly lengthy education, helpful for future productivity gains. Some is no doubt due to depressed conditions in the labor markets and the recent economic crisis. Some may be due to lifestyle changes in which commitment to a job and career no longer appear as attractive as earlier.[9] The youth age bracket has considerable potential to stabilize labor partic-ipation rates, but thus far there has been little progress. It is possible, of course, that with a shrinking labor force and increasing labor scarcity the trend will reverse.

Females in the upper two age groups have made strong gains. At the OECD level, and in the 25–64 age bracket, the female participation rate increased from 62 to 67 percent. For the 65–69 bracket, the rise was sharper, from 13 to 18 percent. Still, there are very large variations in the oldest bracket, with the Japanese and US female participation rates some seven times as high as the Italian rates. And while the gaps between male and female participation rates have narrowed, the female rate remains

9. Clark et al. (2010) cite studies in Japan showing some 9 percent of Japanese age 15–34 (3 million individuals) were outside the formal labor market and were not seeking to join it.

substantially lower in both age brackets. Culture and the compatibility of motherhood and careers are central issues.

These data suggest that there is some scope for blunting the effects of aging on the size of the labor force by increasing youth and female participation rates. But there are also reasons for caution. A year lost to the labor market for a year's more education and training is an investment that *may or may not* have a high social and personal return. But it seems unlikely that the economic and financial challenges of aging will be surmounted by cutting back on education, to gain a few points in youth labor participation. The current critical task is to get a generation of generally well-trained youth into productive employment. The lingering cyclical effects of depressed conditions since 2008 threaten to become structural. This unprecedented unemployment is a clear loss to current and future generations.

Increasing female participation may be desirable, but may backfire by further depressing fertility rates. There is a genuine conflict here. More babies mean more work. To simultaneously press for more children and to press for greater labor-market participation is a stretch. Family-friendly policies are a key: some combination of quality day care, telecommuting, job sharing, paternal leave, and so forth—all in the context of gender equality—is needed (Thevenon 2013). Even then there are limits. Child day care may substitute for home care, but even if it leads to greater participation in the formal labor market, it does not in itself increase real output in an economy, as it shifts home production of child care to the formal sector. GDP is currently defective in not measuring the true value of non-marketed goods and services and can be a poor guide to child-care policy. Much the same can be said about swapping personal care giving for one's elderly parents for installing them in a nursing home, and financing that choice by taking a job. There may be no net gain in economic output. In short, there are real social and economic costs of participating in formal labor markets and ill-conceived policies need to be avoided.

The "early elderly," age 60–70, may offer the greatest scope for productivity gains via labor-market participation. Table 10.1 shows trends are moving in the right direction. On average for males age 65–69, the OECD participation rate moved up from 24 to 30 percent over the period, and the female rate rose from 13 to 18 percent. In Japan, the rate stayed at a remarkably high level of 28 percent. The gains were equally strong for the next younger age bracket, age 60–64. For males, the rate increased from 47 to 55 percent and from 26 to 38 percent for females. Even if the rates of increase dropped by half over the next decade, the OECD labor-force participation rate for males could climb to 60 percent in the 60–64 age bracket and 43 percent for females age 60–64. For the upper range of age 65–69, male participation rates would reach 34 percent and females 22 percent. These increases do not appear unrealistic as some countries are already exceeding them.[10]

Boosting labor-force participation rates, especially within the "early elder" group, could go considerable distance to stabilizing the workforce and maintaining productivity. It would be especially powerful in the next few decades as the baby boom generation reaches this stage of life.[11]

Maestas and Zissimopoulos (2010) argue that the United States is well placed to exploit this coping strategy. There are three justifications for leaning heavily on the early elderly. First, additional years in the workforce produce additional contributions to Social Security systems that could be passed back in higher annual retirement benefits or used to help close unfunded financing gaps. In dependency ratio terms, employment of the elderly improves both the numerator and the denominator, lowering the number of elderly to be supported and increasing the size of the workforce to do the supporting. Second, this cohort is enjoying the benefits of major increases in life expectancy, and equity suggests they pick up part of the tab.[12] Third, following the new metrics of aging and the healthy aging/compressed morbidity concepts discussed in earlier chapters, possibilities for a healthy, active, and productive work life have significantly increased. While some workers may be worn out by their sixties, an increasing number will remain active.

10. Clark et al. (2010) make interesting calculations linking Japan's population decline and aging and economic performance over the period 2005–25. Under the baseline assumptions that age-specific labor-participation rates remain constant and no significant policy changes are made, they find that the employment ratio (total employed divided by total population) falls from 50.0 percent to 45.9 percent. This is mainly due to aging, not population decline. With positive investment, GDP increases until 2020 and then drops about 2 percent in the final five years. GDP per capita rises a total of 16 percent between 2005 and 2020, stabilizes, and then starts to decline in 2024. In a simulation in which all who were not working, but expressed a preference for employment, were in some fashion accommodated, the results were positive but not dramatic. The decline in the employment ratio was blunted, the terminal value of GDP was 2.4 percent above the baseline terminal value, and terminal GDP per capita was 2 percent higher.

11. Clark concludes that, despite Japan's status as having the highest labor-force participations in the OECD, with certain labor market policy reforms and a squeeze on retirement benefits, the ratio of employed males age 60–64 might be increased by 15–20 percentage points over its 2005 level.

12. Judging by trends in retirement age, they have not yet done so. An unweighted average of effective retirement ages in OECD countries shows that they have barely budged since the early 1990s and remain well below retirement ages in the 1960s and 1970s. The OECD reports that postponement of retirement age is underway or planned in 28 of 34 countries (OECD 2012 Pensions Outlook). Nevertheless, it also reports that postponement will keep pace with improved life expectancy in only 6 countries for men and 10 countries for women.

Policy Measures to Boost Participation Rates

Boosting the labor-market participation of the early elderly means manipulating the timing of retirement. If successful, the economic and financial challenges of aging are both eased. Chapter 9 discussed some of the issues in pension reform: inducements to early retirement should be avoided, and disability and unemployment benefits should not be used as disguised early retirement policies. Increasing the age when full benefits are available appears more attractive for closing funding gaps than raising contribution rates, as it would have less adverse impact on private savings. Linking the full benefits age to increases in life expectancy would automate the process. But it is not a free lunch. For those workers with few assets and who work in physically demanding jobs, increasing the age to obtain full benefits can be a heavy physical burden. Mortality differences among socioeconomic groups already reduce the progressivity of OECD pension schemes; although there is no evidence that increasing retirement age *increases* the unfairness to lower income groups (Whitehouse and Zaidi 2008).

Not all measures directly affect the pension system. A number of labor-market reforms could increase the supply and demand for workers in this age bracket (d'Addio, Keese, and Whitehouse 2010). They include scrapping mandatory retirement rules, reducing discriminatory taxation, re-contracting wage agreements, retraining for older workers, improving workforce flexibility (job sharing, telecommuting, etc.), reducing wage gains based on seniority, and redesigning job requirements to fit older workers.

Nudging up labor participation rates will not be easy and painless. There will be political opposition to some of these changes, especially those perceived to reduce retirement benefits. Reform, however, may be advanced by the current economic crisis. Also, if current (elderly) beneficiaries are exempted, and if changes are announced well in advance, the opposition should be less. To date, recent public pension reforms have cut benefits to *future* retirees by some 20–25 percent (OECD 2012). Some observers have suggested schemes to redress the increasing voting weight of the elderly in order to reduce opposition to reform, but this is questionable.[13] Legislation that gave additional voting rights to parents of minor children might itself be blocked by the elderly, and re-jigging voting rights would be generationally divisive.

---

13. See, for example, Demeny (2011). Note that giving triple weight to first-time voters might be better at redressing age imbalances and increasing political participation by youth.

Boosting Productivity per Worker

The complementary policy to participation rates is to increase individual productivity within a possibly shrinking labor force. Productivity gains are "purchased" through investment in human capital (formal education and on-the-job training), public infrastructure (roads and ports), and physical capital, all aided by technological progress and an efficient economic system. These investments must be financed. Countries confronting a shrinking labor force and an increasing number of elderly start with two potential advantages and face two significant obstacles. The first advantage is quasi automatic capital deepening, an increase in the stock of capital per worker. Just as capital shallowing was a concern in an expanding population, a shrinking labor force increases the stock of capital per worker, and presumably increases worker productivity. The positive effect should not be exaggerated. Unlike new investment, the existing stock of capital would not embody the most recent technology. Moreover, much of the capital stock is residential housing and is not easily converted to other productive assets. Nevertheless, housing in the form of bequests to working generations can help boost their savings.

The second advantage is more dynamic and is based on the concept of a second demographic bonus. As explained in previous chapters, and as modeled by Lee and Mason (2011), societal demand for wealth should increase with aging. With fewer children and anticipating longer lives, people may save more over their working years. These additional savings could provide the funds for productivity-augmenting investment and help finance workers' consumption as they pass from the workforce into retirement.

The first obstacle is that to capture the bonus, consumption need be controlled during working years. Pay-go public pensions and excessive reliance on financial support from one's family during retirement undermine the process. The second, speculative, obstacle is the issue of rising health-care costs. Even if the thesis of healthy aging and compressed morbidity is correct, the combination of unavoidable health costs at the end of life, the uncertain impact of technological change on these costs, and the long-term care for "old elderly" may eat up funds that otherwise might have gone to enhancing worker productivity.

If the more optimistic view toward capital deepening and savings prevails, the full set of investment opportunities is made available. Increases in worker productivity can then reinforce increases in labor-force participation in maintaining economic growth.

Compensatory Immigration

Immigration has a positive but limited role in the toolbox for aging.[14] At a high level of abstraction and setting aside social and other frictions, international migration, like free trade and capital movements, contributes to global efficiency. Differences among countries in age structure, skill sets, and income levels point toward substantial potential gains. There are also several practical advantages. Selective immigration could start to address the decline in the workforce almost immediately—unlike fertility rates there is no 25-year lag; as soon as the immigrants are employed social tax receipts should rise, easing fiscal strains; the skill set of immigrants could be matched to perceived needs—geriatric health and long-term care workers for example;[15] some of the human capital investment costs are picked up by the country of emigration; and finally, depending on the country of origin, immigration may give a short-lived boost to fertility rates (Harper 2011).

But there are problems with using immigration as the principal coping strategy. The size of the flows can be daunting. Robert Holtzmann (2005) has estimated the annual net immigration flows that would be needed to keep the labor force constant in various regions of the world for the period 2005–50. For Europe and Russia, he estimates a net *annual* immigration flow of 3.3 million for 2005–25 and an annual flow of 4.1 million for 2025–50 would be needed—well above current levels. The *gross* annual flow would have to be considerably higher to account for non-active working age immigrants and non-working dependents. Considering also returning and circulating migrants, Holtzmann estimates the cumulative gross number of migrants in this region over the 2005–50 period to be between 279 and 566 million, and the net to be perhaps 200 million. (The population of the region in 2005 was 745 million.)

The shortfall in the labor force is not only among the rich. China is identified as facing a decline of 85 million workers by 2050 and would need an estimated net replacement migration of 121 million persons, concentrated in the years 2025–50. Other studies show replacement

14. We consider immigration, not migrant labor. Certain oil-rich economies have been depending on the latter for decades. Still, many long-term immigrants return to their homeland when they grow old so that the distinction is blurred.

15. Cortès and Pan (2013) estimate that the availability of (temporary) foreign domestic workers—maids, nannies, caregivers—has increased the formal labor-force participation rate of native Hong Kong women with young children by 8–13 percentage points, and generated a monthly consumer surplus for each of US$130–$200. This may be thought of as the in-country outsourcing of household and family care production.

migration in the richer countries would further depopulate certain regions including Eastern Europe and Russia (Tyers and Qun Shi 2007).

The magnitude of compensatory immigration is not the only problem. The fiscal contributions of low-skilled workers will be low and perhaps negative. Not all domestic workers will welcome labor competition from immigrants with similar skills. Not all domestic employers will agree on the same desirable skills set. Immigrants themselves will age and have legitimate claims on government pensions and health care. Cultural, ethnic, and religious frictions can become significant and divisive. If excessive, a loss of national identity may threaten. Immigrants themselves often pay a high psychological price in leaving their homelands. Countries experiencing large-scale emigration of the young, the strong, and the bright may stunt their own growth prospects. This is especially problematic when immigration laws favor the highly educated. Unlike poaching salmon from the streams of the laird, the poacher of talent and the talent that is poached may both gain, but the country being poached in may lose.

Although governments may appear to have more direct control over the immigration tool than over the fertility or labor-force participation tools, in practice there are serious political and social limits. Small, multicultural countries with a history of successful assimilation, such as Singapore, may be an exception. Even in that success story, the road forward in not assured. There is a tightrope to be walked between increasing social tension associated with immigration and prolonged economic stagnation that could lead to emigration and a collapsing population. For most countries, immigration will be at best a useful supplementary policy.

As an alternative to labor moving internationally, the outsourcing of certain labor- intensive services may flourish. "Medical tourism" is already well established and likely to grow. Outsourcing "retirement services" via emigration of the elderly to sunny countries with long coastlines and low living costs may be a partial substitute to immigration. Neither directly solves the declining elderly support ratio in rapidly aging countries, and both tend to weaken the balance of payments of the outsourcing country, but they can contribute efficient use of global resources.

Acquiring Rentier State Status

Accumulating ownership of productive assets is a traditional and respectable means of weaning oneself off labor income. This holds for individuals and countries. The advantage of holding net *international* assets is that it allows a country to consume more than it produces. Thus, if the main threat of aging is shrinking output from a shrinking labor force, income from international assets (portfolio and direct investments, patents and royalties, etc.) can help maintain consumption levels. Assuming shrewd investments and prudence, the yield on the assets can provide a permanent source of income. The pertinent questions are how to acquire rentier status and how important is it.[16]

The first question is straightforward. Net international assets are acquired by running a current account surplus in the balance of payments, and this requires selling more goods and services abroad than are purchased. The difference, with some minor accounting changes and barring adverse exchange rate changes, are equal to a country's annual net acquisition of foreign assets. The ownership and form of the assets varies. Some are purely private, some are accumulated by central banks presumably to manage currency values, some are held in sovereign wealth funds. A rough idea of the importance of these assets in maintaining consumption, despite a declining labor force, is obtained by estimating their per capita earning power. Considering only the eight countries with sovereign wealth funds exceeding $100 billion, and assuming a conservative 4 percent real rate of return, the unweighted average annual per capita income from these assets is about $2,500.[17] Six of the eight countries are oil exporters and presumably the principal purpose is to compensate for depleted oil assets. Thus, the funds are not necessarily net gains in wealth. Norway tops the potential per capita income list at $5,896; China is the lowest at $36. Singapore, the only other non-oil-exporting country, would earn $3,164 per person. If central bank foreign exchange holdings were also included, China's annual per capita income from the assets would rise by about $135, but would fall short of Japan's $400.[18] These numbers suggest that a small group of low population, oil-exporting countries can aspire to rentier status, but the main purpose would be to replace oil income. Singapore is the only obvious example of building international assets that might moderate the effects of population decline.

16. As used here, a rentier state is a country that acquires international assets, often via a sovereign wealth fund, for the purpose of earning returns and maintaining its consumption level in the face of depleting domestic assets. The domestic assets may be depletable natural resources but can also be its labor force.
17. Central bank holdings of foreign assets are mainly for prudential and foreign exchange smoothing purposes, and are held in low yield instruments.
18. Fund assets sourced at http://www.swfinstitute.org/fun-ranking.

CAN LESS BE MORE? THE DE-GROWTH ALTERNATIVE

How hard should countries struggle to maintain economic growth in an era of aging and declining population? When does the satisfaction of needs yield to a never-ending creation of new wants? When is enough enough? Should we abandon the religion of everlasting growth? Is there a case for fewer people leading longer, better lives? These questions are only relevant to the rich, group 1, countries, and perhaps not even for them. Middle-income countries still have substantial material needs, made even more difficult to meet when they are aging and facing population decline.

The Commission of the European Communities has staked out an expansionist position on this question. It states that "never in history has there been economic growth without population growth" (European Union 2005, p. 5), and then lists as its first essential priority a "return to demographic growth." This is not very satisfactory logic. In support of its demographic aspirations, it cites surveys which show a large gap between the numbers of children Europeans say they would like and the number they actually have. This, too, is shaky logic. There are many things that many of us would like. If we choose not to "purchase" them, should society pick up the tab?

An intellectual case for yielding to the inevitability of aging and accepting some decline in per capita income or its growth would rest on three arguments. First, a large swath of the environmental community would welcome it as complementary to, and supportive of, the peaking and prospective decline of population. Green growth is a good slogan but green de-growth might be more practical and satisfactory. World population in 1920 was under two billion. Would a world of two billion people at current OECD income levels be such an undesirable place?

Second, there has been continuous increase in income inequality in OECD countries. The average Gini index, a measure of inequality, has trended upward since the mid-1980s, with the sharpest movement in the most recent years. Higher incomes go to fewer pockets. The argument is not that economic growth has been responsible (or the converse), but that priority should now be reset on distribution and economic security. The theoretical bases for concentrating on distribution, not per capita growth, are the venerable diminishing marginal utility argument (the third glass of wine argument) and the relative income hypothesis—utility derives from one's *relative*, not actual income. Closely related, there are a number of well-known defects in national income accounts that weaken their status as economic welfare indicators. Leisure and volunteer activities are given zero value. The costs of pollution are largely ignored. In short, economic growth can be oversold and greater income does not always mean a better life. Securing greater equality and economic security are major planks in the de-growth program.[19]

Third, there are real opportunity costs to many of the coping strategies discussed above. It may be that, on reflection, the costs of at least some of these measures outweigh the putative benefits. For example, there are real costs in terms of money, time, and effort, in rearing children. These costs do not disappear even if their financing is shifted from one parent to another, or to the state, or to employers. Shifting costs changes the calculus for the prospective parents and may increase the fertility rate. But the basic question remains—do the social benefits of an additional birth exceed the costs? It is not clear that they always do.

As another example, governments certainly have tools to increase the labor-force participation rate, especially by modifying retirement schemes. The additional participation and output mitigates the economic challenge and relives the public financing burden. Some measures are costless and correct distortions in the labor market; others are coercive and oblige workers to override their work-leisure preferences. These carry a real cost. Immigration provides a final example. It can make direct contributions to the economic and financial challenges posed by aging and a declining workforce, but the indirect costs, including social frictions and a weakening of national identity, can be large.

A balancing of costs and benefits should inform coping strategy, and countries will stitch together several approaches. A deliberate de-growth policy may not be declared with fanfare because it will be characterized as a failure and be a tough sell. To put a more positive gloss, one could talk of altered, not diminished, expectations. If wrapped together with policies promoting equity and economic security it may have better prospects. In any event, because de-growth may indeed be the least costly response and may increase well-being, it deserves attention.

19. De-growth implies shifting priorities from maximizing per capita income growth to distribution and economic security. Some would argue that the latter are easier to secure in a high economic growth context.

CHAPTER 11

☙

Concluding Thoughts

IN RETROSPECT

Much has changed in the 200 plus years since Malthus took on the Utopians in his famous essay. The primary problem is no longer growing population pressing on food supplies. Today's problem centers on aging and imminent population decline in much of the world. This is Malthus upended! The reversal has been shockingly swift. It was only 50 years ago that runaway population was making apocalyptic headlines. From baby boom to baby bust in less than a lifetime! Two mostly unanticipated developments underlie the reversal. First, despite an eightfold increase in world population over the 200 years, per capita food production is at an all-time high. Agriculture has trumped procreation. Second, and against eighteenth-century expectations, as incomes rose, fertility fell. Both should be considered as great successes.

Oddly enough, Malthusianism has survived, thanks to the concept of environmental limits to growth. The absorptive capacity of the atmosphere, not land, is now the binding constraint; the seemingly insatiable appetite for fossil-fuel-based energy consumption replaces sex as the motive force; and the potentially catastrophic biophysical effects of global warming are stand-ins for Malthus's preventative and positive checks. Time will tell.

The increase in real incomes coupled with the decline in fertility has had consequences that were poorly foreseen and that set up today's problems. The first issue is that declining fertility tilts society toward the higher age brackets—the aging of the population. At the same time, increasing income is spent in part on better health (longer lives) and in part on longer retirements, which are real rewards, but which require funding. Reconciling retirement and health funding needs in an aging population with a shrinking labor force is fraught with difficulties. Doing so in a fashion that sustains the intergenerational "bargain" and also accommodates different views on the role of the welfare state in social spending compounds the difficulties.

A second issue arises from sustained sub-replacement level fertility rates. Setting aside immigration or implausible large increases in life expectancy, this implies continuing population decline. This is a new issue with no close precedent in human history. It was not seen initially as part of the demographic transition. An economic case for allowing population decline can be made as the "economies of scale" argument appears weak in an integrated world economy. A decline could also be strongly supported on environmental grounds. But political, social, and cultural considerations may dominate the discussions. In any event forecasting long-term fertility has a poor track record, and serious decline may not materialize.

Certain threads have linked various chapters in this story. One is the interaction of economic and demographic analysis. There have been several high points. First, both Adam Smith and Malthus gave full play to labor, and thus population, in their economic frameworks (but with very different conclusions). Although attention to population then lapsed for a century or so, it was rediscovered in the Depression years, in the postwar development literature, and now in the context of new growth theory. Economics and demography are being reintegrated. Second, as discussed in chapter 6, a unified theory has been constructed that attempts to endogenize both economic and demographic variables, and to account for the demographic transition, in a modern growth model. This is an advance over the Classical Model, which led to a stationary economy. But a satisfactory theory of long-term population—either stable or in continuous decline—has yet to emerge. Third, microeconomic analysis of family and fertility decisions brought economics into demography and offered new insights in both disciplines. Finally, the exposition of changing age structure in the demographic transition laid the groundwork for the idea of a demographic bonus and a subsequent demographic burden. This has helped bring demography into growth economics. Each approach has been nurtured by the other.

Another thread involves drawing the correct line between private and public interests. Childbearing is a private matter with societal consequences. What are the guidelines for government intervention? The seemingly easy economic answer is when the social cost–benefit calculus departs sharply from the private calculus—in other words in situations of strong externalities. But are the externalities of childbearing positive (increasing the labor pool to help support future retirees) or negative (increasing atmospheric CO_2 loadings)? Can they be quantified? Are there more precise tools for policy interventions? Remember that Adam Smith's support for free markets rested on an invisible hand that guides economic actions toward maximum welfare, but there is no invisible hand in the making of babies. In the absence of very compelling evidence, a cautious policy is appropriate in using state powers to either suppress or encourage greater fertility.

The public–private balance for funding retirement is also disputed. The trend is to reduce public pension benefits and shift retirement responsibility to individuals. Should this be accompanied by mandatory savings schemes? If not, will private-sector prudence and foresight be adequate? In broader terms, aging will test the welfare state in advanced countries and bring great challenges to those developing countries in which social spending and intergenerational transfers remain mainly at the family level.

Finally, looking back underscores the frequently alarmist and orotund language in which population matters have been presented to the public. Malthus set the tone but many followed. What explains this? The views are divided between those who see a teeming, overpopulated world— Robert McNamara who fingered rampant population growth as the greatest obstacle to development; the ecologist Garrett Hardin who asserted that freedom to breed will bring ruin to us all—and those who foresaw demographic suicide—the eminent French statistician Jacques Bertillon, who, at the end of the nineteenth century, thought he saw firm proof of the imminent disappearance of France; and, following Oswald Spengler a century earlier, the modern-day prophets of Western decline. Keynes himself first saw the Malthusian devil of overpopulation, but later the equally fierce devil of population decline. What accounts for the exorbitant language and dire views? The easy answer, that exaggeration and peril sell books, may be a sufficient explanation for some contributions. Indeed, the demographer James Coleman speaks of a moralizing apocalyptical tradition of popular American "disaster demography." But this is insufficient to account for the strong views of men of the stature of Malthus, McNamara, Hardin, Bertillon, and Keynes.

One can only speculate. The second most obvious answer is that indeed there have been perilous points in population history, whose resolution was at the time difficult to foresee. The wolves were circling but did not strike. Grain from the New World powered the European population that made the Industrial Revolution, and in the process raising living standards and decreasing fertility. The Green Revolution arrived when world population growth hit its peak but the dire warnings had been heeded and population planning was embedded in many developing countries. The unexpected and extended baby boom following World War II reversed the declining birth rate in the West and, via population momentum, delayed any serious population decline and aging issues in advanced countries until well into the twenty-first century. That testing is still in front of us, however, and to blithely assume it will be successfully met is premature. Thrice saved from population explosion or implosion does not deliver us for all time.

A final explanation for alarmism is that the most visual population policy is immigration policy. By its very nature, immigration stirs strong feelings and may account for the shrill tone of much of the popular writing on population.

IN PROSPECT

It would be relatively easy to cobble together some of the more extreme economic and demographic estimates, add in generational, ethnic, and political frictions, misconstrue GDP as a complete and accurate measure of well-being, and produce a bleak and dysfunctional future. But that would not convey an accurate description of our prospects. At the same time, to dismiss population decline and aging as inconsequential would be equally inaccurate. A modestly positive tone best fits our view.

The negatives are well known and need not be repeated here. Support for a modestly positive outlook can be summarized in the following points.

1. Using the new metric of aging based on remaining life expectancy (chapter 8), the number of the aged and the speed of aging shrinks substantially. Old age is being continually postponed.
2. Closely related, the compression of morbidity (healthy aging) thesis supports increased labor-force participation by the early elderly. This slows or reverses shrinkage of the labor force and reduces pension obligations, a double win for economic and public finance objectives.
3. Other labor-market reforms can potentially increase labor supply at little cost, as for example scrapping mandatory retirement requirements, establishing flexible work conditions, reducing involuntary unemployment, and speeding youth into first jobs. Greater investment in physical and human capital can increase productivity of the workforce.

4. Studies suggest that aging is not the primary driver of health-care costs (although old age itself is costly). Some advanced countries have found means to stabilize these costs as a share of GDP, offering hope to others.
5. Because countries are at different stages of the demographic transition, international movement of goods, services, capital, technology, and people will improve productivity and reduce aging costs. International differences in age structures are a legitimate source of comparative advantage and promote gains from trade.
6. Population decline per se is unlikely to involve large economic costs.
7. With appropriate policies, many people will indirectly benefit from an environmental bonus associated with a smaller population (unless dissipated by rising consumption).
8. The remaining costs of aging, after appropriate coping strategies have been taken, should be set against the real welfare gains of longer and healthier lives. As conventionally measured, these welfare gains are omitted from growth statistics.

If, after careful consideration of the real welfare costs of deploying some coping measures, and if, after considering the diverse benefits that have already accrued from the demographic transition, including the earlier demographic bonus, countries remain concerned about any remaining slowdown in per capita income growth, they may wish to consider a deliberate de-growth strategy. That might involve switching emphasis from growth to equitable distribution and economic security.

REFERENCES

CHAPTER 1

Bell, F. and M. Miller n.d. "Life Tables for the United States Social Security Area 1900–2100." Actuarial Study 120. Table 10. Accessed at www.ssa.gov/oact/ NOTES/as120/LifeTables_Body.html

Goldewijk, K. 2005. "Three Centuries of Population Growth: A Spatially Referenced Population (Density) Database for 1700–2000." *Population and Environment* 26(4): 343–367.

Lam, D. 2011. "How the World Survived the Population Bomb." Population Studies Center, University of Michigan Report 11–743. www.psc.isr.umich.edu/pubs/ abs/7325

Lee, R. 2003. "The Demographic Transition: Three Centuries of Fundamental Change." *Journal of Economic Perspectives* 17(4): 167–190.

Maddison, A. 2010. "Statistics on World Population, GDP and Per Capita GDP 1–2008AD." Available at http://www.ggdc.net/maddison/orindex.html.

McEvedy, C., and R.Jones. 1978. *Atlas of Population History*. Middlesex, UK: Penguin.

Scherbov, S., W. Lutz, and W. Sanderson. 2011. "The Uncertain Timing of Reaching 8 Billion, Peak World Population, and Other Demographic Milestones." *Population and Development Review* 37(3): 571–578.

UN Department of Economic and Social Affairs. 2004. "World Population to 2300." New York, NY. www.un.org/esa/population/publications/longrange2/ WorldPop2300final.pdf

United Nations. 2012a. "UN Population Aging and Development Report." New York, NY. www.un.org/population/publications/2012PopAgeingDev_Chart/ 2012AgeingWallchart.html

United Nations. 2012b. "UN World Population Prospects." Revision. New York, NY.

US Census Bureau. 2010. International Data Base. Accessed at www.census.gov/ population/international/data/idb/informationGatateway.php

CHAPTER 2

Collard, D. 2001. "Malthus, Population, and the Generational Bargain." *History of Political Economy* 33(4): 697–716.

Corry, B. A. 1959. "Malthus and Keynes—A Reconsideration." *Economic Journal* 69(276): 717–724.

Crafts, N. F. R., and T. C. Mills. 1994. "Trends in Real Wages in Britain, 1750–1913." *Explorations in Economic History* 31: 176–194.

Cummins, N. 2009. "Marital Fertility and Wealth in Transition Era France, 1750–1850." Paris School of Economics Working Paper No. 2009–2016.

Dorfman, R. 1989. "Thomas Robert Malthus and David Ricardo." *Journal of Economic Perspectives* 3(3): 153–164.

Gilbert, G. 1980. "Economic Growth and the Poor in Malthus' *Essay on Population*." *History of Political Economy* 12(2): 83–96.

Hardin, G. 1968. "The Tragedy of the Commons." *Science* 162(3859): 1243–1248.

Johnson, D. G. 1997. "Agriculture and the Wealth of Nations." *American Economic Review* 87(2): 1–12.

Keynes, J. M. 1937. "Some Economic Consequences of a Declining Population." *Eugenics Review* 29(1): 13–17.

Lam, D. 2011. "How the World Survived the Population Bomb: Lessons from 50 Years of Extraordinary Demographic History." *Demography* 48(4): 1239–1262.

Langer, W. 1975. "The Origins of the Birth Control Movement in England in the Early Nineteenth Century." *Journal of Interdisciplinary History* 5(4): 669–686.

Lee, J., and W. Feng. 1999. "Malthusian Models and Chinese Realities: The Chinese Demographic System 1700–2000." *Population and Development Review* 25(1): 33–65.

Lindert, P. 1998. "Poor Relief before the Welfare State: Britain versus the Continent, 1780–1880." *European Review of Economic History* 2: 101–140.

Malthus, T. 1798. *An Essay on the Principle of Population.* London: J. Johnson. Available at http://www.econlib.org/library/Malthus/malPop.html.

Ohlin, G. 1992. "The Population Concern." *Ambio* 21(1): 6–9.

O'Rourke, K. 1997. "The European Grain Invasion, 1870–1913." *Journal of Economic History* 57(4): 775–801.

Petersen, W. 1955. "John Maynard Keynes's Theories of Population and the Concept of 'Optimum.'" *Population Studies* 8(3): 228–246.

Petersen, W. 1979. "Malthus and the Intellectuals." *Population and Development Review* 5(3): 469–478.

Robbins, L. 1929. "Notes on the Probable Consequences of the Advent of a Stationary Population in Great Britain." *Economica* 25: 71–82.

Schofield, R. 1983. "The Impact of Scarcity and Plenty on Population Change in England, 1541–1871." *Journal of Interdisciplinary History* 14(2): 265–291.

Seidl, I., and C. Tisdell. 1999. "Carrying Capacity Reconsidered: From Malthus' Population Theory to Cultural Carrying Capacity." *Ecological Economics* 31: 395–408.

Smil, V. 1994. "How Many People Can the Earth Feed?" *Population and Development Review* 20(2): 255–392.

Spengler, J. J. 1936. "French Population Theory since 1800: II." *Journal of Political Economy* 44(6): 743–766.

Spengler, J. J. 1945. "Malthus's Total Population Theory: A Restatement and Reappraisal." *Canadian Journal of Economics and Political Science*, February and May issues.

Tomlinson, R. 1985. "The 'Disappearance' of France, 1896–1940: French Politics and the Birth Rate." *Historical Journal* 28(2): 405–415.

Toye, J. 1997. "Keynes on Population and Economic Growth." *Cambridge Journal of Economics* 21: 1–26.

Weyl, W. 1912. "Depopulation in France." *North American Review* 195(676): 343–355.

Wrigley, E. A., and R. S. Schofield. 1981. *The Population History of England 1541–1871.* London: Edward Arnold.

CHAPTER 3

Boserup, E. 1976. "Environment, Population, and Technology in Primitive Societies." *Population and Development Review* 2(1): 21–36.

Jevons, W. S. 1866. *The Coal Question: An Inquiry Concerning the Progress of the Nation, and the Probable Exhaustion of Our Coal Mines.* London and Cambridge: Macmillan and Co.

Kelley, A. C. 1988. "Economic Consequences of Population Change in the Third World." *Journal of Economic Literature* 26: 1685–1728.

Lee, J., and W. Feng. 1999. "Malthusian Models and Chinese Realities: The Chinese Demographic System 1700–2000." *Population and Development Review* 25(1): 33–65.

Pearson, C. 2000. *Economics and the Global Environment.* Cambridge, UK, and New York: Cambridge University Press.

Singer, H. 1941. "The Coal Question Reconsidered: Effects of Economy and Substitution." *Review of Economic Studies* 8(3): 166–177.

Spengler, J. 1966a. "The Economist and the Population Question." *American Economic Review* 56(1): 1–24.

Spengler, J. 1966b. "Was Malthus Right?" *Southern Economic Journal* 33(1): 17–34.

World Bank. 1984. *World Development Report.* Washington, DC: World Bank.

CHAPTER 4

Accinelli, E., and G. B. Brida. 2007. "Population Growth and the Solow-Swan Model." *International Journal of Ecological Economics and Statistics* 8(S07): 54–63.

Arrow, K. 1962. "The Economic Implications of Learning by Doing." *Review of Economic Studies* 29(3): 155–173.

Barkai, H. 1969. "A Formal Outline of a Smithian Growth Model." *Quarterly Journal of Economics* 83(3): 396–414.

Becker, G., E.Glaeser, and K. Murphy. 1999. "Population and Economic Growth." *AEA Papers and Proceedings* 89(2): 145–149.

Becker, G., K. Murphy, and R. Tamura. 1990. "Human Capital, Fertility, and Economic Growth." *Journal of Political Economy* 98(5): S12–S37.

Birdsall, N. 1988. "Economic Approaches to Population Growth." In H. Chenery and T. N. Srinivasan (eds.), *Handbook of Development Economics*, 1:478–542. Amsterdam. Elsevier Science Publishers B.V.

Boserup, E. 1976. "Environment, Population, and Technology in Primitive Societies." *Population and Development Review* 2(1): 21–36.

Cellarier, L., and R. Day. 2011. "Structural Instabilities and Alternative Development Scenarios." *Journal of Population Economics* 24: 1165–1180.

Chenery, H. B., and A. M. Strout. 1966. "Foreign Assistance and Economic Development." *American Economic Review* 56(4.1): 679–733.

Coale, A. J., and E. M. Hoover. 1958. *Population Growth and Economic Development in Low-Income Countries.* Princeton: Princeton University Press.

Domar, E. D. 1946. "Capital Expansion, Rate of Growth, and Employment." *Econometrica* 14(2): 137–147.

Easterly, W. 1999. "The Ghost of Financing Gap: Testing the Growth Model of the International Financial Institutions." *Journal of Development Economics* 60(2): 423–438.

Enke, S. 1966. "The Economic Aspects of Slowing Population Growth." *Economic Journal* 76(301): 44–56.

Enke, S. 1971. "The Economic Consequences of Rapid Population Growth." *Economic Journal* 81(324): 800–811.

Enke, S. 1974. "Reducing Fertility to Accelerate Development." *Economic Journal* 84(334): 349–366.

Feen, R. 1996. "Keeping the Balance: Ancient Greek Philosophical Concerns with Population and Environment." *Population and Development: A Journal of Interdisciplinary Studies* 17(6): 447–458.

Fei, J., and G. Ranis. 1964. *Development of the Labor Surplus Economy: Theory and Policy*. Homewood, IL: Richard A. Irwin, Inc.

Grossman, G., and E. Helpman. 1994. "Endogenous Innovation and the Theory of Growth." *Journal of Economic Perspectives* 8(1): 2–44.

Harrod, R. F. 1939. "An Essay in Dynamic Theory." *Economic Journal* 49(193): 14–33.

Johnson, G. 1997. "Agriculture and the Wealth of Nations." *American Economic Review* 87(2): 1–12.

Jones, C. 1995. "R & D Based Models of Economic Growth." *Journal of Political Economy* 103(4): 759–784.

Kelley, A. C. 1988. "Economic Consequences of Population Change in the Third World." *Journal of Economic Literature* 26:1685–1728.

Lavezzi, A. 2003. "Smith, Marshall, and Young on the Division of Labor and Economic Growth." *European Journal of the History of Economic Thought* 10(1): 81–108.

Lewis, W. A. 1954. "Economic Development with Unlimited Supplies of Labor." *Manchester School of Economic and Social Studies* 22: 139–191.

Lucas, R. 1988. "On the Mechanics of Economic Development." *Journal of Monetary Economics* 22: 3–42.

Malthus, Thomas Robert. 1798. *An Essay on the Principle of Population*. 1st ed. London: J. Johnson. Available at http://www.econlib.org/library/Malthus/maPop.html.

Mill, J. S. [1848] 1909. *Principles of Political Economy*. 7th ed. London: Longmans, Green and Co. Available at http://www.econlib.org/library/mill/mlP61.html#Bk.IV,ChV6.

National Research Council. 1986. *Population Growth and Economic Development: Policy Questions*. Washington, DC: National Academy Press.

Nelson, R. 1956. "A Theory of the Low-Level Equilibrium Trap in Underdeveloped Economies." *American Economic Review* 46(5): 894–908.

Ranis, G., and J. Fei. 1961. "A Theory of Economic Development." *American Economic Review* 50(4): 533–565.

Romer, P. 1986. "Increasing Returns and Long-Run Growth." *Journal of Political Economy* 94(5): 1002–1037.

Romer, P. 1990. "Endogenous Technological Change." *Journal of Political Economy* 98(5): S71–S102.

Samuelson, P. 1977. "A Modern Theorist's Vindication of Adam Smith." *American Economic Review* 67(1): 42–49.

Samuelson, P. 1978. "The Canonical Classical Model of Political Economy." *Journal of Economic Literature* 16(4): 1415–1431.

Sanderson, W. 1980. "Economic-Demographic Simulation Models." Research Report, International Institute for Applied Systems Analysis, 112. Vienna.

Sato, R. 1964. "The Harrod-Domar Model vs the Neo-classical Growth Model." *Economic Journal* 74(294): 380–387.

Scott, M. 1992. "A New Theory of Endogenous Economic Growth." *Oxford Review of Economic Policy* 8(4): 29–42.

Sinding, S. 2009. "Population, Poverty and Economic Development." *Phil. Trans. R. Soc B* 364: 3023–3030.

Smith, Adam. 1776. *An Inquiry into the Nature and Causes of the Wealth of Nations.* 5th ed. London: Methuen & Co. Ltd. Available at http://www.econlib.org/library/Smith/sm WN.html.

Solow, R. 1956. "A Contribution to the Theory of Economic Growth." *Quarterly Journal of Economics* 70(1): 65–94.

Solow, R. 1974. "The Economics of Resources or the Resources of Economics." *American Economic Review* 64(2): 1–14.

Swan, T. 1956. "Economic Growth and Capital Accumulation." *Economic Record* 23: 344–361.

Turner, A. 2009. "Population Priorities: The Challenge of Continued Economic Growth." *Phil. Trans. R. Soc. B* 364: 2977–2984.

CHAPTER 5

Alcott, B. 2012. "Population Matters in Ecological Economics." *Ecological Economics* 80: 109–120.

Arrhenius, G. 2003. "The Very Repugnant Conclusion." In K. Segerberg and R. Sliwinski (eds.), *Logic, Law, Morality: 13 Essays in Practical Philosophy in Honour of Lennart Aquist.* Uppsala: Uppsala Philosophical Studies, Department of Philosophy. p. 167–180.

Arrow, K., B. Bplin, R. Costanza, P. Dasgupta, C. Folke, C. S. Holling, B-O. Janssen. S. Levin, K_G. Maler, C. Perrings, D. Pimental.1995. "Economic Growth, Carrying Capacity, and the Environment." *Science* 268: 520–521.

Arrow, K., P. Dasgupta, L. Goulder, G. Daily, P. Ehrlich, G. Heal, S. Lavin. K-G. Mäler, S. Schneider, D. Starrett, B. Walker 2004. "Are We Consuming Too Much?" *Journal of Economic Perspectives* 18(3): 147–172.

Atkinson, A. B. 2014. "Optimum Population, Welfare Economics, and Inequality." In I. Goldin (ed.), *Is the Planet Full?* Oxford: Oxford University Press.

Birdsall, N. 1988. "Economic Approaches to Population Growth." In H. Chenery and T. N. Srinivasan (eds.), *Handbook of Development Economics*, Vol. 1. Amsterdam: Elsevier Science Publishers. p. 478–542.

Blackorby, C., and D. Donaldson. 1984. "Social Criteria for Evaluating Population Change." *Journal of Public Economics* 25: 13–33.

Bohn, H., and C. Stuart. (forthcoming). "Calculation of a Population Externality." *American Economic Journal: Economic Policy*

Broome, J. 2005. "Should We Value Population?" *Journal of Political Philosophy* 13(4): 399–413.

Cohen, J. 1995. "Population Growth and Earth's Human Carrying Capacity." *Science* 269: 341–345.

Cowen, T. 1996. "What Do We Learn from the Repugnant Conclusion?" *Ethics* 106: 754–775.

Dalton, H. 1928. "The Theory of Population." *Economica* 22: 28–50.

Dasgupta, P. S. 1969. "On the Concept of Optimum Population." *Review of Economic Studies* 36(3): 295–318.

———. 1998. "Population, Consumption and Resources: Ethical Issues." *Ecological Economics* 24: 139–152.

Ehrlich, I., and F. Lui. 1997. "The Problem of Population and Growth: A Review of the Literature from Malthus to Contemporary Models of Endogenous Population and Endogenous Growth." *Journal of Economic Dynamics and Control* 21: 205–242.

Fenn, R. 1996. "Keeping the Balance: Ancient Greek Philosophical Concerns with Population and Environment." *Population and Environment: A Journal of Interdisciplinary Studies* 17(6): 447–458.

Gottlieb, M. 1945. "The Theory of Optimum Population for a Closed Economy." *Journal of Political Economy* 53(4): 289–316.

Hardin, G. 1986. "Cultural Carrying Capacity: A Biological Approach to Human Problems." *BioScience* 36(9): 599–606.

Lee, R., and T. Miller. 1990. "Population Policies and Externalities to Childbearing." *The ANNALS of the American Academy of Political and Social Science* 510: 17–32.

Meier, V., and M. Werding. 2010. "Ageing and the Welfare State: Securing Sustainability." *Oxford Review of Economic Policy* 26(4): 655–673.

Mulgan, T. 2002. "The Reverse Repugnant Conclusion." *Utilitas* 14(3): 360–364.

O'Neill, B., and L. Wexler. 2000. "The Greenhouse Externality to Childbearing: A Sensitivity Analysis." *Climatic Change* 47: 283–324.

Overbeek, J. 1973. "Wicksell on Population." *Economic Development and Cultural Change* 21(2): 205–211.

Parfit, D. 2004. "Overpopulation and the Quality of Life." In J. Ryberg and T. Tännsjö (eds.), *The Repugnant Conclusion*. Dordrecht, The Netherlands: Kluwer. p. 7-22.

Pearson, C. 2000. *Economics and the Global Environment*. Cambridge, UK, and New York: Cambridge University Press.

Pearson, C., and A. Pryor. 1978. *Environment North and South: An Economic Interpretation*. New York: John Wiley & Sons.

Pimentel, D., R. Harman, M. Pacenza, J. Pecarsky, M. Pimentel, 1 994. "Natural Resources and an Optimal Human Environment." *Population and Environment* 15(5): 347–367.

Razin, A., and E. Sadka. 1995. *Population Economics*. Cambridge, MA, and London: MIT Press.

Renstrom, T., and L. Spataro. 2011. "The Optimum Growth Rate for Population under Critical Level Utilitarianism." *Journal of Population Economics* 24: 1181–1201.

Samuelson, P. 1975. "The Optimum Growth Rate for Population." *International Economic Review* 16(3): 531–538.

Samuelson, P. 1976. "The Optimum Growth Rate for Population: An Agreement and Evaluations." *International Economic Review* 17(2): 516–525.

Shiell, L. 2008. "The Repugnant Conclusion and Utilitarianism under Domain Restrictions." *Journal of Public Economic Theory* 10(6): 2011–1031.

Van den Bergh, J., and P. Rietveld. 2004. "Reconsidering the Limits to World Population: Meta-analysis and Meta-Prediction." *BioScience* 54(3): 195–204.

Wilkenson, L. P. 1978. "Classical Approaches to Population and Family Planning." *Population and Development Review* 4(3): 439–455.

Wolf, D., R. Lee, T. Miller, G. Donehower, A. Genest 2011. "Fiscal Externalities of Becoming a Parent." *Population and Development Review* 37(2): 241–266.

CHAPTER 6

Andersson, B. 2001. "Scandinavian Evidence on Growth and Age Structure." *Regional Studies* 35(5): 377–390.

Angles, L. 2010. "Demographic Transitions: Analyzing the Effects of Mortality on Fertility." *Journal of Population Economics* 23: 99–110.

Basten, S., W. Lutz, and S. Scherbov. 2013. "Very Long Run Population Scenarios to 2300 and the Implications of Sustained Low Fertility." *Demographic Research* 28(article 39): 1145–1166.

Becker, G., K. Murphy, and R. Tamura. 1990. "Human Capital, Fertility, and Economic Growth." *Journal of Political Economy* 98(5) Part 2: S12–S37.

Birdsall, N. 1988. "Economic Approaches to Population Growth." In H. Chenery and T. N. Srinivasan (eds.), *Handbook of Development Economics*, Vol. 1. Amsterdam: Elsevier Science Publishers. p. 477–542.

Bloom, D., D. Canning, G. Fink, and J. Finley. 2009. "Fertility, Female Labor Force Participation, and the Demographic Dividend." *Journal of Economic Growth* 14: 79–101.

Bloom, D., D. Canning, and J. Sevilla. 2003. *The Demographic Dividend: A New Perspective on the Economic Consequences of Population Change*. Santa Monica, CA: Rand.

Bloom, D., and J. Williamson. 1998. "Demographic Transitions and Economic Miracles in Emerging Asia." *World Bank Economic Review* 12(3): 419–455.

Bongaarts, J. 2009. "Human Population Growth and the Demographic Transition." *Phil. Trans. R. Soc. B* 364: 2985–2990.

Bongaarts, J. 2010. "The Causes of Educational Differences in Fertility in sub-Saharan Africa." *Vienna Yearbook of Population Research* 8: 31–50.

Bongaarts, J., and J. Casterline. 2012. "Fertility Transition: Is sub-Saharan Africa Different?" *Population and Development Review*. 38 (Supplement): 153–168.

Bongaarts, J., and T. Sobotka. 2012. "A Demographic Explanation for the Recent Rise in European Fertility." *Population and Development Review* 38(1): 83–120.

Cellarier, L., and R. Day. 2011. "Structural Instability and Alternative Development Scenarios." *Journal of Population Economics* 24: 1165–1180.

Couzin-Frankel, J. 2011. "A Pitched Battle over Life Spans." *Science* 333: 549–550.

Demeny, P. 2011. "Population Policy and the Demographic Transition: Performance, Prospects, and Options." *Population and Development Review* 37 (Supplement): 249–274.

Eastwood, R., and M. Lipton. 2011. "Demographic Transition in sub-Saharan Africa: How Big Will the Economic Dividend Be?" *Population Studies* 65(1): 9–35.

Eggleston, K., and V. Fuchs. 2012. "The New Demographic Transition: Most Gains in Life Expectancy Realized Late in Life." *Journal of Economic Perspectives* 26(3): 137–156.

Ehrlich, I., and J. Kim. 2005. "Endogenous Fertility, Longevity, and Economic Dynamics: Using a Malthusian Framework to Account for the Historical Evidence of Population and Economic Growth." *Journal of Asian Economics* 16(5): 789–806.

Galor, O. 2005. "From Stagnation to Growth: Unified Growth Theory." In P. Aghion and S. Durlauf (eds.), *Handbook of Economic Growth*. Amsterdam: North Holland. p. 171–293

Galor, O., and O. Moav. 2002. "Natural Selection and the Origins of Economic Growth." *Quarterly Journal of Economics* 117(4): 1133–1191.

Galor, O., and D. Weil. 2000. "Population, Technology, and Growth: From Malthusian Stagnation to Demographic Transition and Beyond." *American Economic Review* 90(4): 806–828.

Goldstein, J., T. Sobotka, and A. Jasilioniene. 2009. "The End of the 'Lowest Low' Fertility?" *Population and Development Review* 35(4): 663–699.

James, K. S., V. Skirbekk, and J. Van Bavel. 2012. "Education and the Global Fertility Transition—Forward." *Vienna Yearbook of Population Research* 10: 1–8.

Jones, G. 2012. "Late Marriage and Low Fertility in Singapore: The Limits of Policy." *Japanese Journal of Population* 10(1): 89–101.

KC, S., and H. Lentzer. 2010. "The Effects of Education in Adult Mortality and Disability: A Global Perspective." *Vienna Yearbook of Population Research* 8: 201–235.

Lee, R. 2003. "The Demographic Transition: Three Centuries of Fundamental Change." *Journal of Economic Perspectives* 17(4): 167–190.

Lesthaeghe, R. 2010. "The Unfolding Story of the Second Demographic Transition." *Population and Development Review* 36(2): 211–251.

Lutz, W. 2010. "Education Will Be at the Heart of 21st Century Demography." *Vienna Yearbook of Population Research* 8: 9–16.

Lutz, W., S. Basten, and E. Striessnig. 2013. "The Future of Fertility: Future Trends in Fertility Size among Low Fertility Populations." In E. Kaufman and W. B Wilcox (eds.), *Wither the Child?: Causes and Consequences of Low Fertility.* Boulder, CO, and London: Paradigm Press. p. 205–233

Lutz, W., and Samir KC. 2010. "Dimensions of Population Projections: What We Know about Future Population Trends and Structures." *Phil. Trans. R. Soc. B.* 365: 2779–2791.

Lutz, W., B. O'Neill, and S. Scherbov. 2003. "Europe's Population at a Turning Point." *Science* 229: 1991–1992.

Lutz, W., S. Scherbov, G. Y. Cao, Q. Rem, X. Zheng. 2007. "China's Uncertain Demographic Present and Future." *Vienna Yearbook of Population Research*, 37–59.

Mascarenhas, M., S. Flaxman, T. Boerma, S Vanderpoel, G. Stevens 2012. "National, Regional, and Global Trends in Infertility Prevalence since 1990: A Systematic Analysis of 277 Health Surveys." *PLOS Medicine* 9(12), e1001356. doi: 101371.

Mason, A., and R. Lee. 2006. "Reform and Support Systems for the Elderly in Developing Countries: Capturing the Second Demographic Dividend." *Genus* 62(2): 11–35.

Meara, E., S. Richards, and D. Cutler. 2008. "The Gap Gets Bigger: Changes in Mortality and Life Expectancy, by Education, 1981–2000." *Health Affairs* 27(2): 350–360.

Navaneetham, K. 2002. "Age Structural Transition and Economic Growth: Evidence from South and South East Asia." National University of Singapore, Asian MetaCentre Research Paper Series 7.

Oeppen, J., and J. Vaupel. 2002. "Broken Limits to Life Expectancy." *Science* 296: 1029–1031.

Olshansky, S. K., D. Passaro, T. Brody, L. Hayflick, R. Butler, D. Allison D. Ludwig. 2005. "A Potential Decline in Life Expectancy in the United States in the 21st Century." *New England Journal of Medicine* 352(11): 1138–1145.

Peeters, A., J. Barendregt, F. Willekens, J. Machenbach, Abdull Al Mamun, L. Bonneux. 2003. "Obesity in Adulthood and Its Consequences for Life Expectancy: A Life-Table Analysis." *Annuals of Internal Medicine* 138: 24–32.

Pijnenburg, M., and C. Leget. 2007. "Who Wants to Live Forever? Three Arguments against Extending Human Lifespans." *Journal of Medical Ethics* 33(10): 585–587.

Razin, A., and E. Sadka. 1995. *Population Economics*. Cambridge, MA, and London: MIT Press.

Reher, D. 2011. "Economic and Social Implications of the Demographic Transition." *Population and Development Review* 37 (Supplement): 11–33.

Shapiro, D. 2012. "Women's Education and Fertility Transition in sub-Saharan Africa." *Vienna Yearbook of Population Research* 10: 9–30.

Sobotka, T., V. Skirbekk, and D. Philipov. 2011. "Economic Recession and Fertility in the Developed World." *Population and Development Review* 37(2): 267–306.

Spengler, O. [1918] 1928. *The Decline of the West*, Vol. 2. Translated by C. F. Atkinson. As quoted in *Population and Development Review Archives* 28(4) (2000): 787–796.

UN. 2012. World Population Prospects, the 2012 Revision.

Van Bavel, J. 2010. "Subreplacement Fertility in the West before the Baby Boom: Past and Current Practices." *Population Studies* 64(1): 1–18.

Wang, F. 2011. "The Future of a Demographic Overachiever: Long-Term Implications of the Demographic Transition in China." *Population and Development Review* 37 (Supplement): 173–190.

Westoff, C. 2012. "The Recent Fertility Transition in Rwanda." Population and Development Review 38 (supplement): 169-212.

Wusu, O. 2012. "A Reassessment of the Effects of Female Education and Employment on Fertility in Nigeria." *Vienna Yearbook of Population Research* 10: 31-48.

Zemac, J., D. Hallberg, and T. Lindh. 2010. "Low Fertility and Long Run Growth in an Economy with a Large Public Sector." *European Journal of Population* 26: 183–205.

CHAPTER 7

Ackerman, F., and E. Stanton. 2013. "Climate Impacts on Agriculture: A Challenge to Complacency." Global Development and Environment Institute Working Paper No. 13–11.

Alcott, B. 2010. "Impact Caps: Why Pollution, Affluence, and Technology Strategies Should Be Abandoned." *Journal of Cleaner Production* 18: 552–560.

Alcott, B. 2012. "Population Matters in Ecological Economics." *Ecological Economics* 80: 109–120.

Brown, L., G. Gardner, and B. Halwell. 1998. "Beyond Malthus: Sixteen Dimensions of the Population Problem." Worldwatch Institute Paper 143. Washington, DC.

Chakravorty, U., M.-H. Hubert, and L. Nostbakken. 2009. "Food versus Fuel." *Annual Review of Resource Economics* 1: 645–663.

Dalton, M., B. O'Neill, A. Prskawetz, L. Jiang, and J. Pitkin. 2008. "Population Aging and Future Carbon Emissions in the United States." *Energy Economics* 30: 642–675.

de la Croix, D., and A. Gosseries. 2012. "The Natalist Bias of Pollution Control." *Journal of Environmental Economics and Management* 63(2): 271–287.

de Sherbinin, A., D. Carr, S. Cassels, and L. Jiang. 2007. "Population and Environment." *Annual Review of Environmental Resources* 32: 345–373.

Dietz, T., E. Rosa, and R. York. 2007. "Driving the Human Ecological Footprint." *Frontiers in Ecological Economics* 5(1): 13–18.

Fargione, J., J. Hill, D. Tillman, and S. Polasky. 2008. "Land Clearing and the Biofuel Carbon Debt." *Science* 319: 1235–1238.

Gornall, J., R. Betts, E. Burke, R. Clark, J. Camp, K. Willet, A. Wiltshire 2010. "Implications of Climate Change for Agricultural Productivity in the Early Twenty-first Century." *Philosophical Transactions of the Royal Society B* 365: 2973–2989.

Hanemann, W. 2008. "What is the Economic Cost of Climate Change?" Department of Agriculture and Resource Economics, University of California Berkeley, Working Paper 1071.

Jiang, L., and K. Harrdee. 2009. *How Do Population Trends Matter to Climate Change?* Population Action International. Accessed at www.populationaction.org

Lobell, D., W. Schlenker, and J. Costa-Roberts. 2011. "Climate Trends and Global Crop Production." *Science* 333: 616–620.

Murtaugh, P., and M. Schlax. 2009. "Reproduction and the Carbon Legacies of Individuals." *Global Environmental Change* 19: 14–20.

Nelson G., M. Rosegrant, A Palazzo, I. Gray, C Ingersoll, R. Robertson, S. Tokgoz, T. Zhu, T. Sulser, C. Ringler, S. Msangi, and L.You 2010. "Food Security and Climate Change." International Food Policy Research Institute Issue Brief 66.

O'Neill, B., M. Dalton, R. Fuchs, L. Jiang, S. Pachauri, and K. Zigova. 2010. "Global Demographic Trends and Future Carbon Emissions." *Proceedings of the National Academy of Sciences* 107(41): 17521–17526.

Pearson, C. 2011. *Economics and the Challenge of Global Warming.* New York: Cambridge University Press.

Pimental, D., and M. Pimental. 2003. "Sustainability of Meat-Based and Plant-Based Diets and the Environment." *American Journal of Clinical Nutrition* 78(Supplement): 660S–663S.

Schlenker, W., and M. Roberts. 2009. "Nonlinear Temperature Effects Indicate Severe Damage to US Crop Yields under Climate Change." *Proceedings of the National Academies of Science* 106(37): 15594–15598.

Schmidhuber, J., and F. Tubiello. 2007. "Global Food Security under Climate Change." *Proceedings of the National Academy of Sciences* 104(50): 19703–19708.

Shi, A. 2003. "The Impact of Population Pressure on Global Carbon Dioxide Emissions 1975–1996: Evidence from Pooled Cross-country Data." *Ecological Economics* 44: 29–42.

Smil, V. 1994. "How Many People Can the Earth Feed?" *Population and Development Review* 20(2): 255–292.

Sokolov, A. P., et al. 2009. "Probabilistic Forecasts for the Twenty-First-Century Climate Based on Uncertainty in Emissions (Without Policy) and Climate Parameters." *American Meteorological Society* 22: 5175–5204.

Stehfest, E., L. Bouwman, D. van Vuuren, D. Elxen, B. Eickhout. 2009. "Climate Benefits of Changing Diet." *Climatic Change* 95: 83–102.

Wheeler, D., and D. Hammer. 2010. "The Economics of Population Policy for Carbon Emission Reduction." Center for Global Development Working Paper 229. Washington, DC.

Wicksell, K. 1914. "Can a Country Become Underpopulated?" Originally published in *Ekonomisk Tidskrift* 16(6): 195–208. Translated from Swedish and republished (2008) as Knut Wicksell on the Benefits of Depopulation in *Population and Development Review* 34(2): 347–355.

CHAPTER 8

Accinelli, E., and G. B. Brida. 2007. "Population Growth and the Solow-Swan Model." *International Journal of Ecological Economics and Statistics* 8(S07): 54–63.

Aghion, P., and P. Howitt. 1992. "A Model of Growth through Creative Destruction." *Econometrica* 60(2): 323–351.

Becker, G., E. Glaeser, and K. Murphy. 1999. "Population and Economic Growth." *American Economic Review* 89(2): 145–149.

Cellarier, L., and R. Day. 2011. "Structural Instability and Alternative Development Scenarios." *Journal of Population Economics* 24: 1165–1180.

Coleman, D., and R. Rowthorn. 2011. "Who's Afraid of Population Decline? A Critical Examination of Its Consequences." *Population and Development Review* 37(Supplement): 217–248.

Cutler, D., J. Poterba, L. Sheiner, and L. Summers. 1990. "An Aging Society: Opportunity or Challenge?" *Brookings Papers on Economic Activity* 1: 1–73.

Eggleston, K., and V. Fuchs. 2012. "The New Demographic Transition: Most Gains in Life Expectancy Now Realized Late in Life." *Journal of Economic Perspectives* 26(3): 137–156.

Elmendorf, D., and L. Sheiner. 2000. "Should America Save for Its Old Age? Fiscal Policy, Population Aging and National Saving." *Journal of Economic Perspectives* 14(3): 57–74.

Hashimoto, K., and K. Tabata. 2010. "Population Aging, Health Care, and Growth." *Journal of Population Economics* 23: 571–593.

Jones, C., and P. Romer. 2010. "The New Kaldor Facts: Ideas, Institutions, Population, and Human Capital." *American Economic Journal: Macroeconomics* 2(1): 224–245.

Keynes, J. M. 1937. "Some Economic Consequences of a Declining Population." *Eugenics Review* 29(1): 13–17.

Lee, R., and A. Mason. 2010. "Fertility, Human Capital, and Economic Growth over the Demographic Transition." *European Journal of Population* 26: 159–182.

Lee, R., and A. Mason. 2011. "Generational Economics in a Changing World." *Population and Development Review* 37(Supplement): 115–142.

Lindh, T., and B. Malmberg. 1999. "Age Structure Effects and Growth in the OECD 1950–1990." *Journal of Population Economics* 12: 431–449.

Longman, P. 2004. "The Global Baby Bust." *Foreign Affairs* 83(3): 64–79.

Lutz, W., W. Sanderson, and S. Scherbov. 2008. "The Coming Acceleration of Global Population Ageing." *Nature* 451: 716–719.

Maestra, N., and J. Zissimopoulos. 2010. "How Longer Work Lives Ease the Crunch of Population Aging." *Journal of Economic Perspectives* 24(1): 139–160.

Malmberg, B., T. Lindh, and M. Halvarsson. 2008. "Productivity Consequences of Workforce Aging: Stagnation or Horndal Effect?" *Population and Development Review* 34(Supplement): 238–256.

Mason, A., and R. Lee. 2006. "Reform and Support Systems for the Elderly in Developing Countries: Capturing the Second Demographic Dividend." *Genus* 62(2): 11–35.

Overbeek, J. 1973. "Mercantilism, Physiocracy and Population Theory." *South African Journal of Economics* 41(2): 108–113.

Prskawetz, A., T. Fent, and R. Guest. 2008. "Workforce Aging and Labor Productivity: The Roles of Supply and Demand in the G 7 Countries." *Population and Development Review* 34: 298–323.

Reher, D. 2007. "Towards Long-Term Population Decline: A Discussion of Relevant Issues." *European Journal of Population* 23(2): 189–207.

Romer, P. 1986. "Increasing Returns and Long-Run Growth." *Journal of Political Economy* 94(5): 1002–1037.

Romer, P. 1990. "Endogenous Technological Change." *Journal of Political Economy* 98(5): S71–S102.

Sanderson, W., and S. Scherbov. 2008. "Rethinking Age and Aging." *Population Bulletin* 63(4): 3–26.

Sanderson, W., and S. Scherbov. 2010. "Remeasuring Aging." *Science* 329: 1287–1288.

Sanderson, W., and S. Scherbov. 2013. "The Characteristics Approach to the Measurement of Aging." *Population and Development Review* 39(4): 673–685.

Skirbekk, V. 2004. "Age and Individual Productivity: A Literature Survey." *Vienna Yearbook of Population Research* 2: 133–153.

Skirbekk, V. 2008. "Age and Productivity Capacity: Descriptions, Causes, Policy." *Ageing Horizons* 8: 4–12.

Tyers, R., and Q. Shi. 2007. "Demographic Change and Policy Response: Implications for the Global Economy." *World Economy* 30(4): 537–566.

UN 2012. *Population, Ageing and Development Report.* New York: United Nations.

Weil, D. (1999). "Population Growth, Dependency, and Consumption." *American Economic Review* 89(2): 251–255.

CHAPTER 9

Aaron, H. 2011. "Social Security Reconsidered." *National Tax Journal* 64(2, Part 1): 385–414.

Adema, W., P. Fron, and M. Ladaique. 2011. "Is the European Welfare State Really More Expensive? Indicators of Social Spending 1980–2012." OECD Social. Employment and Migration Working Papers, No. 124, OECD Publishing.

Alemayehu, B., and K. Warner. 2004. "The Lifetime Distribution of Health Care Costs." *Health Services Research* 39(3): 627–642.

Auerbach, A., and R. Lee. 2011. "Welfare and Generational Equity in Sustainable Unfunded Pension Systems." *Journal of Public Economics* 95: 16–27.

Baicker, K., and J. Skinner. 2010. "Health Care Spending Growth and the Future of U.S. Tax Rates." NBER Working Paper 16772.

Barr, N., and P. Diamond. 2006. "The Economics of Pensions." *Oxford Review of Economic Policy* 22(1): 15–39.

Bommier, A., R. Lee, T. Miller, and S. Zuber. 2010. "Who Wins and Who Loses? Public Transfer Accounts for U.S. Generations Born 1850–2090." *Population and Development Review* 36(1): 1–26.

Breyer, F., J. Costa-Font, and S. Felder. 2010. "Aging, Health, and Health Care." *Oxford Review of Economic Policy* 26(4): 674–690.

CBO 2012. *The 2012 Long Term Budget Outlook.* Washington, DC: Congressional Budget Office.

Chandra, A., J. Holmes, and J. Skinner. 2013. "Is This Time Different? The Slowdown in Health Care Spending." Paper Presented at Fall 2013 Brookings Panel on Economic Activity, September 19–20.

Chomsik, R., and E. R. Whitehouse. 2010. "Trends in Pension Eligibility and Life Expectancy, 1950–2050." OECD Social, Employment and Migration Working Papers No. 105. Paris: OECD Publishing.

D'Addio, A. C., M. Keese, and E. R. Whitehouse. 2010. "Population Aging and Labor Markets." *Oxford Review of Economic Policy* 26(4): 613–635.

Fogel, R. 2009. "Forecasting the Cost of U.S. Health Care in 2040." *Journal of Policy Modeling* 31: 482–488.

Fries, J., B. Bruce, and E. Chakravarty. 2011. "Compression of Morbidity 1980–2011: A Focused Review of Paradigms and Progress." *Journal of Aging Research* 2011(Article ID26702): 1–10.

Fuchs, J. 1984. "'Though Much is Taken': Reflections on Aging, Health and Medical Care." *Milbank Memorial Fund Quarterly: Health and Society* 62(2): 143–166.

Gruenberg, E. 1977. "The Failures of Success." *Milbank Memorial Fund Quarterly: Health and Society* 55(1): 3–24.

Hagist, C., and L. Kotlikoff. 2009. "Who's Going Broke? Comparing Growth in Healthcare Expenditures in Ten OECD Countries." *Revista de Economica Publica* 188(1): 55–72.

Hall, R., and C. Jones. 2007. "The Value of Life and the Rise of Health Spending." *Quarterly Journal of Economics* 122(1): 39–72.

Heijdra, B., and W. Romp. 2009. "Retirement, Pensions, and Ageing." *Journal of Public Economics* 93: 586–604.

Hurd, M., P Martorell, A. Delavande, K, Mullen, and K. Langa. 2013. "Monetary Cost of Dementia in the United States." *New England Journal of Medicine* 368(14): 1327–1334.

Lee, R., and A. Mason. 2011. *Population Aging and the Generational Economy: A Global Perspective*. Cheltenham, UK: Edward Elgar.

Maisonneuve, C., and J. Martins. 2013. "Public Spending on Health and Long Term Care: A New Set of Projections." OECD Economic Policy Paper No. 6. Paris: OECD.

Manton, K., L. Corder, and E. Stallard. 1997. "Chronic Disability Trends in Elderly U.S. Populations: 1982–1994." *Proceedings of the National Academy of Sciences* 94: 2593–2598.

Manton, K., X. Gu, and V. Lamb. 2006. "Changes in Chronic Disability from 1982 to 2004/2005 as Measured by Long Term Function and Health in U.S. Elderly Population." *Proceedings of the National Academy of Sciences* 103(48): 18374–18379.

Manton, K., X-L Gu, A. Ullian, D. Tolley, A. Headem, and G. Lowrimore. 2009. "Long-term Economic Growth Stimulus of Human Capital Preservation in the Elderly." *Proceedings of the National Academy of Sciences* 106(50): 21080–21085.

Martin, A., M. Hartman, L. Whittle, and A. Catlin. 2014. "National Health Spending in 2012." *Health Affairs* 33(1): 67–77.

Martin, J. P., and E. R. Whitehouse. 2008. "Reforming Retirement-Income Systems: Lessons from the Recent Experience of OECD Countries." OECD Social, Employment and Migration Working Papers, No. 66. OECD Publishing.

Mason, A., R. Lee, A.-C. Tung, M.-S. Lai, and T. Miller. 2009. "Population Aging and Intergenerational Transfers: Introducing Age into National Accounts." In D.

Wise (ed.), *Developments in the Economics of Aging*. Chicago: University of Chicago Press and NBER. p. 89–122.

Meier, V., and M. Werding. 2010. "Aging and the Welfare State: Securing Sustainability." *Oxford Review of Economic Policy* 26(4): 655–673.

Murphy, K., and R. Topel. 2006. "The Value of Health and Longevity." *Journal of Political Economy* 114(5): 871–904.

National Research Council. 2012. *Aging and the Macroeconomy: Long Term Implications of an Older Population*. Washington, DC: National Academies Press.

Pearson, C. 2011. *Economics and the Challenge of Global Warming*. New York: Cambridge University Press.

Tyers, R., and G. Shi. 2007. "Demographic Change and Policy Response: Implications for the Global Economy." *World Economy* 30(4): 537–566.

Whitehouse, E. R. 2007. "Life-Expectancy Risk and Pensions: Who Bears the Burden?" OECD Social, Employment and Migration Working Papers, No. 60. OECD Publishing.

Zweifel, P., S. Felder, and M. Meiers. 1999. "Ageing of Population and Health Care Expenditures: A Red Herring?" *Health Economics* 8: 485–496.

CHAPTER 10

Ashraf, Q., D. Weil, and J. Wilde. 2013. "The Effect of Fertility Reduction on Economic Growth." *Population and Development Review* 39(1): 97–130.

Balbo, N., F. C. Billari, and M. Mills. 2013. "Fertility in Advanced Societies: A Review of Research." *European Journal of Population* 29: 1–38.

Basten, S., W. Lutz, and S. Scherbov. 2013. "Very Long Range Global Population Scenarios to 2300 and the Implications of Sustained Low Fertility." *Demographic Research* 28(39): 1145–1166.

Bloom, D. E., D. Canning, G. Fink, and J. E. Finlay. 2009. "Fertility, Female Labor Force Participation, and the Demographic Dividend." *Journal of Economic Growth* 14: 79–101.

Chapple, J. 2004. "The Dilemma Posed by Japan's Population Decline." *Electronic Journal of Contemporary Japanese Studies* 4(1).

Clark, R. L., N. Ogawa, M. Kondo, and R. Matsukra. 2010. "Population Decline, Labor Force Stability, and the Future of the Japanese Economy." *European Journal of Population* 26: 207–227.

Cortez, P., and J. Pan. 2013. "Outsourcing Household Production: Foreign Domestic Workers and Native Labor Supply in Hong Kong." *Journal of Labor Economics* 31(2): 327–371.

D'Addio, A. C., M. Keese, and E. R. Whitehouse. 2010. *"Population Aging and Labour Markets." Oxford Review of Economic Policy* 26(4): 613–635.

Demeny, P. 2011. "Population Policy and the Demographic Transition: Performance, Prospects and Options." *Population and Development Review* 37 (Supplement): 249–274.

European Union. 2005. "Confronting Demographic Change: A New Solidarity between the Generations." Brussels: Commission of the European Communities, COM (2005) 94.

Goldstein, J., M. Kreyenfeld, A. Jasilioniene, and D. K. Orsal. 2013. "Fertility Reactions of the 'Great Recession' in Europe: Recent Evidence from Order-Specific Data." *Demographic Research* 29(4): 85–104.

Harper, S. 2011. *Environment Migration and the Demographic Deficit.* Commissioned for UK Government Office of Science Project on Migration and Global Environmental Change.

Holtzmann, R. 2005. "Demographic Alternatives for Aging in Industrial Countries: Increased Total Fertility Rate, Labor Force Participation, or Immigration." Institute for the Study of Labor (IZA) Discussion Paper No. 1885.

Howe, N., and R. Jackson. 2011. "Global Aging and the Crisis of the 2020s." *Current History* 20–25.

Jackson, R., and N. Howe. 2008. *The Greying of the Great Powers: Demography and Geopolitics in the 21st Century.* Washington, DC: Center for Strategic and International Studies.

Lee, R., and A. Mason. 2011. "Generational Economics in a Changing World." *Population and Development Review* 37 (Supplement): 115–142.

Maestas, N. and J. Zissimopoulos. 2010. "How Longer Working Lives Ease the Crunch of Population Aging." *Journal of Economic Persp 24ectives* 24(1): 139-160.

McKibben, W. 2006. "The Global Macroeconomic Consequences of a Demographic Transition." *Asian Economic Papers* 5(1): 92–134.

OECD (2012), OECD Pensions Outlook 2012, OECD Publishing. http://dx.doi.org/10.1787/9789264169401-en

Sinding, S. 2009. "Population, Poverty and Economic Development." *Philosophical Transactions of the Royal Society B.* 364: 3023–3030.

Striessnig, E., and W. Lutz. 2013. "Can Below-Replacement Fertility be Desirable?" *Empirica* 40: 409–425.

Thevenon, O. 2013. "Drivers of Female Labor Force Participation in the OECD." OECD Social, Employment and Migration Working Papers, No. 145, OECD Publishing.

Tyers, R., and Q. Shi. 2007. "Demographic Change and Policy Response: Implications for the Global Economy." *World Economy* 30(4): 537–566.

Wang, Feng. 2011. "The Future of a Demographic Overachiever: Long-Term Implications of the Demographic Transition in China." *Population and Development Review* 37(supplement): 173–190.

Whitehouse, E. R., and A. Zaidi. 2008. "Socio-Economic Differences in Mortality: Implications for Pension Policy." OECD Social, Employment and Mitigation Working Papers No. 71, OECD Publishing.

NAME INDEX

Note: locators followed by n refers to footnotes.

SUBJECT INDEX

Note: locators followed by 'n' refers to footnotes.